From the Fiery Furnace to the Promise Land

From the Fiery Furnace to the PROMISE LAND

STORIES OF A TENNESSEE RECONSTRUCTION COMMUNITY

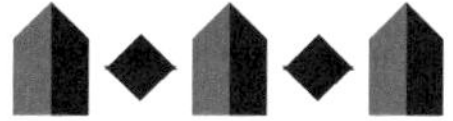

SERINA K. GILBERT

and

LEAROTHA WILLIAMS JR.

VANDERBILT UNIVERSITY PRESS

Nashville, Tennessee

Copyright 2025 Vanderbilt University Press
All rights reserved
First printing 2025

Library of Congress Cataloging-in-Publication Data

Names: Gilbert, Serina K. author | Williams, Learotha, Jr., author
Title: From the fiery furnace to the Promise Land : stories of a Tennessee Reconstruction community / Serina K. Gilbert and Learotha Williams Jr.
Description: Nashville, Tennessee : Vanderbilt University Press, [2025] | Includes bibliographical references.
Identifiers: LCCN 2025006529 (print) | LCCN 2025006530 (ebook) | ISBN 9780826508102 hardcover | ISBN 9780826508119 epub | ISBN 9780826508126 pdf
Subjects: LCSH: Freed persons--Tennessee--Dickson County--History--19th century | Freed persons--Tennessee--Dickson County--History--20th century | African Americans--Tennessee--Dickson County--Biography | Reconstruction (U.S. history, 1865-1877)--Tennessee--Dickson County | Collective memory--Tennessee--Dickson County | LCGFT: Biographies
Classification: LCC F445.B53 G55 2025 (print) | LCC F445.B53 (ebook) | DDC 976.8/44051009--dc23/eng/20250606
LC record available at https://lccn.loc.gov/2025006529
LC ebook record available at https://lccn.loc.gov/2025006530

Front cover images, clockwise from top:
Bobbye and Beverly Gilbert, Leslie Edmondson, Farmie Della Vanleer Bowen

We dedicate the book to the life and memory of Essie V. Gilbert, a lifelong resident, sage, griot, memory keeper, and teacher of the Promise Land Community. Her careful consideration of the stories she was told about the formerly enslaved people and their descendants who created a community between Charlotte and Cumberland Furnace, Tennessee, stories that she valued, inscribed upon her heart, and shared with her children, is the inspiration for this work.

The stories from Promise Land persist today because of her leadership and the commitment of Tamar Primm, Betty Ruth Edmondson, Lizzie Edmondson, and Beverly Gilbert Williams to institutionalize the collection, teaching, and sharing of this history on the land where their ancestors first tasted freedom.

It is our belief that they saw this book when they created what would become the Promise Land Heritage Association.

CONTENTS

Acknowledgments *ix*
Foreword by Frederick Murphy *xi*
Preface *xv*

INTRODUCTION 1
1 Embracing the Story 5
2 The Promise Land Community 9
3 On the Banks of the Jordan 27
4 Soldiers' Stories 35
5 Jumping Jim Crow 65
6 Taking Possession of the Promise Land 69
7 Faith and Resilience 95
8 Community Building and Great Migrations 115
9 Miss Essie's House 131
EPILOGUE Counted Among the Living and Not the Dead 161

Notes *165*
References *169*
Names Index *173*

ACKNOWLEDGMENTS

WE ARE PROFOUNDLY GRATEFUL for the past and present members of the Promise Land community whose lives and memories inspired this work. Your wisdom, joy, strength, and sense of community animate the stories in this book.

We are deeply indebted to the Promise Land Heritage Association for their commitment to ensure that the history of Promise Land is not overwhelmed by shadows of forgetfulness as was the case with similar African American communities that arose after the Civil War in Middle Tennessee. You have faithfully answered and honored the call issued by Essie Gilbert, Tamar Primm, Betty Ruth Edmondson, Lizzie Edmondson, and Beverly Gilbert Williams. Because of your efforts, their call is now our praise song.

A special thank you to Vanderbilt University Press and our editor, Betsy Phillips, who believed in this work from the start and provided insightful feedback and guidance on this project. Your expertise and patience have been invaluable and have shaped this work into what it is today.

Last, we would like to thank you, Gentle Reader, for taking the time to engage with this work. It is our hope that this book will contribute to a greater understanding and appreciation of the rich history of the Promise Land community and the effort of African Americans to define and live as free people in Middle Tennessee.

FOREWORD

IN THE SHADOW OF THE CIVIL WAR, as the nation grappled with the remnants of its most agonizing chapter, a group of men who had fought for freedom and forged steel in the heart of America decided to claim a piece of it for themselves and their descendants. These were no ordinary men; they were formerly enslaved Union soldiers and iron workers enslaved at the local iron furnaces in the heart of Middle Tennessee, bound together by their shared struggles and unyielding resolve. Out of the ashes of a splintered country, Nathan Bowen, Washington Vanleer, and two brothers, John and Arch Nesbitt, laid the foundation of what would become the Promise Land Community—a beacon of hope, resilience, and self-determination. I am a descendant of many people in the Promise Land community and for years marveled at the sheer unwavering commitment to assure its legacy is cemented in our collective memories—memories not only in the "Volunteer State" of Tennessee, but other states and communities alike.

From the Fiery Furnace to the Promise Land: Stories of a Tennessee Reconstruction Community is not just a chronicle of a place but a testament to the enduring spirit of those who built it. This book traces the lineage of a people who refused to let their history be defined by chains and oppression. Instead, they crafted a narrative of their own—one of strength, unity, and a vision for a better future. Through their hands, once bound by servitude, they shaped not only iron but also the very soil that would nurture generations to come.

In the pages that follow, you will discover a story told through the eyes of those alive and deceased, who inherited this legacy. Their gaze carries the weight of their ancestors' sacrifices, the pride of their achievements, and the dreams of those who dared to imagine a community where freedom was more than a word—it was a way of life. As we delve into the rich history of the Promise Land Community, we honor not only the founders but also the descendants who have preserved their story, ensuring that the lessons and legacies of the past continue to guide the future.

This book is a tribute to the indomitable human spirit, to the power of collective action, and to the enduring promise that every person, no matter their beginning, can carve out a place in history. As you read *From the Fiery Furnace to the Promise Land* you will not only learn about the birth of a community but also about the unwavering belief that freedom is a promise worth fighting for—and keeping.

The authors of *From the Fiery Furnace to the Promise Land*, are staples in the fabric of Tennessee's historical education and preservation efforts, thoughtfully highlighting the span of decades and generations in this written masterpiece.

Ms. Gilbert's and Mr. Williams's ability to foster relationships with descendant communities has been the hallmark of their progression, laminating their tireless efforts rooted in humanity and selflessness. The sentiments of both authors help us remember that the legacy of the Promise Land Community is not confined to the past—it lives on in every person who carries its story forward.

To honor the memory of our formerly enslaved ancestors is to recognize the immense courage, sacrifice, and hope that fueled their vision for a better life in this sacred community. Their struggles laid the foundation for the freedoms we enjoy today, and their grit carved a path that we are duty-bound to continue, in which this art depicts clearly.

For those of us who choose to walk in the footsteps of the righteous, the commitment to this legacy is not one of passive reflection, but of active stewardship. It is a call to preserve the history, protect the values, and uplift our communities so many tirelessly built. With every generation that rises, we renew the promise made by our ancestors—that their fight for dignity, justice, and belonging was not in vain.

This book is not just a history; it is a reminder that we are the living testament to our ancestors' dreams. May we all strive to carry forward their unwavering spirit, ensuring that their legacy remains a guiding light for the future.

It has been a pleasure to glean priceless information from these esteemed storytellers and unwavering community pillars.

—Frederick Murphy, founder of History Before Us

PREFACE

ON JANUARY 16, 1865, after an eventful meeting with twenty local African American ministers in Savannah, Georgia, General William T. Sherman issued his Special Field Order Number 15. This order created a reservation, partitioning confiscated and abandoned lands located south of Charleston, South Carolina, to just north of Jacksonville, Florida, the sea islands of Coastal Georgia and South Carolina, and land stretching from thirty miles in from the Atlantic coast for settlement by the African Americans who had followed him from Atlanta to Savannah, Georgia, and others who witnessed his arrival in the city during the fall and early winter of 1864.

Although Sherman's order was not spurred on by any benevolence on his part, the legion of freedom-seeking African Americans that followed his troops to Savannah proved to be a drain on his army's much-needed resources. The biblical undertones of the reservation were inescapable. For many of the more than forty thousand formerly enslaved and their families that received forty-acre plots as a result of Sherman's order, this land was the "New Jerusalem" foretold in scripture; it was their Promise Land.

More than five hundred miles away, in the community of Cumberland Furnace, Tennessee, whispers about this land grant reached its enslaved population. For some, the city of Savannah, Georgia, may have had a familiar ring to it as more than two dozen of their ancestors departed Savannah during the winter of 1853 seeking their own Promise Land on African soil in Liberia. While it is uncertain how they received notification of this gift to freedmen—the grapevine and newly enlisted United States Colored Troops carried news of the war far and wide across the country—by the early spring of 1865, it must have seemed as if their receipt of a promised land was nigh and they would finally live to see the arrival of the Year of Jubilee. For many enslaved Africans in America, slavery was a *hell on earth*. The enslaved who worked the furnaces in Middle Tennessee literally felt its heat each day, laboring under those conditions with no reprieve from almost the moment Tennessee entered the Union until the beginning of the Civil War. The news of the imminent demise of their enslavement must have been welcome news for those that labored in the iron mills and their families.

The history of the people who would call Promise Land home, according to one family historian, can be traced back to a young Fulani man in Africa who was captured and enslaved in America. Born a year after America declared its independence from England, the African who would be known as Billy by his captors was sold to the Nesbitt family in what was believed to have been the second slave auction in the recently created Dickson County. Although the details of his journey from West Africa remain a mystery, it is likely that he was brought from Virginia or North Carolina—two states that had well-established slave systems for almost a century before he was born—to Dickson County. This new land was a place that had been inhabited by Native Americans for centuries, but it was also an area whose geography now stood on the brink of being transformed into something that would make many of its new arrivals some of the wealthiest men in the state. Although agriculture would remain an important part of the county's economy it would be the production of iron that would come to define the area for much of Tennessee's territorial and antebellum period.

The iron industry that would eventually dominate the area was controlled by Montgomery Bell. Born in 1769 in Chesterfield County, Pennsylvania, Bell purchased Cumberland Furnace shortly after he arrived in Middle Tennessee in 1804 from James Robertson, one of the founders of Nashville. An astute businessman, Bell began to establish iron furnaces throughout Middle Tennessee, playing a significant role in Tennessee becoming the third-largest iron-producing state in the nation by 1840. As his iron interests proliferated, his commitment to the enslavement of Africans and their descendants followed a similar trajectory. By 1850, Bell enslaved as many as 272 men, women, and children, making him one of the largest enslavers in the state. Many of those he held in chains would become some of the earliest residents of Promise Land.[1]

The median age of these bond persons was twenty while the 115 women enslaved by Bell represented just over 42 percent of the population. For these women, early signs of pregnancy would have been accompanied by both a sense of joy and dread. Under the legal code *partus sequiter ventrem*, each child born by these women became the property of Bell as soon as they were conceived, a reality that served to increase his wealth and the angst the women felt about bringing their children into a world where their lives would be controlled by violence. Another curious and extraordinary feature of Bell's enslaved population was the fact that 61 percent of the men, women, and children he enslaved were listed as mulatto. Bell remained a bachelor throughout his life, a fact that caused much speculation that many of the women he enslaved bore his children.

Many historians have described Bell as being a benevolent enslaver, citing his being open to some of his enslaved obtaining an education and his lifelong relationship with James Worley, an enslaved African American companion whom he had known since childhood and trusted with his business dealings as an example of his kindness. In 1844, Bell named his last furnace after his faithful agent and companion.

The lack of personal accounts from the enslaved during Dickson County's antebellum period prevent us from painting a picture of the world Promise Land's forebearers inhabited using their gaze, thoughts, and feelings, it is still possible to reimagine their experiences by centering them in extant sources and scrutinizing the culture and experiences of the descendants.

The type of labor enslaved men and women engaged in was diverse in Dickson County. Promise Land's ancestors who labored in the furnaces that dotted Middle Tennessee included the miners who extracted raw materials from the Tennessee countryside, foundry workers, engineers, teamsters, and blacksmiths.

For those employed in the cultivation of wheat, corn, and cotton, a typical day for the men and women most likely entailed them rising in the morning at the sound of a bell or horn, and their making their way to the fields. Working as a gang from "can't see to can't see" their entire day would be centered around the cultivation and care of their respective crops. For those employed in the cultivation of tobacco, their days involved the completion of various tasks. Once they completed their assigned tasks, the remaining time in the day would be their own. Tobacco, however, was a very labor-intensive crop and any enslaved person who could find a spare moment after the completion of their task could consider themselves to be fortunate. Domestic workers would not have enjoyed the highly regimented day of those who worked in the fields. The maids, cooks, wet and dry nurses, and personal servants were typically on call around the clock catering to their enslaver and his family's needs. Although domestic work typically sheltered them from the intensity of the sun during the hottest parts of the day, their proximity to their enslavers led to increased supervision, potential for punishment, and for women an increased likelihood of sexual violence.

Indeed, any discussion of slavery in America must include an exploration of the violence needed to maintain it. Advertisements for enslaved men and women who absconded in search of freedom reveal the violence of the institution. These ads bear witness to scars, exposure to weather, branding, and mutilations. These ads from Middle Tennessee demonstrate that the enslavement of African Americans in the South would not have existed a day had it not been for violence to the enslaved and those they cared about. Enslavement was the primary condition for Promise Land's forebearers during the antebellum period as free African Americans made up a very small part of Dickson County's African American population, representing only seven of the 2,208 residents in 1860.[2] As the nation moved toward war in 1861, in became increasingly difficult to be Black and free in Tennessee.

As was the case in most areas of the South, free African Americans posed a threat to slavery in the minds of many enslavers. Less than a decade after Montgomery Bell sold Cumberland Furnace to Anthony Van Leer in 1825, it became increasingly more difficult to be Black and free in Tennessee. When word of Nat Turner's 1831 rebellion in Southampton, Virgina—and the death of an estimated fifty-five white people at their hands—reached the Volunteer State, state politicians moved quickly to deal with the perceived threat free Black citizens posed to their ability to maintain slavery. Legislation mandating that the manumission of enslaved men and women result in their exile from the Volunteer State quickly emerged from the state house. By the 1850s, a law was passed that required their removal to Africa after manumission.[3]

As Montgomery Bell approached the end of his life, he resolved to free his enslaved population and began planning to send two hundred to Liberia after emancipation. Liberia was established in 1822 by the American Colonization Society as a place where America's free Black population could settle if they desired to return to the land of their ancestors.

Among the group that Bell sent to the African nation before his death, the Sinou region of Liberia became their Promise Land. Their friends and families they left behind after 1853 and others sold by the Bell estate after his death would have to wander in the metaphorical wilderness of antebellum America for another decade.

Although Dickson County was a small rural county, African Americans living there were not insulated from the sectional crisis that was building in the country during the decade of the 1850s. Accounts circulated of self-emancipated African Americans roaming the countryside and using the Harpeth and Cumberland rivers as avenues for freedom. Even those who worked and lived near the iron furnaces often found themselves in the midst of paranoia and racial violence initiated by fears of a slave revolt. The *National Era* reported,

> Our city yesterday was rife with rumors in relation to the insurrection at different points along the river. We understand that six Negroes, who had been found guilty at the iron works, and who threatened a second outbreak, were killed a few days since, and that two white men, known accessories in the matter, had been arrested, and nearly whipped to death. It is also reported that four Negroes will be hung in Dover today, and a number of others have been arrested as implicated in the affair.[4]

These rumors and related outbreaks of racial violence typically occurred during the Christmas holidays, a time of the year where African Americans enjoying more freedom to travel to visit family and loved ones. Noted abolitionist Frederick Douglass recalled, "From what I know of the effect of these holidays upon the slave, I believe them to be among the most effective means in the hands of the slaveholder in keeping down the spirit of insurrection."[5] Primary sources reveal, however, the holidays and the sight of enslaved African Americans enjoying greater freedom of mobility did little to alleviate white fears of slave rebellions during 1850. Often the enslaved laboring at the ironworks such as Cumberland Furnace and the surrounding areas faced scrutiny as possible coconspirators in these plots.

As the decade progressed, the mere presence of African Americans in the Volunteer State meant this sense of paranoia continued, reaching a point of hysteria after John Brown's 1859 failed raid on Harper's Ferry Virginia. Believing free Blacks posed an imminent threat to the security of slavery, the Tennessee General Assembly contemplated legislation that would require free African Americans residing in the state to leave or risk enslavement. One observer supported the passage of this legislation, arguing that if this step was not taken, "free negroes would be at liberty to preach rebellion in their daily and nightly intercourse with the slaves."[6] Less than a year later, this law became a moot point when South Carolina officially withdrew from the Union in December 1860. Tennessee would follow suit when it ratified its own ordinances of secession on June 8, 1861, joining the Confederate States of America, an entity whose constitution explicitly prohibited passage of any "bill of attainder, ex post facto law, or law denying or impairing the right of property in negro slaves."[7] In early 1863, in the aftermath of the implementation of the Emancipation Proclamation, Jefferson Davis, President of the Confederacy, put the issue of free African Americans in the South to rest when proclaimed "On and after February 22, 1863, all free negroes within the Southern Confederacy shall be placed on slave status and be deemed chattels, they and their issue forever."[8]

For the slave-owning class in the South, the Civil War was seen as a way to preserve slavery indefinitely. But for many African Americans in the South, the war became a way to secure their freedom. For many who lived and would later arrive in Dickson County, it would literally become the metaphorical banks of the river that led to their Promise Land.

Introduction

FROM MY EARLIEST MEMORY, I have always viewed the community of my origin as a source of comfort and security. I am convinced that this sense of well-being is the result of having loving parents, seven devoted siblings, and growing up surrounded by a close-knit group of extended family members. In addition to my parents and siblings, I came into a world that included a beloved great-grandmother, maternal grandparents, several devoted aunts, uncles, and a host of cousins. Everyone in the community was connected in some way. Rarely did I encounter a stranger. The teacher and church pastors may have come from outside the community, however by the time they entered my purview they had been thoroughly vetted and approved by those who buffered my existence. I had learned to feel just as comfortable at church or at school as I did at home. Usually accompanied by siblings or other playmates, I attended school and church; visited neighbors; and explored places in the community without any reservations. This experience was nurturing, sustaining, and created in me a sense of belonging and stabilization. Such genetic memory permeates a place that lives in the bloodstreams and passes down through generations. I believe that my mother and father felt the same. No matter where I have traveled or lived, my soul always carried along my true identity, with my community of origin, family, ancestors, country dirt roads, and humble early life. This community and life source is Promise Land.

Promise Land is a small rural community in Middle Tennessee with the distinction of being purposefully populated by formerly enslaved people and members of the United States Colored Troop (USCT) soon after the Civil War. According to the oral history passed down from generation to generation, the settlement of the community was aided by the Freedmen's Bureau. The Freedmen's Bureau, known formally as the Bureau of Refugees, Freedmen, and Abandoned Lands was created by an act of Congress on March 3, 1865, to assist African Americans in making the transition from enslaved to freed persons. The Bureau accomplished this by issuing more than twenty-one million rations, establishing hospitals, insane asylums, orphanages, negotiating contracts, and assisting with the creation of schools. There was an office operating in perhaps both Cumberland Furnace and Charlotte since both towns are in proximity to the location where the newly freed people were referred to establish their homes. I have been told that the Freedmen's Bureau also administered property that had been confiscated or abandoned during the war. As administrators they were able to refer and distribute plots of land to newly freed people. The people who settled in Promise Land came from nearby farms or from the Cumberland Furnace iron plantation where they had been enslaved. Like the others who settled in the community, some had served as members of the USCT.

The United States Colored Troops were regiments of African American soldiers who served in the Union army during the Civil War. They participated in all aspects of the Union's war effort including infantry, cavalry, artillery, and engineers. The regiments containing 185,000 soldiers accounted for 10 percent of the Union army. First mustered during the fall of 1862, and authorized by President Abraham Lincoln for unilateral use in the war when he stated in the Emancipation Proclamation that "such persons of suitable condition, will be received into the armed service of the United States to garrison forts, positions, stations, and other places, and to man vessels of all sorts in said service," they served in many conflicts in Tennessee, including the Battle of Nashville. Their casualty rate was extremely high. Nearly forty thousand Black soldiers died during the war with approximately thirty thousand of that number dying from infection or disease. Their death rate was 35 percent higher than that of white soldiers. This information is included here to demonstrate the sacrifice, courage, and gallantry that the Black men experienced to gain freedom for themselves and their people. It gives me a great sense of pride to recognize that some of the men who served with the USCT escaped local farms and the Cumberland Furnace to join the Union army.

While the origin of the name Promise Land remains uncertain, it has several origin stories. However, I believe that it had to do with the relationship with the USCT veterans who settled in the area and the Freedmen's Bureau as much of the land in the Promise Land area was heavily wooded and not in use.

Many of the early settlers in Promise Land came from the Cumberland Furnace, located about five miles from Promise Land. The Cumberland Furnace name derived from the two large ironworks that operated in the village. The Cumberland Furnace was established in 1797 by James Robertson, the founder of Nashville. Not only did the major iron plantation operate in the Cumberland Furnace village, but it was an emerging city within the county with a train depot, stores, schools, and churches. The iron plantation was the largest in Dickson County. Its ownership was passed from Montgomery Bell to Anthony Wayne Vanleer in 1825. Vanleer became a very wealthy ironmaster with a large workforce comprised primarily of slave labor. It is reported that at the peak of operation, Vanleer enslaved 114 people. In 1862, after the fall of Fort Donelson, the Union army forced the closure of the furnace. Vanleer died before the war ended and his furnace was inherited by his granddaughter, Mary Florence Kirkman. Kirkman married Union army officer James Pierre Drouillard, who had been stationed in Nashville. Following the close of the war, the couple moved to Cumberland Furnace where they reopened the family business.

I had ancestors who were enslaved at the Cumberland Furnace. After emancipation, many continued to carry the last names of their enslavers. My ancestors, the Vanleers, Bowens, Gilberts, and Kirkmans were among those who settled in Promise Land. Others included the Nesbitts, Primms, Grimes, Edmondsons, Robertsons, and many more. These industrious residents worked together to develop a self-sustaining village that within two generations had included at least fifty households, three churches, two general stores, and an elementary school.

The community's population started to decline as part of the Great Migration to the North following WWI and II. By the middle of the twentieth century there were less than ten families remaining in the community. The stores closed as the families moved away, leaving behind the school which closed in 1957 and the remaining church in the early 1990s. The last child born in the community was in 1963. At a community reunion in 1988, a group of descendants, former residents, and the few remaining residents met to form the Promise Land Community Club, which is now known as the Promise Land Heritage Association (PLHA). The goal of this organization was to preserve the history and legacy of the historic community. Included in the organizing mission was to restore the decaying Promise Land School built in 1880 and contribute to the support and help sustain the fledging United Methodist Church, the only remaining house of worship. At that time only five women made up the congregation. The PLHA continues and has grown to become a 501(c)(3) organization whose mission remains the same as it was at formation. The organization has been successful in restoring the historic school building and getting it placed on the National Register of Historic Places. The building has been converted into a historic replica of the school as it was in the nineteenth century, where tours are hosted for the public. Since 2000, the organization has hosted an annual music and arts festival. It also hosts traveling exhibitions and other cultural, educational, and art events.

Today, those who have firsthand memories and knowledge of the community as it was in its heyday are few and are aging, including myself. Therefore, I approach my participation in documenting the community's history, including the sharing of personal memories, with a sense of urgency. I am grateful that Dr. Learotha Williams Jr., professor of African American history, the Civil War, and Reconstruction, has agreed to join in this endeavor. We hope to build upon efforts of others including Sylvia Edmondson-Holt whose memoir *Between the Pews: More Than Sabbath Day's Journey from the Promise Land*, published in 2016, and Sokoto Fulani's *The Ethnos of Promise Land*, an unpublished manuscript written in 2001 and revised in 2006 have served as inspiration toward our goal. In this book it is our desire to provide an overview of the history of the Promise Land Community, including recollections of the people, places, and events that formed and shaped it. This will be achieved through scholarly research by a historian and scholar, and by the personal observations and remembrances of one who was born, nurtured, and came of age under the watchful eyes of the community itself.

1
EMBRACING THE STORY

MOST OF US BORN and raised in the community were aware of our heritage and the people who lived there before us. Whenever we gathered, whether it was for a family reunion or other types of community gatherings, it was sure to bring together residents and former residents. We came with expectations of hearing many amusing and often enlightening tales of the people, places, and events from the community's past. Some of the accounts would be repetitive, while others would be new revelations for some of us. These gatherings were usually intergenerational. The shared recollections were endearing and promoted cohesion. Often these gatherings provided information and facts that were unsubstantiated.

With both parents being descendants of original settlers in the community, my siblings and I were well versed about our early roots. My mother's maternal and paternal great-grandfathers had died before she was born. However, she grew up in the home built by her great-grandfather Joe Washington Vanleer and she had vivid memories of her great-grandmother, although she died before her mother reached the age of five. Mother was especially proud of the fact that she was raised by her maternal grandmother and grandfather. Her grandmother lived to see her grow into adulthood, become a wife, and mother of six children before her death. Her paternal grandfather, who had a great influence on her, died when she was in fifth grade. She was also blessed to have known and spent some time with her paternal grandmother who also lived in the community. My father was not as fortunate to have known his grandparents. They died before his birth and his father died when he was only five years old. My parents' familiarity with their fore-parents and extended families had a great impact on my appreciation for my early ancestors.

By the time I arrived on the scene, the community's early settlers were indeed history. However, as a child, I would often listen to the conversations of my elderly relatives with their peers. They would discuss people and events of the past. There was a saying, "Children should be seen and not heard." I was obedient to this adage. I would quietly listen and soak it all in. Another way the past would be brought into the present was through my father, who had a habit of placing monikers on me, my siblings, and my peers. The names he gave us belonged to people he remembered from his childhood. For example, he called my cousin Birdie "Aunt Parthenia Gregg," another child was called "Blacksmith," and still another was called "Uncle Elijah Suggs." There were many names from past Promise Land residents that he would assign to my peers. When I asked him why he called them by these names, he would say, there's just something about him or her that reminds me of so and so. Years later when I begin to research the census records of 1870s and 1880s, I was not surprised to come across these names that I had heard before. I would visualize how these people may have looked by the appearance or characteristics of my siblings and peers who had unofficially inherited their names.

During my childhood, there were remnants of some of the old houses that were identified by the names of former owners. Most of them had been left vacant by previous occupants who were part of the Great Migration, the movement of six million African Americans from the rural South to the North and Western United States between 1910 and 1970. In addition to the remaining houses, there were springs, graveyards, and roads or paths that carried the name of the individuals or families who had shared a proximity with the place. There were landmarks such as the Ole Garrett House, Hutton Hollow, Dess Grimes Hill, John Wesley's Store, Harriet's Hole, and other such places that gave us a glimpse into the past. I often explored these places with my siblings or other kids in the community. Sometimes we would come across them when we were roaming the area gathering mushrooms, hickory nuts, or blackberries; raiding an abandoned orchard; exploring an old house; fetching water; or when fishing for frogs and tadpoles. The names of these places enabled us to give an exact location of where we had been when relaying our adventures to friends, parents, teachers, or others.

My dad would often tell us scary tales of the haunted Hutton Hollow located near the foot of Promise Land Road going north. It was at the flat of the Dess Grimes Hill, with two graveyards, the Hutton and Nesbitt cemeteries on each side of the road. These stories, handed down from generation to generation, would include the names of the unfortunate haunted victims. Like the landmarks, there were springs that served the residents of the community. Each spring was named after the early Promise Land settler who owned the property on which it was located. We fetched water for our household from the Garrett Spring. It was located on the property which had been owned by USCT / Union army veteran Clark Garrett. Our house was just a short distance through the woodpile to the Mt. Olive Baptist / African Methodist Episcopal (AME) Church. The house where we lived had belonged to early Promise Land settler Lias Jackson and his family. The property on which the church was built in 1884 had also belonged to Mr. Jackson; he donated it to the Baptist congregation. Of course, Lias Jackson and his wife had died before our family became occupants of the house and his heirs had moved away during the height of the Northern migration.

The aforementioned landmarks, people, places, and events are fused with my precious memories of the Promise Land community. Sharing the name of the various places in the community reminds me of an imprint that a member of the PLHA had printed on a T-shirt for the annual reunion about twenty years ago. On the back of the shirt were listed various Promise Land Landmarks, and on the front was printed the words, "It's a Promise Land Thing. You Won't Understand." Hopefully as more people become aware of the community's history, they will also become acquainted with the landmarks that meant so much to its residents.

2
THE PROMISE LAND COMMUNITY

THE PROMISE LAND COMMUNITY is formed by a route that originally served as a stagecoach road leading from Dickson County to Montgomery County. Before the formation of the community, it was called Clarksville Stage Road. From my remembrance as a child, the main artery intersects at St. Paul Road located at about two miles from the Charlotte city limits. At the foot of what is called today Promise Land Road and on St. Paul Road is a building that was once the St. Paul Presbyterian Church. This church, established in 1901, had served the white residents in its area. The doors of the church closed about 1980. Today it is the headquarters for the Sons of Confederate Veterans W. H. McCauley Camp 260. The St. Paul Road intersects with a once-dirt road that snakes its way for about one and a half miles through the Promise Land community to Staton Road near Cumberland Furnace. During the warm, dry seasons, this road would be very dusty; with heavy rain it would become extremely muddy. I can remember cars getting stuck in the mud and the men in the community running to help the motorist dislodge the vehicle. It was a narrow road that not only accommodated the stagecoach, but also wagons and buggies pulled by mules or horses and foot traffic. During the turn of the twentieth century, as more people became owners of automobiles, they became common on the roadway as well. The Post Office designation for it was Rural Route 2. The traffic along the route had created smooth parallel tracks that ran down the middle of the roadway. Outside and between the smooth tracks were rocky ridges created when they were pushed over from the surface by the tires of vehicles. The county road services came out periodically to grate and apply fresh creek bedrocks to keep the road up. These rocky surfaces proved to provide some respite for pedestrians at times when the surface was muddy. For a child, the road held certain threats including encounters with strangers, chances of being struck by a car, and the dust/mud that would mess up your shoes.

As kids we learned to avoid the road altogether and take paths that branched off the road. We preferred to take the woods to get to our destinations. The woods were a better alternative because they provided shortcuts, they were safer from vehicle traffic and much better for exploration. There were many paths from the main road that led to homes, crops, barns, springs, and forest attractions. Our parents cautioned us regarding taking shortcuts through the woods. We were warned to never travel alone or in the dark; to avoid insect and snake bites by covering our extremities well; to beware of wild animals; watch for hunters; to watch for pits, sink holes and animal traps; not to wander inside abandoned buildings; and to always let your parents know where you were going and the route you would be taking.

Most of the families in Promise Land received their mail along Rural Route 2; a box number was assigned to each household. Our address was Route 2 Box 211A. The people who lived along the road had mailboxes in front of their homes. There was also a bank of mailboxes where the Promise Land and the Reddon Crossing Roads met. This was so that mail could be left for families who lived in homes off the road. The bank of mailboxes was located close to the school. Students would congregate at the mailboxes after school to collect their family's mail before they would disperse onto one of the intersecting roads off the main road to their respective homes. The students who lived along Promise Land Road would proceed past the mailboxes to their homes, where there would be individual mailboxes in front.

In the 1940s, most of the homes in Promise Land dated back to houses built by the early settlers. Coming up Promise Land Road from St. Paul Road, near the area known as the Hutton Hollow was a house on the right side of the road. It once belonged to Rev. William Hutton, who was a pastor of the St. John Methodist Church. His farm was in the vicinity of the house. As far as I can remember, the only evidence of the farm was the house. There were no barns or sheds left standing. The house was an old weatherbeaten, wood-framed, charcoal-colored building. When newly built, the house was probably the color of the natural timber from which it came, but over the course of years and exposure to the elements the unpainted building had become nearly black. Typical of many houses in the community, it was a small A-frame structure that measured about fifty feet across. There was a porch that ran completely across the house that stood at least two feet from the grounds, with rickety wooden stairs leading to the porch. The interior of the house had three to four rooms. The entrance led to the parlor, which also doubled as a sleeping room. The adjoining room was a bedroom, and the back room was a kitchen. A back porch was attached to the kitchen. The whole house was covered by a wood shake roof. When I visited this home, Mr. Hannah Collier, a prominent barber in the community, lived there with his wife, my cousin, Ethel Garrett, and their four children.

Next to the house located on a hill was the Nesbitt Cemetery where two USCT veterans, brothers, and early settlers John and Arch Nesbitt are laid to rest. This cemetery is still used today by Nesbitt, Primm, and Edmondson descendants. Adjoining the cemetery was the Hutton cemetery, which is currently inactive and overgrown. In recent years, a building has been constructed extremely near the Hutton cemetery and some of the tombstones were dismantled and destroyed in the development by the property owner. On the right of the cemetery was a clearing, where I am told was once the homesite of Arch Nesbitt, USCT veteran, and his family. More than twenty years ago, a new home was built in the clearing. Leading north from the cemeteries along the road is the only hill of any significant size. It was the source of several automobile accidents when I was growing up. It was called the "Dess Grimes Hill." The Grimes family had property on the left side of the hill. At the top of the hill was the homesite of early settlers Sol and Mandy Cunningham. I remember a woman living there who was known to me as Miss Betty Cunningham and her two brothers, Mr. Lev and Mr. Noye; they were first-generation descendants of Sol and Mandy Cunningham. The Cunningham farm occupied both sides of the road. Their house was on the left side of the road and a barn was on the right side. The Cunninghams raised tobacco and hogs. There was a tobacco field, smoke house, and hog pen on the left side of the road in proximity to the barn. Located on the left side of the road, behind their house was a large vegetable garden, smokehouse, and outhouse.

Going north up the road from the Cunningham farm was a path on the left side of the road that led into the woods. This path led to a spring where my family would go to get water for our household. I would sometimes accompany my brothers to the spring. They carried zinc-galvanized or ceramic gallon buckets, while I would carry a half gallon repurposed molasses can. It was the same one I would carry to pick blackberries. I enjoyed going to the spring. I would play and skip along the path picking wildflowers and watching for small animals such as rabbits or ground hogs as they scurried about. We shared this spring with the Cunninghams. The spring water was very cold and perpetually flowing. The Cunninghams would store their freshly churned butter in the spring to keep it cold. Homes in Promise Land didn't have electricity or refrigerators then. There were so many in our family, we rarely had butter leftover to be stored. We did have an icebox where we kept food cold for as long as the ice lasted. The icebox was kept cold with a large block of ice placed in the ice compartment. Our dad would purchase a block of ice from the icehouse in Dickson on Saturdays. The ice would last in the icebox for about two or three days before melting.

Sometimes we would run into Mr. Noye, who I guess was the water bearer for his household. He was the only one from his household who came to fetch water. Mr. Noye was a pleasant man in his late forties. He was small in stature, standing about five feet six with a smooth dark complexion. He was not one to start a conversation but always seemed pleased to talk with us. My brother Joe would usually be the one to initiate a conversation with him. Joe might ask him about his tobacco crop or ask when they planned to start killing hogs. Mr. Noye sems to have enjoyed the opportunity to talk or perhaps that someone had shown interest in him. He would show a broad grin as he rattled off and moved from one subject to another once he had gotten started. Perhaps because of his age or small frame, Joe would offer to help him carry his water buckets home. Mr. Noye would gladly accept my brother's offer by replying, "much obliged." I remember only him using that phrase. I adopted it and still use it today. Whenever I hear myself saying it, I think of Mr. Noye. For Joe's assistance, Mr. Noye would promise him, "Next time I go to Charlotte, I'll bring you back a bottle of soda water." While waiting for Joe to return, Bill and I would skip rocks or catch little insects that would swim on the surface of the spring. They were called spring keepers. They were little insects that would gracefully glide on top of the spring. This made it easy for us to pick them up from the water surface. It would not be long before Joe would return. When he did, we would walk home, teasing him that he would never get that soda water that Mr. Noye had promised.

From the path to the spring, going north, just up the road was our house on the right side of the road. The old house that we lived in had a lot of history. The original owner of it was Lias Jackson. The exterior looked very much like the house where the Collier family lived, except that it did not have a front porch or back porch. When you stepped out the front door, you stepped onto a plank that led from the house to a big maple tree that stood at the edge of the yard. Our dad would pull his car into the yard from the road and park beneath the maple tree. The plank ran just short of where the car was parked. The plank was to protect our shoes from the mud as the yard was bare and dusty. About forty feet south of the maple tree stood an old oak tree. This tree looked to have been centuries old. From the trees to the house was an ample playground for us. We used this play area to the extent that it was bare of vegetation. It was a dust bowl. Mother would have us sweep the yard in front of the house in the evening, so we would not track the dust into the house. The house had served at least two generations with children playing outside to keep the ground bare of grass. There was a lovely lilac tree that bloomed with the sweetest fragrant lavender blooms in the spring. At the edge of the yard were more flowers, sweet peas, a rose bush, and the Tennessee state flower, flags, or iris in an assortment of colors but mostly purple. There were always blooming plants throughout the spring and summer seasons. There were remnants of Mr. Jackson's old farm that still remained. In the rear of the house was a large garden space. There was a brooder house and pen for the chickens, along the north rear side of the house and on the north rear was a large pear tree that yielded the most delicious yellow pears. It was also great for climbing with limbs so large that you could sit there and read or lie back and fall asleep. Across the road from the house were two major attractions for me. Directly across from the old oak tree was a fenced in field for Cousin Bubba's mules, Hat, and Rodie. Cousin Bubba lived in the house a little farther up the road going north with his widowed mother. His real name was "Beatress," but I did not know that then. I heard some adults call him by the initial, "B" which I thought stood for "Bubba." He used the mules for plowing. They were a handsome pair of tan colored mules with beige manes and tails. One was slightly darker than the other. To me, they were horses. My brother said that they were a mixed breed. They were mild-mannered animals who would romp in the field and would stay near each other. They would sometimes bray, which was intimidating to me, so I would keep my distance from them. A path between the fenced field led into the woods. This path was a shortcut to my great-grandmother's house.

Next to the path was an old corn crib. My sister and I convinced our brothers to help us convert the crib into a playhouse. We loved this playhouse. During the summer months, we spent many hours from early morning until dawn playing, stopping only to go to the house for actual meals. We coexisted in the crib space with lizards, of which I was terrified and despised. They would scurry and slither between cracks in the floor, walls, and ceiling. They were as fearful of us as we were them. In the crib we found a couple of old framed pictures. One of them was a picture that looked like it was taken in earlier times of a Black man and woman. There were also some old household items like cooking utensils and iron pots that we discovered in the crib. One of the most interesting things that we found was a quart jar of canned yellow peaches. The peaches were bright and firm as though they had been recently canned. They were on a shelf that was out of my reach. My mother who had known the Jacksons and had played with their grandchildren, said that she thought that the people in the framed portraits were probably Mr. Lias Jackson and his first wife, and the canned peaches were likely canned by his second wife, Mrs. Francis Talley Jackson. Mother told us to leave the peaches alone. Mother described Mrs. Francis Jackson as a very regal-appearing woman who was tall, slim, and beautiful. She died in the 1930s in the old house where we lived. When my brother was a little boy, he told us one morning during breakfast that he woke up during the night and saw a tall woman standing near his bed. Then she suddenly disappeared. My mother responded to his statement in a very matter fact way, "That was Miss Francis Jackson." We accepted her explanation without question. The descendants of the Jacksons continued to live in the house until 1938 when they migrated to Indianapolis, Indiana. One of Lias granddaughter's name was Mable. She married my mother's cousin, Richard Jenkins, who was also raised by mother's grandmother. He was like a brother to my mother, so we called him Uncle Richard. Mother, Richard, and Mable remained close throughout their lives. After moving to Indianapolis, Uncle Richard would bring his whole family to stay with us during the annual Charlotte Picnic.

The Charlotte Picnic was an annual event sponsored by the Lone Star Masonic Lodge of Charlotte. The Picnic was recognized a few years ago by the local Chamber as the longest recurring annual event in Dickson County. Some believe that it was originally an emancipation celebration. It is held on the third Friday in August in a Black settlement that was originally known as "Cedar Grove," located in the city of Charlotte. The time of the annual event corresponds to the date, August 8, 1863, when then

US president Andrew Johnson freed his personal slaves. Other slaveholders in Middle Tennessee followed suit. Other Black communities in this region would celebrate this time as the "Day of Freedom." It is believed that when Jim Crow became the law of the land, Black people feared retribution if they openly celebrated their freedom, and they discontinued associating the event with emancipation. It was just dubbed "the Picnic." The event, however, is and was well-known by the Black communities around the county and descendants of this region. People would travel from the places that they had migrated back to Charlotte for the event. It was like a holiday for us when I was growing up. It would be planned and discussed for months before the day arrived. My mother said that she remembered people traveling to the event in horse-driven wagons. During the event, we would expect family from out of town to come and stay with us. The question often asked by neighbors was "Who do you have coming in for the Picnic?" We would get new outfits to wear. It was a big deal. Today it has lost much of its appeal as many of those who moved away and would return each year are no longer with us. The event does not appeal to the second and subsequent generations as it did for the first generation of migrants. Nor does it hold the same appeal for local descendants as it did for my generation.

Next door to the Jackson House was Mt. Olive Baptist / AME Church. The land on which the church was built was donated by Mr. Lias Jackson. Mr. Jackson and his family were of the Baptist faith. The church was originally built for residents of the community. It was a simple one-room A-framed wooden structure covered with gray brick siding and a tin roof. It was completed about 1884. Prior to opening, the church's leadership were approached by community residents who identified as members of the African Methodist Episcopal Church. The AME members had been holding church services in homes of various members. Two of these members were my maternal grandfathers. The Baptist congregation agreed to share the facility with the AME congregation. Members of the two churches worked together in building the three-slatted wooden pews for the sanctuary and the podium. The two congregations amicably shared expenses for the upkeep of the facility and alternate Sundays for worship services.

My mother recalled attending Mt. Olive when she was a child. She said that some Sundays when the St. Paul Presbyterian Church located south at the foot of Promise Land and St. Paul Road, would dismiss, the members traveling north would pass Mt. Olive. They would stop to listen to the worship services. Service would be going strong at Mt. Olive and the uninvited visitors would be out in front of the church in wagons or on horseback. Some who were on horses would come to the open windows of the church and allow their horses to poke their heads inside. Mother said that this would frighten the children. If they were sitting by the windows, they would move and sit next to their parents or other adults. No one inside the church would say anything to the intruders. After a while, the unwelcome visitors would move along to their homes.

About the mid-1940s the Baptist congregation had grown so small that they had to disband as a congregation. Many members had died or moved away and the number who remained were inadequate to sustain their share for church. Mt. Olive AME continued to be an active church in the community until 1963, when it closed due to an insufficient number of members. Although our maternal great-grandmother and great-aunts belonged to the AME Church, our nuclear family belonged to the St. John Methodist Church located farther north down the road, as this had been the church [to which] my paternal grandparents belonged. It was nice living next door to Mt. Olive. It seemed that every time the doors of the church were opened, the Gilbert family was there. The Methodist Episcopal Church met on the first, third, and fifth Sundays. The AME Church met on the second and fourth Sundays. I do not think it mattered to my brothers and sisters which church we attended. We participated in programs and events at both churches. I remember my Uncle Baxter Robertson, who was married to my father's sister Ruby, serving as chairman of the Trustee Board at Mt. Olive. Uncle Baxter usually occupied the first pew in the "Amen Corner." The Amen Corner was the section of the church that was usually reserved for the deacons or trustees. Uncle Baxter sitting on the corner of the pew, with one of his legs crossed over the other, would straighten his shoulders, put his head back, while gazing out the window, and belt out his favorite congregational hymn, "Pass Me Not O Gentle Savior." This would usually be the song that would lead into the sermon. His singing was soul stirring but mostly humorous to us children, whom he liked to tease when we were called on to sing or recite. This was an opportunity for us to giggle and make fun of him.

In addition to church services, there were special events held there. There was a path that led from our woodyard right to the church. I remember the church having a carnival, organized by my Aunt Mabel, in the yard of the church. She asked her husband, Uncle Peony, to build a platform. On the platform there was a shelf that contained toys. Included among the toys were colorful wind-up cars, tin clowns, and rubber kewpie dolls. There was one item that I really admired. It was a little royal blue plastic piggy bank. My aunt must have noticed me looking at it. I did not have the money to purchase it and I don't recall asking anyone to buy it for me. The carnival was held during the early fall. At Christmas, my aunt really surprised me by gifting me with the little royal blue piggy bank.

Just past the Mt. Olive Church, going north and on the right side of the road, was Cousin John Wesley's Store. The proprietor of the store, John Wesley Edmondson, lived across the road from it. He was the father of "Cousin Bubba," mentioned earlier. John Wesley Edmondson was one of the first generation of children born in Promise Land to formerly enslaved parents. His parents were Jeff and Violet Gilbert Edmondson. Unfortunately for me, Cousin John Wesley died in 1946, the same year I was born. I had heard so many good things about him. I regret that I never got to know him. He was a well-respected community leader, merchant, carpenter, and farmer. His son Bubba continued to run the store for several years after his father's death. By the time I was old enough to explore the community, the store had been closed. However, remnants that would support its identity as a store remained. It was a large, wood-frame building that was graying from age. The design of the structure was similar to other buildings in the community. It was a large rectangular structure covered by an A-shaped tin roof. The entrance to the building was a door at the center with a small platform extending from it. Over the door was a large rectangular sign with white lettering and an orange background. On the sign were the words, "Drink Pop Cola." I am told that it was a general store that sold dry and canned goods, fabric and sewing essentials, coal oil for lamps, non-electric lamps and chimneys, powdered laundry detergent, soft drinks, snuff, and hard candy. Inside the building were a couple of glass-covered display counters and wooden barrels that had held dry goods like beans, rice, cookies, and crackers.

Behind the store was a large tobacco barn, smoke house, corn crib, and a hog pen. I remember going with my brother to watch Cousin Bubba slop the hogs. It was fun listening to the sounds the hogs made as they doggishly slurped up the food. Cousin Bubba was a kind, friendly man who laughed easily. Unmarried, he was in his forties and lived with his widowed mother. He would allow us to follow him around and talk with him as he did his chores. In fact, he seemed delighted to have our company. He would ask us about school and would share stories about his school days with us. We thoroughly loved hearing these stories, even if he had told them to us before. From his stories he was a mischievous child and would get into lots of trouble with his brother, Arthur. Arthur died as a young adult. Even then I sensed that Cousin Bubba found pleasure in remembering the time that he spent with his brother. One of the stories he told was about a time he had done something that displeased the teacher, "Miss Ross." He said that she sent a student outside to get a switch for her to whip him. He said that more than the whipping, he hated being whipped in front of the other students. However, Miss Ross showed no mercy on him. The more he screamed and cried the more she whipped him. He said that finally our grandmother Molly Bowen, who was a few grades ahead of him, slammed a book on the floor and yelled at Miss Ross, "That's enough!" Molly was stout and appeared older than her chronological age. She got out of her seat and approached the teacher, forcibly taking the switch from her. She told the teacher if she dared try to take the switch from her, then the two of them would have to "fight it out." Miss Ross did not want to confront Molly Bowen, at least not in front of the other students. Miss Ross regained her composure and told Cousin Bubba that he could be dismissed to go home, saying to him, "You may be excused." She said to Molly, "I will speak with you after school."

Directly across the road from the store was the house where Cousin Bubba lived with his mother, Emma Hutton Edmondson. Like her deceased husband, Cousin Emma was a remarkable woman. When I came to know her, she was an elderly woman. She was the daughter of early settlers Rev. Will and Althea Hutton. The Huttons were prominent citizens of the community. Cousin Emma often reflected the prominence of her parents. Although she would sometime stutter, she was well-spoken. She was the Sunday School superintendent and pianist at St. John Methodist Church. She also served as a substitute teacher at Promise Land School. The house where they lived was not at all like the other houses that I described earlier. It had at least five sides. It was a large wood-frame structure designed and built by Cousin John Wesley about 1905, shortly after he and Cousin Emma married. It was a two-story building with a front porch that ran from the center of the house's front, then wrapped around to the side of the house. The side section of the porch faced the intersecting road that is known today as the Redden Crossing Road. A swing was on the side section of the porch, which faced what is now the Promise Land Road. A copula tin roof covered the house. The main entrance to the house was located at the end of the front section of the porch. The entrance was not visible until you had climbed the steps to the porch and looked to the left. The door led to a hallway that separated the rooms on the first level of the house. In the hallway facing the entrance was an impressive cuckoo clock. The rooms on the lower level of the house included two bedrooms on the right of the hallway. On the left of the hallway was a parlor. In the parlor there was a piano that Cousin Emma played. Also left of the hallway was a kitchen. Off the kitchen on the left side of the house was a back porch. The dining room was adjacent to the kitchen and the stairwell to the bedrooms upstairs. There was another bedroom off the dining room. Underneath the house in the back was an entrance way with stairs leading to the cellar. In the cellar was where they had gathered items for the store. They also stored vegetables and fruit that had been canned by Cousin Emma. I am told that some of the homemade canned goods may have belonged to store customers who had used them as barter for store goods. Near the entrance to the cellar was a wellhouse that was a free-standing small building that resembled an outdoor toilet except the wood frame was built with slats that crossed each other, allowing one to view inside the small structure. The well itself was as interesting as the building that housed it. It was a small four-foot iron pipe protruding from the ground with an opening about the circumference of a large grapefruit. It was just large enough to allow a long, rusted tin cylinder tube to fit through it to draw the water up. To draw the water, the cylinder tube, which was attached to a rope on a wheel, would be inserted into the protruding pipe until you heard a sinking thud sound from the well. Then you would wait to hear at least two burbles from the tube. The burbling sound was an indicator that the cylinder was filled to its two-gallon capacity. The tube would then be pulled up by turning the wheel on which the tube was attached. When the tube was drawn up from the protruding pipe, it was placed over a bucket, then the lever on the side of the cylinder was to be released to allow the water to flow into the bucket. The water released would be cold but discolored with a brownish tinge from the rusty tube. Despite the discoloration the water was considered safe for drinking, cooking, bathing, washing, and whatever purpose was deemed necessary. Other structures in the backyard were a chicken coop and pen, a smokehouse, an outdoor privy, a garden area, and a grape arbor.

Cousin John Wesley built all the structures on his farm, including his house and store. He built a boxed style house slightly similar to his for his sister-in-law, Josie Gilbert Edmondson, my paternal grandmother. He was also known for building barns in the community. His brother, James, often assisted him in his carpentry work. According to family sources the brothers inherited their carpentry skills from their father Jeff Edmondson. Next to his house was a lane that had been created by wagons and pedestrian travel. There were several homes located along and near the lane. Years later the lane was named in honor of Plummer "Boss" Redden, who lived along the lane and was known to be a frequent pedestrian on the road. The first farm located immediately behind John Wesley Edmondson's farm belonged to USCT veteran Clark Garrett. By the time I was born, Clark Garrett had long been deceased. The last family who I remember living in the house was Pugh and Mary Bea Jackson and their sons Hershell and Leroy. They moved to Indianapolis, Indiana, about 1950. I do not recall anyone living in the house after they moved. The house remained empty for many years. It eventually collapsed to the ground. In the distance, across was a large field and sitting far from the lane was another house. According to my mother this house also belonged to Clark Garrett's farm. My mother said that Garrett's brother John had been the primary resident of this house when she was a child. After the Garrett family had passed away or moved from Promise Land, the property was purchased by a white farmer who used the land for cattle grazing. When I was a child, the house was barely visible due to overgrowth. Mother said she remembers that Clark Garrett's grave was in the front yard of the house with a marker to indicate that he was a member of the USCT in the US Army during the Civil War.

My maternal great-grandfather, Joe Washington Vanleer, owned the neighboring farm to the Garretts. He divided parcels of land between his descendants, and they owned property along the lane. Included on the property is the graveyard where Joe Washington Vanleer, his wife, and most of their children are buried. It is called the Vanleer Cemetery. It is an active cemetery where both my parents and two of my siblings are buried. The cemetery is located just down the lane from the site where Joe Washington Vanleer's primary homesite was established. This was the site inherited by his daughter and my maternal grandmother Farmie Della and her husband George Bowen. Basically, that was the only home that Farmie Della ever knew. It is the home where my mother grew up and the home where I spent most of my life. It held many fond memories for me and my family. Next door to this house was the house that my great-grandmother's younger sister Milley Vanleer Redden had occupied with her husband Plumber "Boss" Redden. Milley died as a young woman, leaving Boss a widower with small children. With the blessings of Milley's parents, Redden remarried and continued to live in the house with his new wife, Georgia "E" Weakley until his death. The lane on which the house was located would eventually bear Redden's name, the "Redden Crossing Road."

The last house along the lane was occupied by a lady I knew as Aunt Sally. I had known her as an independent, elderly, unmarried woman. I was surprised to find that she had actually been married three times. Her name was Sally Edmondson Vanleer Suggs Garrett. She was the daughter of second-generation descendants Jeff and Charlotte Bowen Edmondson. Her first husband was my great-grandmother's brother, Daniel Vanleer. Daniel built the house where she lived just a short distance down the lane from his father's home. Unfortunately, Daniel and Sally's marriage was cut short when he was murdered. After his death, Sally married a man in the community whose name was John Suggs. This marriage ended in divorce after six years. Her last marriage was to John Garrett of the Garrett Farm just up the road from where she lived. She had four children and four grandchildren. However, by the time I came to know her, all three husbands had died and her children and grandchildren—all but one—were adults and lived elsewhere.

I remember Aunt Sally as a petite aging woman who walked with a gait that made her rock from side to side. She would grunt the words "Ah Lawdy," as though saying those words aided in her ambulation. It was something about her that I always found amusing and comical. Her house was the last one along the lane before reaching the State Highway 48 North. We called it "The Highway." Aunt Sally's little house was covered in gray brick siding, with a front porch that ran completely across the house. I can't recall how the house looked inside. I am not sure if I ever went inside. Aunt Sally was usually outside on the porch, breaking beans, hulling peas, or walnuts. She seemed to always be in motion. There was a garden in the rear of the house and there were chickens who would meander from behind the house to the front. The thing I remember most was Aunt Sally physically relocating her outdoor privy independently. That was something that the kids would talk about. We would say "Aunt Sally is moving her toilet again." Her granddaughter Jean, who was in high school, lived with her. I vaguely remember her living there before she moved away to Nashville after graduation. She was a beautiful girl who looked like an *Ebony Magazine* fashion model. We would pass Aunt Sally's house on our way to the highway to watch the cars go by. Other times we were on our way to visit our Uncle James and Aunt Betty Ruth's house near The Highway. They lived with their six children in the house that Cousin John Wesley had built for our grandmother Josie Gilbert Edmondson. Grandma Josie passed away in 1946.

This lane leading to Highway 48 generated almost as much traffic as the Promise Land Road. There was foot traffic from Promise Land residents who would walk to and from the highway to catch a ride to Charlotte or Dickson. There was also automobile traffic. It was a shorter route into the community than the St. Paul Road route for many of the travelers. However, it was a narrow road and only wide enough for one car to pass at a time. It was also not as well maintained by the county road system as was the road that ran through the community. The county would grade the road three to four times a year. Other times the road would wreak havoc for commuters during inclement weather.

There was another roadway that ran east and intersected Promise Land and Redden Crossing Road. This roadway or lane ran between John Wesley Edmondson's Store and a large lot where Cousin John Wesley would host an annual gathering when he was living. Today, the lot is known as the Bowen Lot. In the lot, a marker stands in memory of Nathan Bowen and his descendants buried in a nearby cemetery. This lane had less traffic use than the Redden Crossing Road. It was traveled mostly by pedestrians, wagons, and occasionally by automobiles. It was a sizable lane with paths that branched off from it leading to homes. Just past Cousin John Wesley's barn, there was a bend to the left of the lane where there was a clearing located near the large, wooded lot. This was where my ancestor Nathan Bowen had settled. I remember, during the 1950s two brothers Levi and Robert Britt, third-generation descendants of Nathan Bowen, started to build a house on the lot. For some reason the brothers abandoned the project. It was never finished. In the early 1960s, Levi Britt purchased land from John Thomas Vanleer, the grandson of Joe Washington Vanleer. He built two houses there, one for himself, and another for his daughter, Margaret.

Across the road from the location of Nathan Bowen's home site, the lane forks to the right. This path led to USCT veteran John Nesbitt's house and farm. Continuing further down the lane from the Bowen's place, under the hill was a little rust-colored wood-frame house that had been inhabited by Bowen family descendants. During my lifetime, the house was occupied by Calvin Robertson, his wife Christine, and their four children. Robertson was a descendant of Jeff and Charlotte Bowen Edmondson. The Robertson family migrated to Columbus, Ohio, in the early 1950s. The house remained empty for several years before a white family headed by a man named Wed Gill purchased the home. Gill worked for the Dickson County Road Service. In the 1980s, the County Commissioners named the rural roads in Promise Land. They named this lane "Wed Gill Road." I assume it was named in his honor because he had lived on the lane and had worked for the county roads system. It would have been great if the commissioners had consulted some of the original descendants of the community who were residents of Promise Land at the time. I am sure that they would have recommended that the roadway be named in honor of Nathan Bowen or John Nesbitt, who were early settlers of the community. This roadway stopped at the little red or rust-colored house, which is no longer standing. However, if you walk toward the house and make your way through the woods, you arrive at the home sites of early Promise Land settlers Jerry Robertson and USCT veteran Landin Williams. When I was a child, it was a shortcut to my Aunt Ruby and Uncle Baxter Robertson's house (now the homesite of Bettye Robertson). From the Robertson homesite, you could see the homes of William and Tamar Primm and home of Tamar's grandparents, John and Elvie Cunningham. Neither of these homes remain. The access to the properties were paths leading from the White Oak Flat Road, which is now the Promise Land Road.

On return to the main artery of Promise Land and the Redden Crossing Road continuing north, the next building on the left is the historic Promise Land School building. Th Promise Land School opened about 1880. It served as a school until 1956. From the time it was built, in addition to serving as a school, it served as a special events and meeting center. Events included dinners, talent programs, dances, plays, and occasions requiring the space and facilities that the building offered. On the right side of the road adjacent to the school is property believed to have been settled by USCT veteran Edward Vanleer. I remember the youngest daughter of Edward Vanleer living in a small house there. Her name was Susie Vanleer, known to me as "Cousin Susie." Further down from Cousin Susie's house was the home of her daughter, Lizzie. Lizzie lived there with her husband Theodore Edmondson and their children. Theodore happened to have been my father's brother. He was the son of James Edmondson and my grandmother, Josie Gilbert Edmondson. Like his father, Uncle Theodore was a carpenter. He built the homes where his mother-in-law lived and where he and his family lived. Across from his house, on the left side of the road was the St. John Methodist Episcopal Church.

Next door to the church was a large white house that had belonged to Ernest Nesbitt, the oldest son of John Nesbitt. The home had also housed a second general store for the community. The store was located in front of the house. According to my older sister Della Bryant, the store was in operation until about 1943. I only remember the house and residents vaguely. The occupants moved away to Columbus, Ohio, when I was very young. I recall the vacant building, with its close proximity to the church. The children would often venture into the premises surrounding the house. We would be warned by adults to be cautious of playing in the vicinity of the house because of the old cellar that was underneath the house. Located on the same side, farther down the road stood a little wood-frame house that had turned black from the years and elements. I remember it was also vacant. It had been occupied by another son of John Nesbitt. He was Charley Nesbitt, the second to the youngest of John Nesbitt's children. He lived there with his wife whose name was also Charlie. I would hear my older siblings refer to them as "Mr. Charley and Miss Charlie." They had moved to Nashville sometime during the early 1940s. My sisters Bobbye and Beverly would practice good posture by walking like Miss Charlie. They said that Miss Charlie would walk to the spring to wash clothes. She would place a bundle of clothing on her head and carry two buckets of water in each hand as she walked to the spring. They were convinced that the key to balancing the bundle on the head was a way to gain perfect posture. Not far from the Charley Nesbitt's house was a newer house. It was a small box-shaped house with a tin roof that was set high off the ground. According to my deceased cousin, James Edmondson, this house was built in 1923 by his father, my Uncle Theodore. The house had been built for a newly married couple in the community named Beasley and Beatrice Cunningham. The couple lived in the house only a few years before moving to Cleveland, Ohio. After they moved, another family in the community moved into the house. They were Hersey and Hattie Redden Robertson and their children. I don't remember anyone ever living in the house after the Robertsons, who relocated to Charlotte. They later moved back to Promise Land about 1956. Meanwhile the little box-shaped house stayed empty and remains so today. It is the oldest house in the Promise Land Community.

Within close proximity of that little house is a community landmark known as the "Hickory Flat." It was called the Hickory Flat because a large hickory tree was at the location. The hickory tree has long been gone, but for original Promise Land residents and former residents the landmark designation is well remembered. People from the community would say things like "I'll meet you at the Hickory Flat" or "my car broke down at the Hickory Flat." The road forked at the landmark. It veered right and became unofficially known as "White Oak Flat Road." There was no white oak tree at this junction. However, it led to a community much further away known as White Oak Flat. The continuing northward stretch of the road was the Promise Land Road until it ended at Staton Road in Cumberland Furnace. About a quarter of a mile from the Hickory Flat was an area known as Gilbert Town. Gilbert Town was named after my paternal great-grandfather William Gilbert and his wife Priscilla who settled in the area in 1878. The area encompassed about fifty-nine and a half acres of land located on both sides of Promise Land Road. His home was located on the left side of the front-facing road. The majority of the Gilbert Town acreage was behind the homestead and through the woods leading to Highway 48 North. The Gilbert Cemetery is located in the area. When I was a child, there was little left of this once popular community gathering place. The cemetery was still there and active during my childhood. The last person to be buried there was my dad's sister Ruby Robertson, who was buried there in 1974. The old house where my father and some of his siblings were born was occupied at that time by a peculiar white couple, Bud Hooper and his companion, Miss Myatt. As a child they seemed to me to exhibit odd behavior. They did not have an automobile. They would travel by foot walking along Promise Land Road to Charlotte. Bud, dressed in overalls, with his head bent, would walk several feet ahead of Miss Myatt. I never saw them walking together or conversing with each other. Next door to the house that they lived in was an old vacant general store. I am told that the store served the Promise Land community. An old ledger from the store was donated to the Promise Land Museum by a descendant of the Hoopers a few years ago. South of the store was a path that led into the woods to a clearing where a house had once stood. The house had belonged to William Gilbert's daughter, Fannie "Toad" Gilbert Hampton. Aunt Toad had been the last survivor who carried the Gilbert name. Further down the lane from the clearing was a house built in the mid-1950s. It was the home of Hersey and Hattie Robertson. Hattie Redden Robertson was the daughter of William and Priscilla Gilbert's nephew,

Ed Redden. Cousin Ed had been raised by my great-grandparents from early childhood. He was left an orphan when both his parents, Charles and Rachel Redden, died. His father was the brother of Priscilla. Cousin Ed inherited land from William and Priscilla on which he farmed, built a house, and raised his family. His house was located on the right of Promise Land Road going north to Cumberland Furnace.

As a child, I remember Cousin Ed living in this house with his wife Annie Stringfellow Redden. His wife died and left him living alone on his farm. Cousin Annie was buried in the Gilbert Cemetery. When Cousin Ed's daughter's family moved back to Promise Land, I am sure that he was pleased. He moved into the home with them. My father looked very much like Cousin Ed. Both of them were short in stature, standing about five feet seven. I really saw the resemblance as my father began to age. Their amenable personalities were also similar. Both of them enjoyed making others laugh. Cousin Ed had a large hematoma located on the left of his forehead. He was known for walking the roads and paths in the community. As he aged, he started to show signs of dementia and his walking became more like wandering about the community day and night. I am sure many times his daughter did not know where he was. But in this community, she did not have to worry. People in the community would look out for him. He was able to live out his life in a place surrounded by loved ones. He died about 1962 and was buried next to Cousin Annie. Cousin Ed Redden's original house was the last house that I remembered going north on Promise Land Road. There were other homes that were further north on Promise Land Road that existed before my time. This section of the original Clarksville Stage Road/Promise Land Road was renamed by the county in the 1980s as Harris Hollow Road. Today, Promise Land Road has been re-routed by the county to go right at the "Hickory Flat" bend. It replaces what was once called White Oak Flat Road and now extends to Tennessee State Highway 49 West.

3

ON THE BANKS OF THE JORDAN

THE SOUTHERN CONFEDERACY was devastated by the war. Although the major cities in the Volunteer State escaped the devastation experienced by Richmond, Columbia, and Atlanta, many rural farms and other areas lay in ruins as a result of Tennessee's decision to go to war in 1861. Cumberland Furnace, unlike many ironworks in Middle Tennessee, was not destroyed by Union forces during the war. Nonetheless, it ceased operations from 1862 until the war's end.

For the African Americans who remained there during the duration of the war, Cumberland Furnace was a place that bristled with excitement and uncertainty. Confederate forces moved in and around Charlotte for the duration of the war as Union forces established headquarters in and near the homes of furnace workers' enslavers. The presence of these northern soldiers cultivated fears in the landowners that their property might be destroyed and the men and women whom they had forced to work on their farms, homes, and industrial sites for generations might be freed. While it is almost impossible to determine how many African Americans self-emancipated during the war, it is likely that they heard and looked forward to the demise of slavery as the war progressed. Always acute observers of their surroundings and enslavers, they witnessed and experienced the physical and psychological impact of the war and when the opportunity presented itself, men like Promise Land Civil War veterans John and Arch Nesbitt, Clark Garrett, and Landy Williams actively participated in the destruction of slavery and ushering in the long-awaited Year of Jubilee.

When the generational curse of slavery was finally broken in 1865, there were fewer African Americans living in Dickson County than there were when the war started. According to the 1860 US Census, there were 2,201 free and enslaved African Americans living in the county on the eve of the Civil War. After the Confederacy's defeat, that number had declined by almost 25 percent. While the precise cause of this decrease remains a mystery, there are a few possible facts that can assist in our understanding of this post–Civil War reality. First, it is very likely that some enslaved people used the war as an opportunity to escape. With the disintegration of the agricultural and industrial plantation system and weakening of the formal and informal controls of Black mobility, running away or toward Union lines provided opportunities for freedom during the war. Additionally, more soldiers died from diseases such as dysentery, cholera, pneumonia, infection, and other illnesses than on the battlefield. With troop movement becoming a common feature of life in Cumberland Furnace, Charlotte, and the county, civilian casualties from disease due to the proximity to soldiers may also account for the decrease.

When the war ended in 1865, African Americans who had survived the physical and mental violence needed to maintain slavery in Dickson County began to act upon their own notions of freedom. Among the things they sought to do immediately included locating and reconnecting with families that had been sold away during the antebellum period. The memories of friends and loved ones regarding the sale of one hundred and forty of their friends and family formerly enslaved by Montgomery Bell in 1856 would still be fresh in their minds, and emancipation provided an opportunity to reunite with the understanding that they could not be sold again. Others sought to legalize their marriages as the unions of enslaved men and women were not recognized by law. The creation of independent churches often quickly followed news of emancipation, with Baptist and Methodist denominations enjoying the most support among the recently freed men and women. The African Methodist Episcopal Church, founded in Philadelphia in 1816, also had a significant presence in Dickson County. A second tangible manifestation of freedom that occurred in the county was the creation of schools. One such example was a school that was operated by the Freedmen's Aid Society of the Methodist Episcopal Church. The primary school could boast having fifteen male and thirty female students and being supported by the freedmen community. In her report to the Freedmen's Bureau, the school's teacher, Annie Butler—an African American woman who exposed this group of students to the rudiments of reading, writing, math, and geography—pointed out the need for a different schoolhouse, observing that a nearby church might be used for school, "but we have no way to have fire."

The church and schools would continue to experience a symbiotic relationship as institutions in Promise Land with many of the churches hosting schools during the day and Sabbath Schools on Sunday. Like many of America's four million formerly enslaved African Americans who lived to see the abolition of slavery in 1865, residents who lived in and around the area that would become known as Promise Land believed that an education was needed to enjoy a full measure of freedom. As was the case during slavery, the churches that emerged in the area continued to serve as repositories of their African history and culture before their ancestors arrived in America in chains, and their schools became spaces where they could become equipped with the skills necessary to enjoy a full measure of freedom and learn life skills that would help them negotiate the horrors of Jim Crow. The church and school in Promise Land stand as memorials to these notions of freedom and monuments to their passage from enslaved to freed persons, and later as block, wood, and asphalt memorials to their negotiation through the period known as Jim Crow in America. They would become spaces that would become as symbolic of their freedom and independence as the acres of land its first settlers purchased.

It appears that it was newly emancipated people who settled gradually in the community that would become Promise Land. In an effort to preserve a system of servitude for Black laborers by the white establishment, work contracts were executed. We found labor contracts that were hastily drawn up to include some of the formerly enslaved families who settled in Promise Land. These contracts often did not represent the formerly enslaved in a favorable way. Deed records show the land purchase of the initial settlers took place between 1868 to 1882. They purchased land from white landowners. Although previously owned, the property purchased was not cultivated and unused. Likely the prior owners had obtained the land through land grants or other opportunities, which enabled them to have an excessive amount and the use of it was not urgent. The properties were remotely located and inaccessible by developed roads. There were also no large water sources in proximity to the properties such as rivers, lakes, or creeks for livestock and for the creation of fertile soil for planting. These are just some speculations of why the land was not in use and was therefore available for the newly freed people.

For the new owners, I can only imagine the treasure it was to them.

The properties gave the new occupants an opportunity to re-establish their lives and reconnect with family with whom they had been separated during slavery. This had to be a mixture of emotions including ambivalence, fear, uncertainty, doubt, excitement, joy, and so many more for them. Judging from the oral history and subsequent behavior of descendants, faith in God was a guiding and stabilizing force in the transition. Faith has always been a source of strength, perseverance, and fortitude for the people of Promise Land. There were some ministers of the Gospel among the settlers. I'm told that my second great-grandfather, Nathan Bowen, was a minister of the gospel. Several of his sons followed suit. Even today there are descendants who have followed the occupational path of divinity leadership. Faith was crucial in pursuing the life ahead for the early settlers—considering the choices, decisions, and work required. It is natural that establishing a place for collective worship was among the priorities. Not only was land cleared for homes, but it was also cleared for communal worship services. Worship services were held outdoors and sometimes in temporary shelters made from brush and vines. These shelters were known as brush harbor churches. Brush harbors and worship services in homes sufficed until permanent buildings were erected. Community churches will be discussed in more depth in other chapters.

Much of the redistributed land was in heavily wooded areas. The clearing of this land was obviously an enormous job that required determination and steadfastness to complete. It also required the establishment of bonds and unity between the settlers. Many of the settlers were familiar with each other, as they had been enslaved together or in proximity on farms and at the furnace. Bonds of unity and support were reinforced easily by shared commonalities, including kinship, experiences, hopes, and dreams. The bonded relationship of the early settlers remained evident in the community long after the original settlers ceased existence. As a child I remember how the community worked together on projects, whether it was harvesting tobacco, killing hogs, canning, or quilting. Neighbors would come and help, not expecting compensation, which was just what they expected of each other. The same was true in the case of illness or other calamities. The neighbors were there to prepare meals, care for children, do laundry, fetch water, assure that there was adequate wood supply for heating or cooking, and other types of assistance.

Based on census records and other archival reports, it appears that a village had emerged within a brief period. The 1870 Census was the first time Black households were documented in sizable numbers. Prior census records may have reported some freed Black families or listed Black residents in white households as servants. There are forty-two families recorded in the 1870 Census. This did not include all the families, however. I know for certain that my maternal ancestors were not included. By contrast I found a deed record that put them in the area by 1868. It is likely that many factors contributed to missing or inaccurate census data during that period in history. Other records provide an accounting of the community's population. By the beginning of the twentieth century, the community's population had reached its peak. A 1904 *Enumeration of Scholastic Population* report by the Dickson County School System showed that ninety-two students were enrolled at Promise Land School. The students represented thirty-three households in the community.

There were events that took place in Promise Land that drew people from other communities. One recorded event was reported in the *Nashville Globe* in January 1913. The news article reports that Promise Land celebrated its fifteenth annual event in recognition of the issuance of the Emancipation Proclamation. From the article it appears that the event was a collaboration between Promise Land's St. John Methodist Episcopal Church and the Stone Chapel Methodist Episcopal Church in Cumberland Furnace. During the day of January 1, 1913, Promise Land residents joined their fellow Methodist Episcopal Church in Cumberland Furnace for worship services and a program. Music was provided by "the Bradley Band" and a reading was presented by Nonie (Bradley) Stansfield, who had been a resident of Cumberland Furnace but at that time was a student at Walden University in Nashville. The guest speaker was Nonie Stansfield's husband Rev. J. Stanfield. The reporter quoted Rev. Stansfield saying, "with a retrospective view, he caught slavery and with his eloquence of speech and knowledge of history caused the thinkers to take an introspective view of self, and in a prospective way looking forward and asking what has God wrought?"

That evening the events were shifted to St. John at Promise Land; the program consisted of music by Charley Nesbitt, son of USCT veteran John Nesbitt, and "Messrs." Braden and Hutton. A selected reading was presented by Ernest E. Nesbitt, schoolmaster at Promise Land School and the eldest son of John Nesbitt. Mrs. Rosetta Martin, Mrs. Lula Jackson, and Miss Molly Bowen presented essays. My grandmother, Molly Bowen, was thirteen years old at the time of this event. The names of the other presenters are familiar to me as former residents of the Promise Land community who I had heard others speak of. The keynote speakers included a community original settler, Rev. William Hutton, followed by the church pastor Rev. William T. C. Travis. The title of Rev. Travis speech was "The Momentous Occasion."

Rev. Travis was also the pastor at Stone Chapel. The Nashville area Methodist Conference continued the practice of assigning pastors to share pastoral responsibilities between the two congregations, St. John and Stone Chapel churches, even after the closing of St. John in 1992. The article went on to report that throughout the day, thirty-eight people pledged to give $1 during the year (1913) to the Freedmen's Aid as a "thanks offering." The reporter gave grateful recognition to Rev. Travis, writing, "Too much cannot be said of our pastor, Wm. T.C. Tavis, for carrying out the plans as laid down in our great church; he is a man not of the past but of today. We invoke God's blessings on him."

The Nashville Globe, a Black-owned and operated newspaper founded in 1906, served Nashville and its outlying area. The reporter of the article covered stories of African American people and events in the Dickson County area. He placed an emphasis on stories related to the people of the Cumberland Furnace and Promise Land communities, which lead me to believe that he may have been from one of these communities. Stories from old newspaper articles provide an excellent glimpse into life as it was for Black people of this area. Such documented stories combined with oral accounts and the iconic remnants of the community—the history is easily unfolded.

The backdrop of this amazing event gives impetus to take a closer look at the earlier settlers. Who were they? They were intelligent and capable of planning and executing an inspiring event. As we examine them closer, we will review the men who served with the USCT. By their considerable number among the population, I see them as a foundation of the community. Although their settlement in the community appears to have created little fanfare or recognition, their contribution to making the transition from bondage to freedom is worthy of recognition, even if it is belated. Considering the time and circumstances of the time of settlement, it is understandable why the event flew under the radar. To acknowledge the success of achieving liberty would have been an invitation for greater backlash against the newly emancipated people. Due to modesty around the heroic contributions made by these Civil War veterans, many went to their graves without them being acknowledged for their gallantry. They established homes in the community, raised their families, maintained sources of sustainment, lived out their lives quietly, and died with the knowledge of the USCT service known only to themselves, their families, and perhaps a few others. Generations passed without their identity being disclosed. Growing up in the community, I never heard of the USCT or their service to the Civil War efforts. This was a part of US history that was systematically disregarded. There were no celebrations or school lessons regarding the African American contributions to the war. This void in study was absent from my elementary, high school, and college curriculum. I first learned of the USCT in 1976. At that time, I was twenty-nine years old and working as a docent at the Ford's Theatre, the site where Abraham Lincoln was assassinated.

I first heard of two early settlers who had served in the Civil War from my cousin, Dr. Sokoto Fulani (a.k.a. Charles Nesbitt), who was researching his genealogy. Dr. Fulani, who was a faculty member in the Black Studies department at the Ohio State University, began research on his family's history in 1972. Although as a child he had heard talk in the family that his great-grandfather John Nesbitt was involved in the Civil War, to what extent, he was unaware. He remembered hearing his grandfather say something like, "My daddy fit for our freedom." Unfortunately, as a child he failed to explore the meaning behind his grandfather's musings. There were other indicators that could have revealed more with little more exploration but that did not happen. For example, Dr. Fulani's family of origin lived in the house once owned by his great-grandfather, where an old trunk belonging to him was stored in a closet. He and his siblings were warned by their mother, "Don't mess with that trunk. Papa's papers are in there." He suspects now that the trunk may have contained his great-grandfather's USCT uniform as well as related documents. Unfortunately, the trunk was left behind when the family moved to Columbus, Ohio, in 1952. The house remained empty and mysteriously caught fire and burned down in the 1970s.

In the process of data collection, Dr. Fulani interviewed a descendant of John and Arch Nesbitt's enslaver, J. P. Nesbitt. The descendant, however, misinformed him by stating that the two brothers went to the war as body servants to their enslaver who was with the Confederate army. Later in a conversation with his father, Ernest, and Ernest's father, Charley Nesbitt, Fulani shared what he had been told by J. P.'s descendants. He recalled that his grandfather, who he called "Papa Charley," vehemently disagreed with what he had been told. Papa Charley, the eleventh child born to John and Ellen Nesbitt, was enraged by the claim that his father was a "body servant," otherwise an attendant who accompanied his enslaver, a member of the Confederate army, to the war and returned to the farm with him when he was discharged due to injuries. Fulani recalled him shouting, "T'ain't so, t'ain't so!" Once again, he heard the familiar declaration, "My Daddy fit [fought] for our freedom!" A few years later, on acquisition of his great-grandfather's military records from the National Archives, Fulani discovered what his Papa Charley had said was true. My mother, who was nearly seventy years old at that time, shared that growing up, she had known something about the Nesbitt brothers serving in the Civil War from her grandfather and others. Her grandfather George Bowen was a close friend of John's eldest son, Ernest, who was the namesake of Fulani's father. She also recalled that she heard of another man who in the community who had fought in the Civil War. His name was Clark Garrett.

Over the years, I've heard from descendants of others who they believed "may have been Civil War veterans." With the aid of Ancestry.com and FamilySearch records we have documented proof of some of these Promise Land early settlers. They include John and Arch Nesbitt, Landin Williams, Ed Vanleer, Ransom Vanleer, and Alfred Grimes. There may be others who we have not discovered yet. The following stories and profiles of these men has been gleaned from records and oral recollections. During their lives, there was little recognition given to their heroic and honorable military services. They certainly were not recognized by their military rank as civilians. Out of respect and honor of each of them, I will refer to them by their rank on discharge in each of their profiles.

4

SOLDIERS' STORIES

TENNESSEE APPROVED ITS ORDINANCE of Secession on June 8, 1861, and twenty days later, the Tennessee State General Assembly—after passing acts expelling emancipated Black Tennesseans from the state and the country and considering the enslavement of manumitted persons who did not leave the state during the previous decades—passed the first act in the country to draft free Black men for military service. The irony of the news of them being drafted into military service would have been unavoidable for the more than seven thousand free Black residents in the Volunteer State as most of their lived experiences during the 1850s were being treated as though enslaved by the communities in which they lived. Their roles would be severely limited in the Confederate war effort. They were not called upon to bear arms for the Confederacy, and they would not be issued Springfield Rifles or other firearms. In a bill called An Act for the Relief of Volunteers, the Tennessee General Assembly decreed that all "such free persons of color shall be required to do all such menial service for the relief of the volunteers as is incident to camp life, and necessary to the efficiency of the service, and of which they are capable of performing."[1]

The position of the Union in the war was clear. Although abolitionists such as Frederick Douglass, Frances Ellen Watkins Harper, and others saw this war as one of liberation, they were in the minority when the war began. In an August 1862 reply to Horace Greeley, editor of the *New York Tribune* and critic of his policy regarding emancipation, Abraham Lincoln made the goal of the war clear when he stated,

> My paramount object in this struggle is to save the Union and is not either to save or destroy Slavery. If I could save the Union without freeing any slave, I would do it, and if I could save it by freeing all the slaves, I would do it, and if I could save it by freeing some and leaving others alone, I would also do that. What I do about Slavery and the colored race, I do because I believe it helps to save this Union, and what I forbear, I forbear because I do not believe it would help to save the Union.[2]

On the other hand, the Confederacy was clear that its goals were to preserve its institutions, the most important being the enslavement of African Americans. A month after President Lincoln made his position on slavery clear to Horace Greeley, the Confederate Congress introduced legislation that called for the return to their enslavers or public sale of any African Americans found bearing arms against the Confederacy and the execution of officers leading them into battle.[3]

A little more than one hundred days later, President Lincoln would sign the Emancipation Proclamation, a wartime act that freed enslaved African Americans living in areas that were still in open rebellion against the Union. Although the act was not enforceable when signed on January 1, 1863, the proclamation linked the destruction of slavery with Union victory. Lincoln's statement toward the end of the proclamation would have a dramatic effect on the men who would establish Promise Land, as it provided an opportunity for them to enlist and fight for their freedom. In the Emancipation Proclamation, Lincoln stated, "And I further declare and make known, that such persons of suitable condition, will be received into the armed service of the United States to garrison forts, positions, stations, and other places, and to man vessels of all sorts in said service."[4] John and Arch Nesbitt, Clark Garrett, Landin Williams, and Ed Vanleer heeded this call, joining the 140,000 African American men the Union recruited from slave states. The men who enlisted in USCT units suffered heavy casualties. According to most recent estimates, 2,751 were killed in combat and 65,000 were missing or killed by disease, the most frequent way soldiers met their deaths during the Civil War.[5]

The Confederacy found the sight of these troops and their formerly enslaved supporting the Union intolerable as they represented their worst fears about the people in their midst they had held in chains, people whom they had convinced themselves were loyal. Most prominent among these was the fear that they would one day face violent retribution from the Africans and their descendants whom they compelled to labor for them in the South. In the years preceding the war, several rumors circulated about slave rebellions in Dover and Clarksville that involved enslaved men and women who worked in the ironworks, plots and conspiracies that resulted in mass executions of suspected conspirators.[6] The Emancipation Proclamation made the fears not only possible but probable.

Four days after Lincoln signed the Emancipation Proclamation, the president of the Confederacy, Jefferson Davis, issued a statement that made their policy clear on how they would address the issue of USCT and free Black people living in the Confederacy. In his response Davis proclaimed, "On and after February 22, 1863, all free negroes within the limits of the Southern Confederacy shall be placed on the slave status, and be deemed to be chattels, they and their issue forever." Further, Davis declared that all free Black persons taken prisoner from the non-slave-owning states would be enslaved ipso facto, transforming the Confederate army into an instrument that could be used to increase the numbers of enslaved people in the country. Davis concludes his address by justifying this action:

> In view of these facts, and conscientiously believing that the proper condition of the negro is slavery, or a complete subjection to the white man, and entertaining the belief that the day is not distant when the old Union will be restored with slavery nationally declared to be the proper condition of all of African descent, and in view of the future harmony and progress of all the States of America, I have been induced to issue this address, so that there may be no misunderstanding in the future.[7]

The grim fact for the Black men that put on the blue uniforms of the Union was that the war was a fight for their freedom. There was no going back to the way things were for the Nesbitt brothers, Clark Garrett, Landin Williams, and Ed Vanleer and the other Black soldiers in Tennessee. As the year progressed and word reached the new recruits of the massacre of Black soldiers after they surrendered at Fort Pillow, they realized that the Confederacy had raised a "Black Flag," meaning no quarter would be given when it came to their participation in the war. They were going to emancipate themselves and their families on the battlefield or die trying. By the time the war ended in April 1865, the men of Promise Land served in areas throughout Middle Tennessee, including the Battle of Nashville where they were a part of efforts that kept the capital city out of Confederate hands.

On June 10, 1865, the *Christian Recorder* announced, "The last remnant of the rebel military power has disappeared, and the old flag floats every where from Maine to the Rio Grande."[8] This statement signaled an official end to the war and the dawning of what Lincoln described in his Gettysburg Address as a new birth of freedom for America, one that would be inclusive of the formerly enslaved descendants of Africans whose uncompensated labor served as the foundation for the economic growth of the nation. The nation would enter a period known as Reconstruction, an effort to reshape the economic, social, and political realities for a country that had been rent by war.

Tennessee's rapid fall to Union forces during the Civil War led to it being the earliest state to begin Reconstruction. In March 1862, Lincoln issued his "Ten Percent Plan," a very lenient and controversial policy that allowed Southern states to rejoin the Union once 10 percent of the electorate who voted in the election of 1860 swore an oath of allegiance to the Union. The plan and the Wade-Davis Bill—the congressional Reconstruction plan that followed—had a glaring weakness because they did not define the status of the four million African Americans living in the South. At the war's end, Tennessee, like many of its sister states in the Confederacy, took on a paradoxical stance in determining the status of its Freedpersons. By February 1867, the state had enfranchised more than forty thousand men; African Americans living in Tennessee could enjoy the benefits of citizenship. This was remarkable because it predated the ratification of the Fourteenth and Fifteenth amendments to the US Constitution that defined citizenship and gave Black men the right to vote.[9]

Nonetheless, these progressive changes occurred within a dark period in the history of the Volunteer State as many of the state's more than nine hundred thousand residents refused to see African American as equals, launching a counterrevolution that would result in their former enslaved population occupying a status as close to slavery as possible. Indeed, Tennessee began its retreat from Reconstruction only months after the artillery shells from the battlefield had been silenced.

According to local tradition, the six men who founded the Ku Klux Klan created the organization in Pulaski, Tennessee, at the law offices of Judge Thomas Jones on December 24, 1865.[10] Fancying themselves to be a social order when created, the Ku Klux Klan evolved to using acts of violence and terror to prevent freed persons from enjoying their new rights, especially the newly acquired right to vote. Violence was most pervasive in places where African Americans made up significant percentages of the population, such as Maury, Giles, Williamson, Davidson, and Rutherford Counties. Nonetheless word of increasing violence and outrages committed against African Americans and their allies would have undoubtedly made its way to nearby Dickson County. Perhaps the easiest road to take for many of the rural community's residents would have been to migrate to Nashville, a place that still had a significant military presence and could provide some security. Reconstruction in Tennessee ended shortly after the men who fought in the USCT returned to the area. Two years after the Tennessee General Assembly granted Black men the right to vote, they undermined this freedom with the implementation of a poll tax. A year later residents of the state elected John C. Brown, a known leader of the Ku Klux Klan as governor of the State of Tennessee. Brown's election heralded the end of Reconstruction in the Volunteer State.

Throughout this period of hope, despair, and uncertainty, certain beliefs remained constant for the discharged soldiers that would call the area home. They retained their desire to acquire land as many of them seemed to equate land with liberty, and they—with the assistance of the Freedmen's Bureau—constructed the two most important institutions of the post–Civil War period for them and their families: independent Black churches and schools. Land, churches, and schools would become the blessings and foundation upon which their new community was built. In many ways, they would see and treat this area as a space that had been divinely prepared for them.

PRIVATE JOHN NESBITT, USCT OF THE US ARMY

Since John Nesbitt was the first veteran of the United States Army's United States Colored Troop, I will begin with his story.

John Nesbitt was enslaved at a grist mill/farm owned by Allen Nesbitt. The mill was located on Barton's Creek, which is located between Charlotte and Cumberland Furnace in Dickson County, Tennessee. On his military record, Pvt. Nesbitt's occupation is listed as a miller. Nesbitt was twenty years old when he escaped the mill to Paducah, Kentucky, where he enlisted with the US Army's USCT. On his enlistment form he is described as five feet seven and a half inches in height. His complexion is reported as "yellow" and his hair and eyes as black. He enlisted on October 25, 1863. He was assigned to Company H.4 and Regiment Heavy Artillery. His chief military duty was the maintenance, cleaning, and operation of large ammunitions, including cannons. This assignment led to the development of injuries that would prove to affect his health status and ability to be gainfully employed later in life. He was honorably discharged from his station in Arkansas on February 25, 1866, with the rank of private.

According to legend, John made his way back to Tennessee. The story holds that during his enslavement he encountered a girl named Ellen Clemons who was also enslaved at a neighboring farm. Although they were barely acquainted, he had developed a fondness for her. One day he learned that Ellen had been given to her enslaver's daughter, who had also been her former playmate, as a wedding gift. She moved away with her new mistress to a place where she would become her personal servant. Nesbitt was heartbroken by the fate of Ellen and vowed that he would someday escape the system of bondage. Once he had gained his freedom, he would then find Ellen and free her also to become his wife. This story was family folklore. Ellen was my maternal great-grandmother's sister. Ellen was my mother's great-aunt, whom as a child she got to know. To my mother this was a love story that she would enjoy telling throughout her life.

The story continues that Pvt. Nesbitt was on a mission when he returned home. The mission was to reunite with Ellen and marry her. So, one of the things he did soon after discharge was to go to the farm of his former enslaver. Allen Nesbitt had also served in the Civil War with the Confederate army and was discharged with the rank of Colonel. Pvt. Nesbitt was certain that Col. Nesbitt would be aware of Ellen's whereabouts. Although they had served on different sides of the war and John had escaped slavery from his farm, Col. Nesbitt was amicable and happy to see Pvt. Nesbitt. I imagine that they shared pleasantries, but that Pvt. Nesbitt did not waste any time inquiring about Ellen. He told him that she was in Dover, Tennessee, a town about forty-four miles northwest of Cumberland Furnace. He also told him that Ellen and her mistress had fallen upon hard times during the war. Her mistress's husband had been killed during the Battle of Fort Donelson, and they wanted to return to Barton's Creek to their families. He agreed to let John use a pair of his horses and buggy to go to Dover to get the two women and bring them home. When Pvt. Nesbitt went to Col. Nesbitt's home to return the horses and buggy, he asked the Colonel, who was a Justice of Peace, to perform their marriage nuptials. The Colonel agreed to honor his request. After getting settled, Pvt. Nesbitt and Ellen returned to the Colonel's farm on February 26, 1868, and were married.

Pvt. Nesbitt was informed that he could receive assistance from the Freedmen's Bureau in finding a home for him and his bride. The Bureau referred them to an area where they had been helping other formerly enslaved people to settle. This was land that the Bureau had access to through the Freedmen's Bureau Act of 1866. The adult citizen applying for the property agreed to pay a minimal filing fee and cultivate the land for a home and farming. After five years living on the property, the claimant could secure a deed for the property. John and Ellen settled on a plot that was near where the St. John Methodist Church building is now located.

As an emancipated woman, Ellen had desires of her own. She wanted to ensure that the other newly emancipated people of the community would become literate. During her childhood, she had been given special privileges in the home of her owner. She had been allowed to live in the big house as a playmate of their child, who was only two years older than her. Her enslaver's daughter attended school and wanted to share that experience with Ellen. She started sharing her books and slate with Ellen, teaching her the rudiments of reading, spelling, writing, and arithmetic. This was a well-kept secret between the two girls, as it was illegal for the enslaved to receive educational instruction. When the daughter became engaged to marry, Ellen was given to her as a wedding gift. The couple were married and moved to Dover, Tennessee, where the groom had employment. Ellen moved with them, and the relationship remained the same between the two girls as it had been prior to the marriage. The plan was that Ellen would become the couple's nanny when children were born. However, the daughter was never conceived, which allowed her and Ellen to spend a lot of time together, as her husband was a practicing attorney and was away from home often. When the war broke out, he enlisted with the Confederate army. Ellen and her mistress would write letters and mail them to their family at Barton's Creek.

After emancipation and settling in the new village, Ellen decided that she wanted to exercise her new freedom to make choices. She wanted to help adults and children in her community learn to read, write, and calculate. Pvt. Nesbitt supported her decision. With the aid of other literate members of the village, they begin to hold classes in their small home.

Meanwhile, Pvt. Nesbitt found that he was having difficulty trying to do chores, like cultivating his property. He would easily tire and become short of breath. During medical consultation he was told that he had a severe respiratory disease from inhaling harmful smoke from the ammunition during his military service. He also had scarring on his lungs and visible external scars on his chest from burns sustained from the backfiring of the cannons. He was encouraged by the doctor that he consulted to apply to the Department of Army for disability compensation. This turned out to be an arduous task. It took twelve years of back and forth with the Department of Army before he was finally awarded compensation. Copies of this process were on file in the National Archives. The file was so large that it appeared as a life novel. The last document was filed by his doctor and a friend who had also been enslaved at Barton's Creek. His name was McPherson Lanier. Lanier attested that he had known Nesbitt "since childhood and during the time before he entered the war, he never suffered from any of the maladies that he now has."[11] Lanier also served with the USCT. He moved to a Black settlement in the city of Charlotte known as Cedar Grove and became a headmaster at the Cedar Grove Elementary School for Black students in the late nineteenth to early twentieth century.

Pvt. Nesbitt received his compensation retroactively from the time he was discharged in 1880. This compensation enabled Pvt. Nesbitt to purchase his first 172 acres of land in the community on May 14, 1880, from a white landowner and farmer named W. H. Hooper. From this tract he donated a portion of land for a school. The school, a wood-frame building, was built by the men in the community. At first it was called the Nesbitt School. It served as a literacy training school for children and adults. It was administered by the Nesbitts and others in the church leadership. The community was responsible for providing supplies for the school. Mrs. Nesbitt continued to teach intermittently at the school while sharing the responsibilities with other capable people in the community. In 1889, the Nesbitts along with the community leaders decided that they would deed the school to the Dickson County School System. It was renamed the Promise Land Elementary School and served students aged five to twenty-one years of age. This decision allowed the transference of administrative and fiscal responsibility to the county. On May 19, 1899, the Nesbitts purchased another tract of land from C. C. Collier, a white landowner, and built what at that time was a state-of-the-art farmhouse complete with a well and nearby spring. It was a beautiful home surrounded by apple and plum orchards. It was a large farm where tobacco and corn were raised along with livestock including hogs, mules, horses, chickens, and cattle. Though farming diminished over the years, the house remained occupied by descendants. The last of the descendants occupied the house until they moved away in 1952.

As a child I visited the house often to play with my cousins, "Poodle" (a childhood nickname for Sokoto Fulani) and his sister, Nancy. Poodle and Nancy were the great-grandchildren of John Nesbitt. They lived in the house with their parents, Ernest and Gracie Nesbitt, sisters Minnie and Mary, and brothers Lemuel and Bob. I thought that the house was the grandest that I had ever been inside. It was a large white house with a porch that stretched across the entire facade. On the inside was a large hallway with a tall stairway. Behind and beneath the stairway was a large closet. I suppose that the trunk that held John Nesbitt's "important papers" was stored there. Four bedrooms were upstairs. Downstairs, the rooms were separated by the large hallway, where at the end was a door which led to the back porch. On the right of the hallway were two large rooms. The first was the master bedroom. Next to it was another bedroom. On the left side of the hallway was a large parlor with a huge fireplace. Next to the parlor was a spacious dining room and the next room was the kitchen. There was a door in the kitchen that led to a back porch that stood high off the ground. The tall stairway from the back porch led to a pump well. The well provided water for the household as there was no indoor plumbing. After the Nesbitts moved from the house, my Uncle James and his wife Aunt Betty Ruth Edmondson moved into the house with their seven children and lived there until 1959. The house remained vacant after Uncle James and his family moved. Then sometime in the late 1970s, it mysteriously caught on fire and burned to the ground.

I am sure that it was a relief to move the school from their home as the couple's family was beginning to grow. Their first son Ernest was born June 21, 1870. As an adult, Ernest would become a teacher at Promise Land School. He married a young widow, Lizzie Kirkman, and they lived in the house that was previously owned by his father. On the ground level of the house, he owned and operated the Nesbitt General Store. Ernest was followed in birth by his brothers, Jettie, born in 1872; John Henry, 1875; Manuel, 1877; and James, 1879; in 1881 their first daughter, Susan, was born; followed by sons Earsley, 1884, and Elzie, 1886; another daughter, Kittie, 1888; and the last three children, sons Joseph, 1890; Charley, 1892; and Babe, 1896. They raised all their children in Promise Land. However, by the time the children reached adulthood, most of them had moved away from Promise Land. Their eleventh child, Charley, was the only one who stayed in the community and raised his family, but he moved away after his wife died. I do not remember him when he lived in the community, but I remember the house where he lived. It was a small wood-frame house that stood empty on Promise Land Road for many years. I believe that it eventually collapsed from the wear and tear of the years and fell to the ground. This was probably in the 1970s.

John Nesbitt died January 15, 1919, and Ellen passed away March 25, 1940. Both are buried at the family cemetery on Promise Land Road.

With twelve children, their descendants are many. Some of them were charter and leading members of the PLHA and continue to be actively involved.

CORPORAL ARCH NESBITT, USCT

Arch Nesbitt was the older brother of Private John Nesbitt. He was also enslaved by Col. Allen Nesbitt at the farm on Barton's Creek in Dickson County, Tennessee, where he engaged in domestic labor. Nesbitt was born October 12, 1841. He was twenty-two years old when he enlisted with the USCT and was assigned to the Regiment 12th Infantry of Company G. He is described on his enlistment form as being five feet four inches tall with a dark complexion. His occupation is listed as "servant." On the military records, his name is spelled "Archie." He enlisted at Sullivan's Barracks, near Kingston Springs, Tennessee, on September 1, 1864, almost a year after his brother signed on. Under the command of General James B. Steadman, his unit took part in the fighting around Nashville, culminating in the Battle of Nashville, December 15–16, 1864. Cpl. Nesbitt sustained significant combat injuries from this engagement. He recovered from his injuries and continued his enlistment, where he served in other battles near Decatur, Alabama. Before the end of his tour of duty, he and his unit were assigned along with the 13th Regiment to build and guard the Northwestern Railroad System (once L&N Railroads, now CRX) that runs from Nashville west to New Johnsonville, Tennessee. Corporal Nesbitt was honorably discharged on January 16, 1865.

During a furlough, Nesbitt married his sweetheart, Mahalia Tennessee Hickerson. In a deposition taken by federal authorities and dated March 7, 1908, Corporal Nesbitt reported that he and his wife, Tennessee (known by her middle name), were married near Charlotte on "February 16, 1862, the same night that Fort Donelson fell." Tennessee, born on March 30, 1846, was enslaved at the time of their marriage by Henry Hickerson, whose farm was located just off what is now Highway 48 North near St. Paul Road in Charlotte. The report revealed further that they were married by Rev. Isham W. Leech.

After discharge from the military, Cpl. Nesbitt and his bride settled in Clarksville, Tennessee, and later relocated to Cumberland Furnace. Deed records show that on December 29, 1885, the couple purchased a tract of land in Promise Land from William and Alice Roberts. There was a Roberts family known to my family. They were a white family of modest means who had a farm on the fringe of the city of Charlotte near the Promise Land community. I believe that they may have been the descendants of the Roberts who were the original owners of the land purchased by Cpl. Nesbitt. My Uncle James worked on the Roberts's farm during the fifties and sixties. They owned property next door to my grandmother's house and rented it to a white family and later to my Uncle James and his family.

From the recollections of my mother, Cpl. Nesbitt erected the first brush harbor church in the community. As a testament of their faith, the couple sold a portion of their property to the Methodist Episcopal Church of America for the sum of four dollars on March 28, 1889. Shortly after the sale and purchase of this lot, a Methodist church was erected on it. The original building served the congregation and Middle Tennessee Methodist Conference until 1935 when it was struck by lightning and was burned to the ground. The church was rebuilt and continued to serve community until the Tennessee Conference closed it in 1992 due to low membership. Today it is the location of the Promise Land Heritage Association Cultural Arts Center.

Corporal Nesbitt and his family are reported in the 1870 Census. At that time, they reported five children, and the Corporal was employed at the Cumberland Furnace in the capacity of "wood setter." During the Civil War the Cumberland Furnace was shut down. During the shutdown, the owner Anthony Wayne Vanleer died. After the war it reopened under new management. The new manager was James Pierre Drouillard, the husband of Mary Florence Kirkman, the granddaughter of Vanleer. Drouillard was a Union officer who had been stationed in Nashville, where he met and married Kirkman. When in operation the furnace labor force consisted primarily of enslaved workers. Emancipation called for major changes in staffing for the furnace industries that had been dependent on slave labor. Drouillard made a proposal to the formerly enslaved men and women that was difficult to turn down. He offered them pay for their labor. Many who had been enslaved at the furnace were skilled at the various jobs. So, it was without question that many responded positively to this opportunity. It also attracted those who did not have the furnace background but were willing to accept a paid occupation. I imagine that this was especially appealing to those who had worked as farmers.

Thus, this was a new experience for Nesbitt. There is a glossary of the various furnace job titles. The job title "wood cutter" refers to a labor related to harvesting wood used to fire the furnace. It was imperative that the furnace maintained extreme heat to smelt the iron ore and transform it into iron. The iron would be shaped by blacksmiths into useful products including household utensils, building supplies, ammunition, etc. There were several work assignments directly related to the wood supply. Among these job titles were *wood cutters*, these were men who were responsible for going into the woods and cutting down timber; *teamsters*, who would haul the timber in a wagon driven by a team of mules from the woods to the furnace; and *wood setters*, who were responsible for stacking the lumber/timber for burning at the furnace. The 1880 Census revealed that Nesbitt's son-in-law, seventeen-year-old Alfred Johnson, was also employed at the furnace.

The Nesbitts were the parents of four children, who included a daughter Bettie born 1866, who grew up and married a young man from the community, whose name was Harry Primm; Angeline born 1868, married Alfred Johnson, the young man who worked with her father at the Cumberland Furnace; Johnny Nesbitt born 1870, married Nara Vanleer daughter of Joe Washington Vanleer, another prominent early settler in the community; and Archie T. born 1872. They also raised a grandson, John McKinley, who followed his grandfather's military footprint. He served in the US Army during WWI. Nesbitt's services perhaps had a generational impact on many of his descendants. George Bernard Reddon, Nesbitt's great-grandson, shared much of this history orally as well as in his biography published in the Heritage Book of Dickson County, Tennessee. According to George Bernard, he and all six of his brothers served in various branches of the US armed forces.

In the early part of the twentieth century, Arch and Tennessee Nesbitt moved to the outskirts of the City of Dickson to a place called Hendricks. Soon after relocating there, they became founding members of the Bowman Chapel Methodist Church. Cpl. Arch Nesbitt died on March 29, 1920, and his wife Mahalia Tennessee Nesbitt passed away on April 7, 1939. Both are interred in the Nesbitt Cemetery in Promise Land. Cpl. Nesbitt's grave is marked by a USCT tombstone. Nesbitt and his wife left an impressive legacy. They have many surviving descendants as a testament to their existence. Some are active members of the PLHA.

PRIVATE LANDIN/LANDERS WILLIAMS, USCT

Landin Williams was one of the few early settlers who was not enslaved near the Promise Land settlement. According to his descendant, Leon

Bates of Indianapolis, Indiana, Williams's father Alex Williams was from North Carolina and his mother, Harriet Williams, was from Virginia. Williams was born near Atlanta, Georgia, in 1839. He escaped from slavery as a teen and ended up in Chattanooga, Tennessee, where in 1863 he enlisted with the USCT. At the age of twenty-four he was assigned to Battery A and placed in Regiment 2 Light Artillery. Military records reported his name as "Landin"; this would later pose a problem as will be revealed later. In Regiment 2, he was responsible for handling and maintaining small artillery including guns and ammunition. He was also responsible for transporting munitions and supplies to military bases. Upon enlistment he received the rank of private. He remained at this rank through his honorable discharge in 1866. Pvt. Williams was garrisoned to Charlotte, Tennessee. While serving in Charlotte, he was detailed to Clarksville, Tennessee. During his assignment in Clarksville, he met and courted a young woman whose name was Lucy McCurdy. They married soon after he was discharged.

In 1920 after Pvt. Williams's death, his wife's application for his Civil War pension was disputed due to the discrepancy in the spelling of his name. The federal records reported his name as "Landin" while civilian records such as marriage license listed the spelling as "Landers." The United States Department of Interior requested a hearing to resolve the dispute. The deposition with Mrs. Williams provided some very valuable information for his descendants. In it, Mrs. Williams stated that they met near the close of the Civil War. He was wearing his USCT uniform and appeared so handsome. She was quoted as saying "Yes, he was a Yankee Soldier." She also verified the name of his parents and place of birth and the dates of his service in the United States Army.

The Williamses settled in the Promise Land settlement where he had a small farm. In the 1870 Census, he is reported to be twenty-nine years old, and she is reported as twenty-five years old. They have two children; one was a two-year-old girl named Mary and the other was a five-month-old son named Landers. The census also reveals that Pvt. Williams worked at the Cumberland Furnace. According to Mrs. Williams's deposition, her husband's occupation was that of farmer and teamster at the Cumberland Furnace: "He drove a team of mules carrying iron products from the furnace to the train depot. He was always good with horses and had a natural ability to ride and care for them." The Williams had more children and they remained in Promise Land until their children had grown up and moved away from home.

After the children had left home, the Williams moved to Lone Oak, a rural Black community in Montgomery County, Tennessee, so that Mrs. Williams could be near her family. Pvt. Williams died in 1919. He is buried at the Lone Oaks Cemetery in Montgomery County. After the inquisition by the government, his wife was approved to receive the benefits that he earned from his military service to the United States Army. Mrs. Williams moved to Nashville to live with her daughter after his death. She passed away in 1929 in Nashville and is interred at the Greenwood Cemetery.

Their oldest son, Landers Jr., known as Landy, stayed in Promise Land and married a woman named Sally Washington. His wife was from the Black settlement in Charlotte known as Cedar Grove. Their children attended Promise Land School. One of his sons, Landy III, attended Promise Land School with my mother. She recalled that as a young man he was a creative aspiring artist. She said that he would write plays, enlist, and rehearse players and present the plays at the school. He was also an outstanding vocalist who continued this artistry throughout his life. As a senior citizen, he was a member of an all-male choir in Indianapolis and performed with them at churches, public events, and on television. Mr. Landy would return to Promise Land throughout his life, often accompanied by younger descendants, to make them acquainted with his place of origin. In 2005, Landy Williams III passed away at the age of ninety-four in Indianapolis, Indiana.

PRIVATE CLARK GARRETT

Pvt. Clark Garrett enlisted into the US Army's USCT on December 15, 1863, at the Nashville & Northwestern Railroads, under Lt. Wildy. He was assigned to Company 12, Regiment 48 Colored Infantry. At the age of twenty years, his enlistment profile described him as being five feet four inches tall with a dark complexion. Dickson County was listed as his residence and his occupation was reported as house servant.

The company and regiment assignments indicated that Pvt. Garrett was assigned to work on the railroad that ran from Kingston Springs, running through Dickson to Johnsonville in Humphries County. This railway became an important source for transporting arms and supplies to Union installations. Work had begun on the railway prior to the war. It was intended to extend from Nashville to Hickman, Kentucky, a total of 170 miles. However, before the war broke out the line ran only to

Kingston Springs in Cheatham County, Tennessee. After the federal seizure of Nashville in February 1862, work began to extend the line westward to Johnsonville on the Tennessee River, to provide another supply line for the federal troops. Members of the USCT Regiment 12 and 14 were charged with constructing this railway. After it was completed, the same military units were charged with guarding the trestles, bridges, and blockhouses along the railroad they had constructed. Thus, Private Garrett was likely to have been among the laborers who constructed the railroad and guarded it on its completion. He was honorably discharged from the army with the rank of private on February 8, 1866.

Sometime after discharge, Pvt. Garrett returned to the Charlotte area. He married a young woman whose name was Violet Corlew, and they settled in Promise Land. The 1880 US Census reports the couple residing in the 8th District of Charlotte. He was thirty-eight years old at the time and his wife was thirty-two. Five children are listed in the household, including Rosetta the oldest child born 1870, followed by six-year-old Gertrude, and three boys, Washington, age four, John, three, and McPherson, who was only six months old. Pvt. Garrett's occupation is reported as farm laborer. This implies that he was perhaps working on someone else's farm. Farming was a skill that many of the newly freed settlers were well acquainted with; however as free people, they were paid for their labor. It is also likely that the young veteran maintained a small subsistence farm of his own for his growing family.

Pvt. Garrett died on March 29, 1909, at the age of sixty-seven. Written as the cause of death is "shot himself." I was surprised to find that. There was no explanation as to why. Unfortunately, there is no one around with whom I can inquire. Violet was awarded a survivor's pension for her husband's military service. Twenty-eight years after his death, she passed away at the age of eighty-nine.

My mother often pointed out to me the "Clark Garrett House." She said that she remembered that there was a gravesite on the property near the house. She believed that Clark Garret was buried on the property. In her later life, she recalled that there was a large Civil War veteran headstone on one of the graves. I remember that the house was located far off the road in what then was a cow pasture. We would pass it when we took a shortcut to school from my great-grandmother's house. It was separated from the cut-through by a fence and was surrounded by overgrowth. Therefore, we were unable to get a close-up view of it. The distance from the road seems even greater today. The cut-through path is no longer there. The field is fully used as a cow pasture. From all appearances it seems that there are no remnants of the house. Knowing the location of where it was, I hope to go to the site one day, in search of the gravesite.

I have been told that we are related to Clark Garrett on my dad's side of the family. I think that he may have been a nephew to my great-grandfather, William Gilbert. William Gilbert had many siblings from whom he was separated during slavery. I recall that my father nicknamed one of my playmates "Aunt Gertie." He said that she reminded him of his Aunt Gertrude (Garrett), who was the second daughter born to Clark and Violet.

I also recognize that Clark's oldest daughter Rosetta Martin was a speaker on the Emancipation Day program in Promise Land on January 1, 1913, an event referenced earlier in this text. Other known descendants of Clark would be those of his brother John. John Garrett had a farm in proximity to Clark's. John's home was near the Promise Land School. It was demolished more than seventy years ago. One of his direct descendants was a gentleman whose name was Rev. George Clayton Jenkins (C. D.) He grew up with my dad and his brothers. For many years I thought that he was also one of my dad's brothers. They have a kinship relationship. He became a prominent African Methodist Episcopal minister and was known as Rev. G. C. Jenkins. He was appointed as the first African American Chaplain of the Tennessee State Prison under Gov. Frank Clement's Administration. His granddaughter, Rev. Benessa Sweat, was my pastor at McGavock Chapel AME Church, the church where her grandfather once served as pastor. Rev. Sweat delivered the eulogy at my mother's funeral in 2017.

PRIVATE EDWARD VANLEER

Born about 1820, the military records reveal that Edward Vanleer was forty-three years old when he enlisted in the USCT of the Union army on December 24, 1863. He was considerably older than most enlistees. Records show that most enlisted between the ages of twenty to twenty-five years of age. Vanleer entered in at the rank of private and was assigned to Company F, Regiment 16 Infantry. He served two years, four months, and six days and was honorably discharged with the rank of private on April 30, 1866. In 1997, Pvt. Vanleer and many other African American Civil War veterans were recognized and honored for their service and sacrifice in helping to bring an end to the war and freeing more than four million enslaved Americans. His name is listed on the African American Civil War Memorial Wall located at the Spirit of Freedom Statue in Washington, DC.

Pvt. Vanleer returned to Dickson County after discharge from the army. On August 11, 1870, he married a young woman whose name was Susan McCauley. According to the 1880 US Census, the couple were residing in the Promise Land Community. He was reported to be sixty years old, and she was forty years of age. Pvt. Vanleer is also reported to be working as a woodcutter for the Cumberland Furnace. It is very likely that he had been enslaved at the furnace prior to his military service. This is suggested by the last name that he carried. Most of the people who were enslaved by furnace owner Anthony Wayne Vanleer also carried his last name. Accepting work at the furnace as a paid laborer after emancipation from slavery is another indicator. Because of his knowledge and experience as a slave, he perhaps viewed becoming a paid laborer as an opportunity not to be refused.

From records it appears that Private Vanleer died before 1890. His place of burial is unknown to this writer. It is probable that he was buried in Promise Land as many of his survivors are reported to have been buried there. His wife Susan is listed in the 1890 US Census "Special Schedule of Surviving Soldiers, Sailors, and Marines and Widows" as the beneficiary of his military benefits.

The 1880 and 1890 Census report them having seven children. The oldest was born 1862. Her name was Lou. Unfortunately, my research and data collection yielded no other information about Lou. However, I have a lot of information on the second daughter, who was Sarah, born 1867. As an adult, Sarah would marry a man named John Edmondson. They became the parents of my mother's stepfather. His name was Lesley Edmondson. Sarah and John had other children, my great-aunts and -uncles with whom I was well acquainted. They included uncles Robert, Earl, and John, and aunts Susan, Eolie, Pearl and Hester. My ninety-five-year-old cousin Claytee Mallory, the daughter of my Aunt Pearl, has been very helpful in filling me in and bringing to my memory stories of Sarah and John's family.

Pvt. Vanleer and Susan's other daughters were Lizzie, Mary, Addie, and Suzie. Lizzie was born in 1868 and, like Sarah, I hold close family ties with her. Lizzie married twice; her first husband was named Paton Kirkman. She and Paton had a son whose name was Hersey. As teenagers, he and my maternal grandmother were involved in a relationship that led to the conception of my mother. Although never married to each other, his mother played a prominent role in my mother's life. She was my mother's beloved "Grandma Lizzie." Mother enjoyed spending time with her, although for a short period, as she died when mother was preadolescent. She left her with gifts and fond memories to which my mother treasured to her death.

The fourth daughter Mary Francis was born in 1873, and married a man whose name was Elisha Collier. They had five children whose names were Nora, Jordon (Cardell), Judy, Leona, and Nobie. When I reviewed the names of the children with my cousin Niva Driver Smith, a direct descendant of Mary Francis, she recalled knowing of them all, but recalled best memories of her grandmother Leona, who she referred to as "Big Momma" and Big Momma's brother, Nobie. Leona was born to Mary in 1908. Leona had a daughter who was born on April 19, 1922. Her name was Canara Idessa. Idessa attended Promise Land School. She married a man whose name was Kelly Driver and settled in a community north of Promise Land called Mt. Zion. They were the parents of nine children, four sons and five daughters. I grew up with the youngest five children but was acquainted with all of them. As an adult, Idessa became a minister of the gospel and founded the Faith Apostolic Church, which was built next door to her home. Pastor Idessa Driver passed away on July 7, 2015. The church that she founded continues under the leadership of her granddaughter, Kimberly, and her husband Duple Teravillion. Pastor Driver had many descendants; some are active members of the PLHA.

Addie was the fifth child born to Pvt. Vanleer and Susan. She was born in 1876. The 1890 Census reported Addie to be twenty-four years old. Also in the household were Addie's two sons, seven-year-old Joe and five-year-old Fred. I was assisted in completing the story of Addie by her step-grandson, Thomas Vanleer, a ninety-two-year-old elder of the PLHA. According to him, Addie worked as a domestic and in the early 1900s she relocated from Tennessee with her employer and his family to Evansville, Indiana. Addie's sons moved with her, and she raised them in Indiana. They would return to visit family in Tennessee. It was doing one of those visits that her son Joe became acquainted with Thomas' mother, Beatrice Nesbitt. They courted each other and eventually married. Thomas was in the second grade at Promise Land School when he moved with his mother and stepfather to Evansville. Thomas recalled that "Daddy Joe" who was seventeen years older than his mother, was a good father. He said that his "Grandma Addie" was a kindly reserved woman who kept her home very neat. Although she had been married before he met her, she remained divorced and single most of her life. Addie died in Evansville on February 6, 1957.

The only son reported was Edward, born 1879. Named after his father, Edward grew up in Promise Land. He married a young woman in the community who happened to have been the oldest daughter of Pvt. John Nesbitt and Ellen Clemons. Like Edward's mother, her name was also Susan. Young Edward and Susan had seven children, all of whom were born and raised in the Promise Land Community. Their offspring included: daughters, Laura, Jetti, Bessie and Fannie; sons, Earsley, Elzie, and John. Their last child, Fannie, would become a teacher at Promise Land School during the years of 1949 to 1952. Pvt. Edward Vanleer has a long line of descendants who have impacted significantly on the history and legacy of the Promise Land Community.

The seventh and last child was born in 1881 and reported in the 1890 Census. Her name is listed as "Fanny." As a child, I knew her as "Cousin Susie." Thomas Vanleer confirmed that Fanny was the actual given name to Susie. Fanny/Susie lived in Promise Land all her life. She lived next door to her daughter, Lizzie Edmondson. Lizzie Edmondson was married to my father's brother, Theo. There were two things that I remember most about Cousin Susie. One was that her brother Edward would sometime visit her, and the two of them would sit on her front porch and talk. The second was that in age she developed dementia and would occasionally wander off from her home. My brother, Billy, and I would see her walking down the road in front of our house. Billy was about six years old, and I was about five. We would run out to meet her, position ourselves on each side of her, take her hands in ours and walk her back to her house. Although she lived alone, she was carefully watched by her daughter and grandchildren. She was the first person who I had encountered with dementia, which led to a paper that I wrote in graduate school on the care the elderly received when family units tended to be more extended as opposed to the nuclear family units that were more prevalent during latter years of the twentieth century. Cousin Susie died at the age of seventy-three on February 18, 1955.

SGT. ALFRED GRIMES

The military records of Sgt. Alfred Grimes reveal that he was born in Maury County, Tennessee. At the age of twenty-four, he enlisted at Sulfur Trestle, Alabama, into the US Army's 111 Infantry Regiment of the USCT on March 1, 1864. At the time of enlistment, he was described physically as being five feet eleven inches tall, with a dark complexion. He is reported to have used an alternate name, which was Elbert Grimes. He was enlisted at the rank of private. As an infantryman, he served in Pulaski, Tennessee, Athens, Alabama, and a district of North Alabama until September 1864. He fought in the battles at Sulphur Branch Trestle, Alabama, from September 23 to 27, and October 1, 1864. During combat against Gen. Nathan Bedford Forrest's army, on September 23 and 24, the records state that "most of the Regiment was captured." Fortunately for him, he was not among those captured. After those battles, he was assigned duty in Pulaski, Tennessee, until January 1865, and was later transferred to Middle Tennessee where he was assigned guard duty for the Nashville & Northwestern Railroad until 1866. Sometime during his service, he was promoted to the rank of First Sergeant. Sgt. Grimes was honorably discharged with this rank on April 30, 1866. He is memorialized for his military as part of the African American Civil War Memorial in Washington, DC.

It's not clear whether Sgt. Grimes was enslaved in Middle Tennessee prior to his enlistment, but we are sure that he was discharged in that area. There is evidence that his brother, William settled in District 8, the area that would become known as Promise Land. It is not surprising that he also settled in this community at least for a brief period and later relocated to nearby, Dickson. Following military discharge, he married a woman whose name was Ellen. Ellen was from a Charlotte community known as Bellsburg. Alfred and Ellen had nine children. The oldest was a girl, born in 1864. Her name was Emma. Emma was followed by Rosie, born 1965. Rosie was followed by three brothers born in succession from 1867 to 1871. They were John, Miller, and Henry. Another girl, Mary was born 1873, and she was followed by a boy, Eddie, born 1875, then another girl, Susie, born 1876 and their last child was Samuel, born 1878.

It appears that by the 1880 Census, Sgt. Grimes had relocated to Dickson and was cohabiting with a new partner, whose name was Alice Bell. He married Alice in 1887; however, they had already begun procreation. To them were born three sons, James, born 1878, Percy, 1880, and Emerson, 1885. They also had two daughters, Alberta, born 1890, and Irene, born 1893. Sgt. Grimes's family seems reminiscent of his own family of origin. His father, Isaac P. Grimes, an enslaved man born in 1824, also had two sets of children, affording him as many as twelve siblings. Like Sgt. Grimes, they were born into slavery but were able to live free following emancipation. The majority lived in Dickson County where many of their descendants continue to live today.

According to folklore, the Grimes family may have been one of the first Black families to establish their home in the Promise Land community. An enslaver whose name was John Grimes owned land that bordered the Promise Land settlement. It is said some of the people who had been enslaved on his farm made their homes on land in proximity to his farm. These Grimes were direct descendants of Sgt. Grimes and will be revisited in the next chapter.

Sgt. Alfred Grimes passed away on February 1, 1919. He was reported to have been seventy-eight years old. Reported as the cause of death was influenza, secondary to "old age." His occupation reported on the death certificate was "Stone Mason." His remains were interred at the City Cemetery in Dickson.

A DIFFERENT FORM OF MILITARY SERVICE

To this point, I have discussed men who fought with the USCT. However, prior to May 22, 1863, the creation of the USCT, there were Black men who were hired out by their enslavers for services to the military. This system applied to both the Confederate and Union Armies. These enslaved men gave support to the military as cooks, teamsters, and manual laborers. Such was the case of a man who was called Sam Grimes. Sam was enslaved by a man whose name was John Grimes. John Grimes was the original owner of Sam. He had owned him from the time that Sam was an infant. Since Sam had three different enslavers who were named John Grimes, I will refer to his first owner as John Grimes the First. John Grimes the First died when Sam was a young child. Sam, inherited by John the First's son also called John Grimes, will be referred to as John Grimes the Second. By the time Sam reached young adulthood, John the Second had sold him to his son known as John B. Grimes. John B. Grimes and Sam were close in age. Sam was essentially enslaved by three generations of Grimes. As customary during slavery, Sam carried the last name of his owner. His biological parents were reported to have been Bob and Katie Blacksmith, who were considered mulatto. Mulatto is a racial classification for the first generation of mixed heritage having one Black and one white parent. There is no information in the court deposition that served as the primary source for this story to indicate if the Blacksmiths lived as freed or enslaved individuals.

According to John B. Grimes's wife's testimony, at the outbreak of the Civil War in April 1861, her husband hired Sam as well as another enslaved man named Albert to serve the military as teamsters. Enslaved men were often hired out by their owners to serve the Confederate war effort. This provided a revenue source for the enslavers who suffered financially because of the war. Ten dollars a month was paid for each man hired out. This payment was paid directly to the owner. It is an assumption that John B. Grimes's agreement was with the Confederacy. This assumption is because it appears that the arrangement was accepted by the community. There was nothing stated in any of the testimonies during the trial that would make one think otherwise.

The commitment was that both Sam and Albert were each to drive a team of six mules loaded with pig iron from the Cumberland Furnace to Betsy Town, a nearby village that had grown out of the Vanleer Landing, a port on the Cumberland River where Anthony Wayne Vanleer, owner of the Cumberland Furnace would receive and export cargo. From Betsy Town, the teamsters would load their wagons with supplies and take them to Fort Donelson, which at the time was controlled by the Confederacy. The destination between Betsy Town and Fort Donelson by wagon trail was about thirty miles.

Before the war began, Sam married a young, enslaved woman whose name was Hagar Jackson. Hagar was owned by the widowed aunt of John B. Grimes; she was his father's sister. Her name was Katie Jackson and she lived about four miles north of John B. Grimes's farm. The Grimes's farm was located at "the head of Johnson Creek," just off what was then the Clarksville Stage Road (now Harris Hollow Road) what was then designated as District 6. The Promise Land Community would become included in this location. Katie Jackson's farm was located north of her nephew's farm, closer to Cumberland Furnace.

The marriage between Sam and Hagar was the major factor in this case. Whether or not it would be accepted by the court as a legitimate bond between Sam and Hagar would determine the outcome. Enslaved people were not permitted to marry in accordance with state regulations. If an enslaved man and woman wanted to marry, all that was required was that their owners gave their permission. According to the testimony of Dan Grimes, the son of John B. Grimes, his father and his Aunt Katie had granted permission for Sam and Hagar to marry. He explained that a marriage between an enslaved couple was only recognized when the owners were aware and approved the cohabitation of the couple. He explained further, "It was customary for Sam to go spend the night with Hagar at Aunt Katie's farm on Friday and Saturday night and return back to our farm late Sunday evening." Sam stayed at the farm during the week and only stayed with Hagar on the weekend. When the war started, his father allowed Sam to move to "Aunt Katie's" farm and take the mule team with him, because it was closer to the Cumberland Furnace. Katie Jackson allowed the couple to occupy the "loom house." This was a small building built adjunct to the main residence.

In 1861, Hagar gave birth to their daughter, Patsy. By then the war was in full force, and Sam was away from home for long stretches of time. In 1862, Sam was stricken with a severe case of measles. It was during the fall of Fort Donelson. According to witness Dan Grimes, "My Pa wanted to make sure no harm came to his mule teams and to both boys, he got them out of there."[12] Sam was escorted back to Grimes's farm by Albert. Sam was extremely sick and put to bed soon as they returned to the farm. His condition was complicated by pneumonia and worsened. He died at the home of his enslaver on February 22, 1862, just days after his return from Fort Donelson. Recognizing that Sam would have normally returned to the house that he shared with Hagar, the attorney for the complainants asked Grimes's son, the witness, why Sam was brought to his Pa's farm instead of Katie Jackson's. His response was that "None of the folks at Aunt Katie's farm had had measles and they did not want to put them at harm."

After Sam's death, Hagar and Patsy continued to live at Katie Jackson's farm. Hagar would take Patsy to visit Sam's mother at the grandmother's request. Hagar died in 1870; Patsy was nine years old when her mother died. The deposition did not disclose the cause of Hagar's death. According to witnesses, after Hagar's death, "Kate Jackson raised Patsy as if she were her own child." In the deposition of Mrs. Sack Loggins, stepdaughter to John Grimes the Second, testified that Kate Jackson referred to Patsy as her "granddaughter, though she knew that she really wasn't." During Patsy's testimony, she stated that her father's sisters, Mary and Jane, would sometimes visit her at Katie Jackson's farm or would take her to visit her grandmother Katie Blacksmith. Patsy was unaware that following her father's death, his mother Katie Blacksmith had received a bounty from the government for her father's military service. By the time Patsy became aware of the bounty, Katie Blacksmith had died. However, before Katie Blacksmith's death she purchased land in District 8, near Cumberland Furnace, with the funds that she had received for Sam's military service. There was a deed which showed that the tract of land had been deeded to her daughter Mary Blacksmith.

In 1879, Patsy married William (Bill) Grimes. William was twelve years older than Pasty. He was known as Bill and he was a brother to USCT veteran Sgt. Alfred Grimes. During the years between 1884 and 1899, William and Patsy had seven children, five sons and two daughters. One of their sons was named William, after his father, but was better known by his middle name Dess. Mr. Dess was well-known to my family. He was married to a relative on my father's side of the family. Her name was Minnie Johnson. As a child, I remember visiting their home with my parents and siblings. I had often heard my parents speak of another son of Bill and Patsy; his name was John. John was deceased by the time I was born; however, I know that he was married to our neighbor, Betty Cunningham. There was a steep hill on Promise Land Road just down from where Miss Betty lived. The hill was interchangeably referred to as "the Dess Grimes Hill" or the "John Grimes Hill." I assume that the hill's name was an indication that Dess and John Grimes had lived in proximity to it. During the late 1930s, Mr. Dess and Cousin Minnie moved from Promise Land to an area outside Dickson, Tennessee, called Edgefield. There were other families from Promise Land who moved to Edgefield including USCT veteran Pvt. Arch Nesbitt. Pvt. Nesbitt was the grandfather of Cousin Minnie. It is likely that the offspring of Bill and Patsy remained in Promise Land for at least a couple of generations after their parents' demise. Records indicate that the second generation, George W. Grimes Jr., and his wife Priscilla Horner Grimes, continued to live in the community because two of their children, Arthur Lee, and Katherine, were schoolmates with my mother. My mother said that they moved from Promise Land before they finished elementary school.

Patsy was nearly fifty-five years old when she and Bill decided to act against the paternal side of her family for denying her benefits from her father's death compensation. In June 1916 William and Patsy sued for entitlement to property that had been purchased with money paid for her father's service to the Confederate army during the Civil War. By the time of the lawsuit, Katie Blacksmith had died. She was survived by six children: a son, John, and daughters, Mary, Jane, Sarah, Lovey, and Agnes. It was alleged by some of her children that prior to dying, Katie willed her land to her oldest daughter, Mary. Mary had also passed away by the time of the lawsuit. Somehow the surviving heirs had created parcels of the land prior to Mary's death and divided it among themselves—Mary's only child, Martha, who had married a man by the name of Marshall Collier; Katie's son, John Blacksmith; and the daughters—Jane who had married a man named Riley Collier, Lovey who had married Wash Bly, Sarah who was married to Turner Young, and Agnes

Blackwell—were all included in the land division. Katie's granddaughter, Patsy was not included.

The case was brought before the Chancery Court in Charlotte for Dickson County in Tennessee on June 16, 1816. The Honorable J. W. Stout served as Chancellor Judge. Representing the complainants Patsy and William Grimes was attorney R. L. Leech of Charlotte. The lawsuit was brought against defendants John Blacksmith, Martha and Marshall Collier, Jane and Riley Collier, Sarah Young, Lovey Bly, and Agnes Blacksmith.

The complainant's affidavit submitted by Attorney Leech on behalf of Patsy and Bill Grimes reflected that they sought to show the courts that Katie Blacksmith had received a recompense from the government for the death of her son, Sam Blacksmith Grimes, who had died while in service to the Confederate army during the Civil War. However, she withheld this important information from Sam's wife Hagar and their daughter, Patsy. She never told them about the money she had received. With the money, Katie purchased a tract of land in District 8 near Cumberland Furnace and bordering Promise Land. A copy of the deed to that property was presented to the court and filed as Exhibit A as part of the lawsuit. Leech wanted to further prove before the court that while enslaved and before the war, Sam married an enslaved women whose name was Hagar Jackson. The two were married under the terms and conditions mutually acceptable to their owners and by unwritten societal rules for enslaved people. And that it was in this marriage, their daughter Patsy was conceived and born. Patsy was the child of Sam Blacksmith Grimes and the granddaughter of Katie Blacksmith and was therefore entitled to her father's share in the land that was purchased with the recompense.

In addition to establishing Patsy's birthright to the property, Leech wanted to make the court aware that Patsy and Bill Grimes lawfully married in 1879, before the death of her grandmother, Katie Blacksmith. Yet, Katie still did not share the information of the recompense that she had received with her granddaughter nor her granddaughter's husband. Leech argued that after Katie Blacksmith's death, her biological children divided the land under fraudulent circumstances among themselves. The land was divided between Mary, John, Jane, Sarah, Lovey, and Agnes. "Not withstanding" that Patsy was the only heir of Sam Grimes, she did not receive any parts or proceeds of the land.

Finally, the complainant's affidavit stated that Patsy and Bill wished to show the court that they should own the land in common with the defendants named in the suit. However, the land was located and situated so it could not be equally divided with a seventh party. It would have to be sold and the proceeds be divided between all who were entitled.

The trial was held at the storied Charlotte courthouse, which was built in 1804 and was severely damaged by a tornado in May 1830; many records and furnishings were destroyed. In October 1830 the building was restored on the original foundation and its purpose resumed. During the Civil War the courthouse was taken over and occupied by the Union army from 1863 to 1864. During this period once again records and furnishings were lost. After the war, the county resumed using the facility as designed. Today the old building carries the distinction of being one of the oldest functioning courthouses in the state.

In the summer of 1916, the old courthouse was what would be expected for a rural Southern county. The two-story brick building with the white cupola atop stood majestically in the center of the town square. There were seven large windows on the top and six at the lower landing on the north and south sides of the building and three windows on the top landing and two on the lower level of the building's east and west ends. The grounds on which the building stood were surrounded by a gray-blocked wall with a hitching post in cement mounted on top for hitching horses. The blocks had been meticulously laid years earlier by an enslaved man, whose name was Ben Overton. The courtrooms were small, with highly buffed wood floors and furnished with simplistically built wooden courtroom furniture. There was the expected separate and designated seating in the segregated South. In the courtrooms during the Jim Crow era Black attendees were required to sit in the gallery or balcony. The rooms were probably cramped, especially when they had to accommodate large trials. However, that probably was not the case with this trial.

This was a small trial that probably only attracted a few who were familiar with the case, and the affected family and their acquaintances. The defendants, Katie Blacksmith's surviving children and their spouses, were represented by attorney E. H. Stone of Cumberland Furnace. E. H. Stones's goal was to defend his clients, who claimed that they were legitimate heirs to the land that had belonged to Katie Blacksmith and to disprove that Patsy Grimes had any rights to claim any part of the inheritance.

The case remained active from June 24, 1916, until the retirement of the docket on May 30, 1918. This period includes depositions, where witnesses provided testimony under oath prior to trial, and intermittent chancery court proceedings. Depositions were taken from Mrs. J. B. Grimes, the seventy-five-year-old widow of John B. Grimes, Sam's last enslaver; and

Mrs. Sack Loggins, the daughter of John Grimes, father of John B. In the transcripts, the court and the legal representatives were careful to address the white women as "Mrs." or "Miss." They were usually identified by their husband's initials and last name. With the African American witness there was a noticeable contrast. The women were often referred to as "Auntie or Aunt" and the elder men were referred to as "Uncle" or "Ole" (e.g., "Ole Bob Blacksmith"). There were blatant racist references to African Americans as "darkies" throughout the court proceedings.

The testimonies of J. B. Grimes's wife and her sister-in-law were important because both women had known Sam Grimes from the time that he was a boy. They knew who his birth parents were and about his courtship and marriage with Hagar Jackson. They were also familiar with the circumstances of his death. John B. Grimes's son, Dan Grimes, was also a witness for the complainants. Like his mother and his aunt, he had intimate knowledge of Sam Grimes's life. Several years younger than Sam, he had the opportunity to observe with interest Sam's activities as a young, enslaved man who was also navigating the roles of husband, new father, and Civil War participant. In reading his testimony you can almost detect his admiration for Sam as he responded to the questioning. All the testimonies given by members of Sam's enslavers were helpful in supporting that there had been a committed relationship—in a marriage—between Sam and Hagar. The information that the three witnesses provided was consistent with other witnesses called by the attorney for Bill and Patsy Grimes. Their testimonies were strong, credible, and remained firm during the cross examinations.

The witnesses for the defense included two men, P. Jackson and F. Jackson. They were the nephews of Katie Jackson, Hagar's enslaver. Both men gave brief testimonies, and both denied knowing that Sam and Hagar were lived together as husband and wife. P. Jackson acknowledged that he had heard that Sam was the father of Patsy and he agreed that Patsy looked like Sam. On cross examination of the defense witnesses, Attorney Leech asked if Patsy favored Sam. Jackson replied, "Yes sir. She is as much like him as he is himself." He also acknowledged that Sam was often at Hagar's house on Saturday night and Sundays. This statement was important for the complainants because staying overnight during the weekend was considered a standard characteristic of a marriage between two enslaved adults.[13]

Also called by the defense attorney were two Black, men, Carroll Guerin and Wade Vanleer. Both men had been peers to Sam Grimes. Like the two earlier witnesses, these two men were called to disprove that Sam and Hagar were ever married and that Sam was the biological father of Patsy. From their testimonies it was evident that their relationship with Sam was tenuous. Carroll Guerin acknowledged that he had only known Sam for about "ten or twelve years" before he died. The amount of time that he had known Hagar was inconsistent. At first, he said that he knew her when she was a little girl and later during the cross examination, he said that he first became acquainted with her when the war began. He attempted to characterize Hagar as being promiscuous, stating that he as well as other men had sexual encounters with her. He denied that he had ever been aware that Hagar and Sam were in a committed relationship. Wade Vanleer's testimony was very similar to Guerin's. He stated that he was living at the O.K. Furnace near Montgomery County when he became acquainted with Sam. At that time Sam was driving the mule team from Cumberland Furnace to Fort Donelson. He claimed to have been acquainted with Hagar and to have known other enslaved men in Cumberland Furnace who had sexual relations with Hagar. At one point during the cross examination, it appears that he had become disturbed by the attorney's line of questioning. The attorney for the complainant's questioned him about how long he had known Hagar, as he had originally stated knowing Hagar since she was a child and then later claimed that he had met her after meeting Sam. After asking several questions in succession which led the witness to further contradict himself, the witness abruptly said, "I don't know anything but what I have heard! I don't want to tell you nothing but the truth!"

The inconsistencies and the attacks on Hagar's character led me as the reader of the proceedings to wonder if some of the defense witnesses may have been unduly influenced to testify. Perhaps they may have been intimidated or paid. Guerin acknowledged that he was working as a mail carrier, carrying mail to Cloverdale from Cumberland Furnace when "a few days ago" he was approached by Esquire McCaslin, a member of the defense team. In the words of the witness, "Esq. McCaslin attacked me about what I knew about Sam and Hagar."[14] When this information was revealed, Attorney Leech asked whether the witness knew McCaslin's connection to the lawsuit and if Guerin had gone to see McCaslin or if McCaslin had come to him. This is when Guerin explained the encounter occurred on his mail route. There was nothing else discussed in the court recording relative to this matter. The testimonies of the witnesses for the complainants were convincing in proclaiming that Patsy Grimes was the natural daughter of Sam Grimes and thus entitled to birthrights.

Over the two years of the trial, two of the defendants passed away. Mary's daughter Sarah Young died without any direct heirs within months after the trial began. In 1917, her sister Lovely Bly died, leaving a daughter Becky and her daughter's husband Sam Harvey. Originally, Attorney Leech had informed the court that the land division established by Katie Blacksmith's heirs was situated in a way that to add Patsy and Bill Grimes within the distribution would be impossible. So, he recommended that the plats of land be sold, and profits be divided between the heirs including Patsy Grimes. The tract of land left by Sarah Young created the possibility of redistributing the land that could now include Patsy without having to sell or auction it off.

On May 30, 1918, a settlement of the case was presented. According to the settlement the plan to sell the disputed property was "called off and abandoned." Instead, the land had been redistributed in six tracts. Plat number 6 was awarded to Martha Collier, daughter of Mary Blacksmith, the fifth plat went to John Blacksmith, the fourth to Agnes Blacksmith, Plat three went to Jane Collier, Plat Two went to the heirs of Lovely Bly, and Plat One was awarded to Patsy and Bill Grimes. It further stated that the defendants agreed to pay the court $200. One hundred dollars of this amount would pay the attorney cost for representing Bill and Patsy Grimes. Eighty dollars would be used to cover court costs, and twenty dollars was awarded to Patsy Grimes.

George Bowen, Serina Gilbert's maternal great grandfather, posed between the original home built by Joe W. Vanleer and the home built for his daughter Milley.

Serina & her brother Bill, circa 1947.

From left to right, kneeling are Robert and Jewel Gilbert, standing are James, O. C., Peony, Tom, and Theodore Edmondson, circa 1946.

Bowen Family Reunion, 1986, in Dickson, Tennessee.

Bobbye and Beverly Gilbert, 1955, taken in St. Louis during Christmas break 1955.

Mabel Edmondson, around 1945, in a picture taken in a penny arcade photo booth.

Beverly Gilbert Williams sitting at her desk in her classroom, around 1990. She taught business in the Dickson County school system.

Essie Gilbert and her children, circa 1947.

Leslie Edmondson, Essie Gilbert's stepfather, approximately 1919.

Hattie Bowen Gilbert with brothers Jewel and Robert at their birthplace in Gilbert Town with Robert's grandchildren Robin, Sy and Lateef sitting on the porch. The adults are being are interviewed by television personality Huell Howser in 1976.

Mary (Molly) Edmondson, daughter of George and Farmie Bowen and mother of Essie Gilbert, posed for photo this shortly after arriving in Omaha, circa 1919.

Robert and Essie Gilbert with their daughters and sons-in-law at the New Jersey home of daughter Bobbye in 1982.

Essie Gilbert (left) with siblings Sarah Nelson, Robbie Beason, and Stanley Edmondson (seated) in Omaha, Nebraska, in 1986

Essie Gilbert (Center) with children and grandchildren at a 1996 family gathering in Clarksville, Tennessee.

Essie Gilbert's siblings, Sarah, Stanley, and Robbie, at their home in Omaha, Nebraska, about 1928

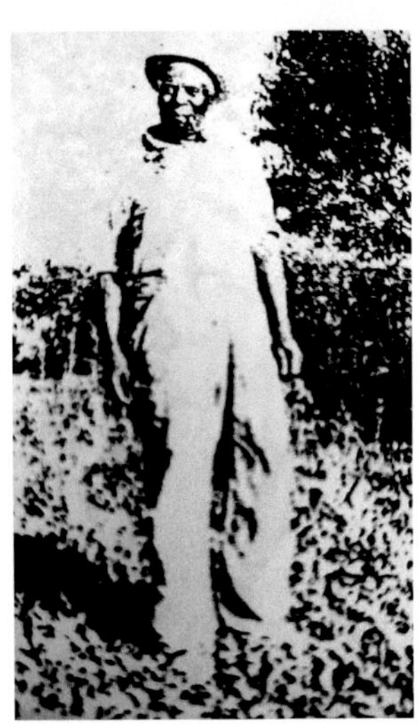

William Plummer "Boss" Redden, well respected Promise Land resident. Redden Road was named in his honor

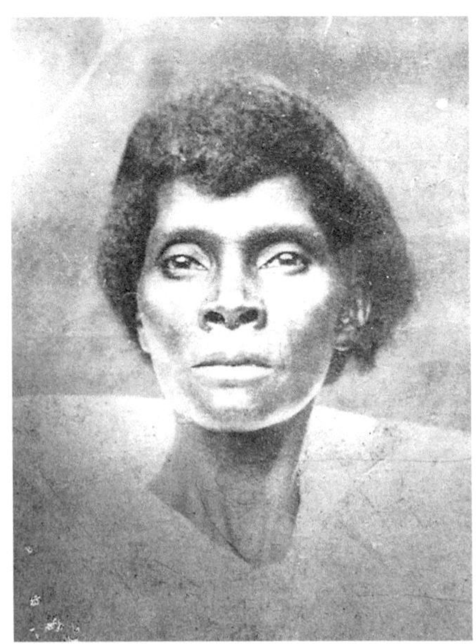

Farmie Della Vanleer Bowen, daughter of Joe Washington Vanleer, wife of George Bowen, and maternal grandmother of Essie Gilbert

AT RIGHT: A map by the authors, of how Promise Land would have looked during the twentieth century, starting around 1930.

1	St. Paul Church	16	William Gilbert House
2	Old Hutton House	17	Toad Hampton Home Site
3	Nesbitt & Hutton Cemeteries	18	Hersey/Hattie Robertson House
4	Harry Primm Home Site	19	Gilbert Cemetery
5	Cunningham House	20	Clark Garrett House
5a	Cunningham Farm	21	Joe W. Vanleer House
6	Lias Jackson House	22	Boss Redden House
7	Mt. Olive AMEC	23	Sallie Vanleer House
8	John Wesley Edmondson House	24	Vanleer Cemetery
8a	Edmondson Store / Jumping Jim	25	Ed Redden House
9	Promise Land School	26	Nathan Bowen Home Site
10	St. John Methodist Church	27	Bowen Cemetery
11	Susie Vanleer House	28	John Nesbitt House & Farm
12	Theo Edmondson House	29	Calvin Robertson House
13	Lizzie & Ernest Nesbitt House & Store	30	Baxter Robertson House
14	Charlie Nesbitt House	31	John Cunningham House
15	Beasley Cunningham House	32	William Primm House

Charter members of the Promise Land Heritage Association Tom and Betty Ruth Edmondson, Essie Gilbert, Robbie Bowen, and James Bowen (kneeling) pose for the dedication of the Promise Land state historical marker in 1992.

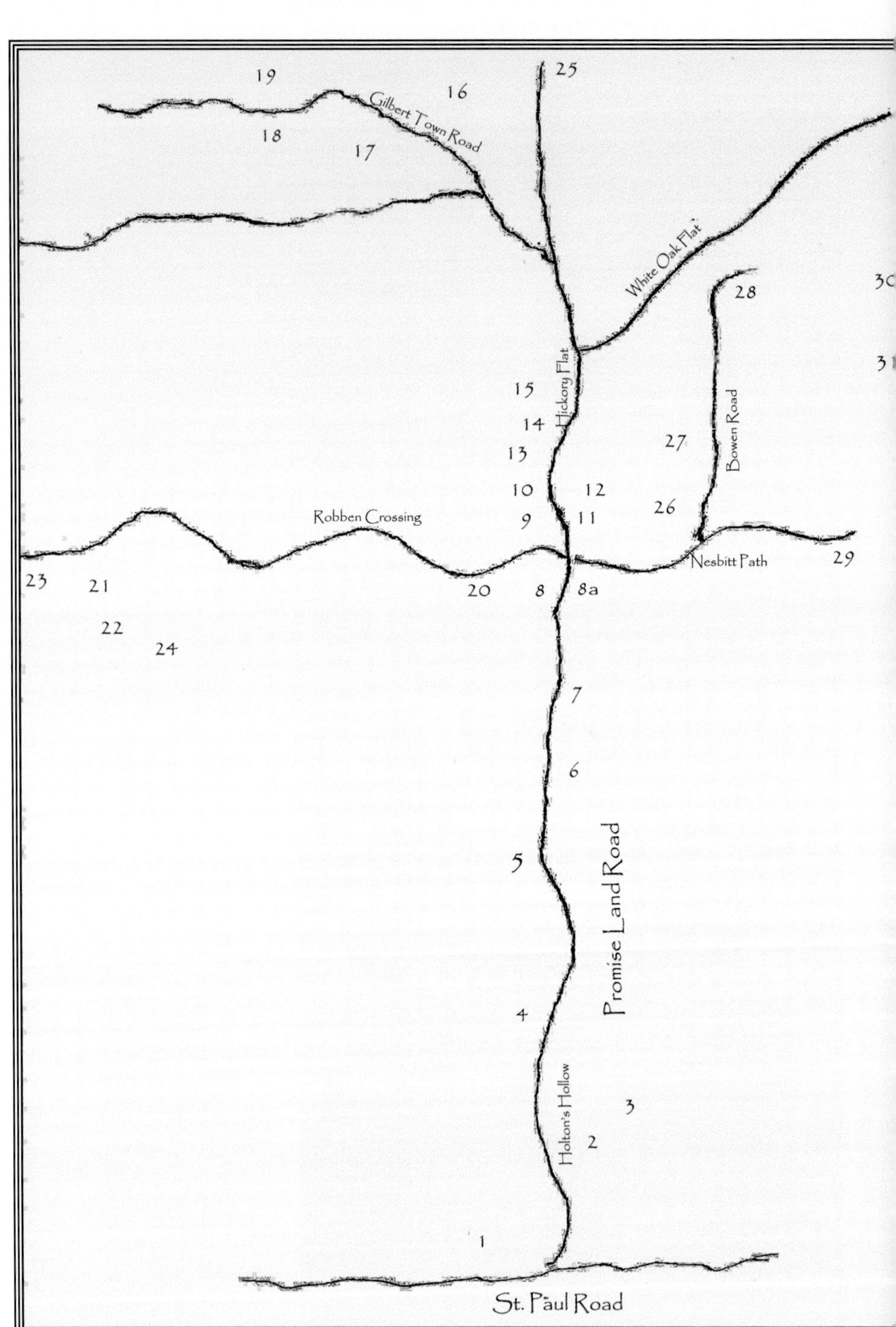

19
16
25
Gilbert Town Road
18
17
White Oak Flat
28
Hickory Flat
15
14
Bowen Road
13
27
10
12
Robben Crossing
9
11
26
Nesbitt Path
29
23
21
20
8
8a
22
24
7
6
Promise Land Road
5
4
Holton's Hollow
3
2
1
St. Paul Road

5
JUMPING JIM CROW

DAN VANLEER AND SALLIE EDMONDSON exchanged wedding vows on June 26, 1900. As the loving couple exchanged vows, the nation appeared to be taking steps to return to some semblance of normalcy. The year the couple exchanged wedding vows marked the eight-year anniversary of Homer Plessy purchasing a first-class ticket on a Louisiana train and being removed from his seat because of his race, and four years since the Supreme Court ruled that racial segregation was consistent with the US Constitution as long as equal facilities were provided for both races. State law clearly defined who a "Negro" was, declaring that this group included mulattoes, mestizos, and their descendants, having any blood of the African race in their veins. Any people who fell into these categories were defined as "persons of color" by the laws of the state and condemned them to lives that would enjoy the least of the best and disproportionately suffer from the worst things life in the Volunteer State had to offer its citizens. The state would spend less on Black pupils than it would white, and this discriminatory funding would extend from the one-room schoolhouse in Promise Land to Tennessee's lone public institution of higher learning for Black students, Tennessee Agricultural & Industrial (A&I) State Normal School for Negroes, which opened its doors twelve years after Dan and Sallie exchanged nuptials.

Life in Promise Land could insulate its residents from the day-to-day indignities of Jim Crow, as the community and its institutions extended them the type of dignity and respect that they would never receive in nearby Charlotte, Dickson, or when they ventured out to Nashville,

Clarksville, or Memphis. Nonetheless, there were many white voters in the state that were as committed to Black inequality as Black residents were to obtaining full citizenship. Sadly, many of these Tennesseans held public office, and their numbers increased while the number of African Americans holding public office declined dramatically by the time Dan and Sally exchanged vows.

In 1903, Senator Edward Carmack, reflecting the fervor and commitment many Tennesseans had to keep African Americans in a position as close to slavery as possible, wrote "The whites of the South are given the alternative of recovering their mastery or abandoning their country."[1] Every aspect of the lives of African Americans in the state was impacted by Jim Crow. Jim and Jane Crow led to the segregation of hospitals, libraries, stores, and public spaces, often with "colored" and "white" signs reminding community members of their respective places in society. In 1850, 62 percent of all the people enslaved by Montgomery Bell were listed as mulattoes or Blacks with both European and African ancestry. At the time when Dan married Sallie, antimiscegenation laws made the unions that produced these people a felony punishable by one to five years in prison.

Since its founding, the desire to obtain an education was one of the most fervent and visible manifestations of freedom, and the rapid construction of schools often outpaced the building of churches in the South. However, it was in the area of education that Tennessee's Black citizens felt the most diabolical forms of Jim Crow, ones that impacted them and their children on a daily basis. According to state law, education was to be segregated, and it was unlawful for Black and white pupils to attend the same schools; this included college. Anyone found violating this law could face a fine of up to fifty dollars for each offense and imprisonment from 30 to 180 days.[2]

The impact of the state's Jim Crow laws would result in unforeseen consequences on Promise Land and other communities throughout the state, causing them to fortify and strengthen the churches and schools in their community, transforming them into spaces that did more than provide education and spiritual direction for the community. Lessons in reading, writing, and arithmetic were to be had in the schools. Some were educated until their labor was needed to support their families, while others completed the twelfth grade and received the opportunity to attend college at Tennessee A&I or another one of America's Historically Black Colleges and Universities. Schools were also places where excellence was emphasized and strategies on how to survive and sometimes thrive in the face of Jim Crow were taught. These institutions became economic, social, and political centers in the community, places that often provided services that could not be found or accessed from state and municipal offices, social spaces, and other areas in Charlotte and Dickson where the indignities and humiliations they suffered under Jim Crow flourished.

Dan and Sallie and other African Americans that called rural Dickson County home in many instances embraced the ideology promoted by noted African American leader Booker T. Washington, from the Tuskegee Institute in Macon County, Alabama. In Washington's Atlanta Cotton Exposition Speech given in 1895, he warned the first generation of free-born African Americans that "Our greatest danger is that in the great leap from slavery to freedom we may overlook the fact that the masses of us are to live by the productions of our hands, and fail to keep in mind that we shall prosper in proportion as we learn to dignify and glorify common labor, and put brains and skill into the common occupations of life; shall prosper in proportion as we learn to draw the line between the superficial and the substantial, the ornamental gewgaws of life and the useful. No race can prosper till it learns that there is as much dignity in tilling a field as in writing a poem. It is at the bottom of life we must begin, and not at the top. Nor should we permit our grievances to overshadow our opportunities."[3] Many in Promise Land took the "Sage of Tuskegee's" advice and pursued commercial, subsistence, and tenant farming, as it was the most readily available way to make a living in rural Dickson County, where 60 percent of all its residents lived and worked on farms.[4]

While many in the community saw Washington's advocacy for an education that focused on vocations that would contribute to them becoming better farmers and tradesmen, the appreciation of their arts and culture persisted and desire for full American citizenship never subsided as Black populations entered the twentieth century. Their actions reveal that many agreed with W. E. B. Du Bois, noted Black intellectual and Washington critic, noting that "the ignorant Southerner hates the Negro, the workingmen fear his competition, the money-makers wish to use him as a laborer, some of the educated see a menace in his upward development, while others—usually the sons of the masters—wish to help him to rise."[5] Many would not fully endorse Washington's ideas as evidenced by Promise Land's producing intellectuals, poets and singers—some that were capable of filling the opera houses Washington encouraged them to eschew—in spite of the limitations Jim Crow placed on the community.

Dan and Sallie's wedding also marked the onset of the Great Migration, one of the largest movements of African Americans in US history. Although, there had been other diasporas of formerly enslaved from the South during and after Reconstruction, the most notable being led by Nashville's Benjamin "Pap" Singleton that encouraged African Americans to leave the South and move to Kansas, this movement would last for more than six decades. During this period, more than six million African Americans left the South for urban spaces in the Northeast, Midwest, and West. For some, growing Southern cities such as Memphis and Nashville became more attractive destinations. On the day the couple exchanged vows in 1900, there were 2,919 African Americans in Dickson County and by 1930, only 1,846 remained. This departure represents a decline of about 10 percent per decade during the start of the twentieth century, but Promise Land survived the departure of its residents. Many areas that emerged in Middle Tennessee—especially those established in Wilson, Rutherford, Williamson, Montgomery, Maury, and other counties with notable antebellum African American populations—did not.[6]

6
TAKING POSSESSION OF THE PROMISE LAND

IN ADDITION TO THE MEN who served in the Civil War, including members of the United States Colored Troop and those who provided services to the Confederate army, there were other formerly enslaved people who moved into the new settlement that included parts of District 6 and District 8 of Dickson County. Both my maternal and paternal ancestors were among these settlers. I have little information that details their lives before emancipation. These newly emancipated people apparently were not readily forthcoming in discussing their lives prior to freedom.

There are thousands of autobiographical firsthand accounts of enslaved Africans in America. However, most of these narratives were enlisted or initiated by abolitionists like Frederick Douglass, and others who authored, edited, and published them to benefit the movement to abolish slavery. In the late 1920s two historically Black universities, Fisk and Southern, begin to collect oral histories. This effort was followed in the 1930s Federal Writers Project, under the Works Progress Administration (WPA), which set out to interview formerly enslaved people in seventeen states. The interviews of 2,500 individuals were organized and published in 1941 as the *Slave Narratives: A Folk History of Slavery in the United States*. To my knowledge there were no interviews with any of the settlers in Promise Land.

My mother was born just fifty-two years after the end of slavery. I am sure she may have known a few people who had been enslaved. She told me that she was never able to engage anyone including her grandparents, great-aunts, or great-uncles to discuss their knowledge or perhaps experience with slavery. I agree with my mother, who believed that her elders preferred to live in the present rather than to revisit that painful history. I imagine that these were sorrowful, distressing memories for those who experienced it directly. This was the dreadful fate of both my maternal and paternal grandparents. I can only imagine what it was like for them to become free from the shackles of slavery. My third grandparents were as follows: on the maternal side were Joseph Washington Vanleer and his wife Rebecca Stokes Leech Vanleer, and Nathan Bowen and Lucy Carr Bowen. On my paternal side were William Gilbert and Violet Vanleer Gilbert, and James and Harriet Blair Armstrong.

Joseph Washington Vanleer, who became known as Wash, was about twenty-one years old when he was emancipated. He was born in the Cumberland Furnace; his mother's name is unknown to us. Apparently, he was separated from his mother at a young age and did not develop any type of relationship with her. He acknowledged and recognized an older brother, whose name was Ransom. Ransom lived in Promise Land for a while but moved back to the furnace where he worked as a paid laborer at the Cumberland Furnace after emancipation. The majority of those enslaved at the furnace were men; however, there were roles for women as well. They were washerwomen, cooks, and cleaning women. Family folklore was that Wash was fathered by the furnace owner, Anthony Wayne Vanleer. Vanleer was from Chester County, Pennsylvania and was heir to the Reading Iron Works. He purchased the Cumberland Furnace from Montgomery Bell along with two partners, Isaac H. Lanier and Wallace H. Dickson, in 1825. By 1840 Cumberland Furnace had become the nation's third-largest iron-producing furnaces. It operated continuously with a labor force consisting primarily of enslaved men and women.

Born about 1844, Joseph was likely enslaved at the furnace until he was freed. The furnace operations were shut down in 1862 when the Union army occupied Nashville and its surrounding areas, including Dickson County. Several major things happened during this brief period. Anthony Wayne Vanleer died in 1863. The war ended and the furnace reopened under new ownership. Before his death Vanleer had willed the furnace to his granddaughter, Mary Florence Kirkman. Kirkman was living in Nashville during the war where she met and married a Union officer, Major James P. Drouillard. Drouillard resigned his commission and moved with

Florence Kirkman to Cumberland Furnace, where he built her a mansion that still stands today. He reopened the furnace and hired people who were once enslaved there to return as paid laborers.

As changes were being made at the furnace, Joseph Washington Vanleer was also making some major life changes. It does not appear that he was waiting to see what would happen with the furnace. I am not sure if Wash remained in bondage during the furnace shut down or not. From family records, I found that during this period he united with Rebecca Stokes Leech, a young woman also from Cumberland Furnace. Like Wash, she had been enslaved and was fathered by a white man. The practice of slave owners and other white men fathering children by enslaved women was not uncommon. It was another way for the enslaver to demonstrate dominance, exert control, demean the victims, and to increase their personal wealth. Yes, producing children by enslaved women resulted in profit for the slave owner. There has been much written on this topic so, to avoid giving the practice more credence, I will not discuss it further here. Rebecca was born in 1847. She was the sister to Ellen Clemons, the wife of Private John Nesbitt of the USCT discussed earlier in this book. In 1864, the first child was born to Joseph and Rebecca. Named after his father, he was called "Little Joe." Less than two years later, his sister Ellen was born. Ellen, born in 1865 was nicknamed "Sis." It was and still is customary for Black parents to nickname their oldest female "Sister," "Sis," or "Baby Sis." The older son might receive the nickname of "Brother," "Baby Brother," or "Bubba." Throughout this text you will see this pattern as other family units are described. The records show that Cumberland Furnace was the birthplace for both Little Joe and Sis.

At the age of twenty-four, on January 6, 1868, Joseph Washington (Wash) Vanleer purchased 132 acres of land in a wooded area in District 6 of Charlotte, Tennessee. The handwritten deed reads, "We Thomas Overton and A. S. Gill, have this day bargained so and do hereby transfer and convey to Joe Vanleer (Colored Man) and his heirs forever for the consideration of four hundred dollars to us paid as follows to wit: Two hundred dollars cash; and two hundred dollars payable 25, day of December 1868." The document proceeds to describe the location of the purchased property. In summary, this young, formerly enslaved man made his first land purchase less than six years after the signing of the Emancipation Proclamation. This had to be one of the happiest and most significant occasions in the life of Wash and his young family. The site itself was an uncultivated, heavily wooded rural area located about five miles from

Cumberland Furnace and about three miles from the city of Charlotte. The land was rugged and long unattended. It had some small hills and slopes with a lovely spring and other streams. It was about a half a mile from the Old Clarksville Stage Road, which is now Promise Land Road. Today it sits just off State Highway 48 North. This roadway did not exist at the time of Wash's land purchase.

Wash was apparently a successful subsistence farmer, raising crops and livestock enough to support his fast-growing family. Growing up I remember the orchards, with apple, plum, and peach trees that dotted the property. There were also hickory nuts and walnut trees throughout the tracts of land. Joseph and Rebecca had seven more children after moving into Promise Land. The children were born in succession. In 1869, their son Isham was born. He was followed by daughters Panthera in 1870 and Nara in 1873. In 1874 their son Daniel was born, and daughter Milley was born in 1876. It seems that there was a brief respite before my great-grandmother Farmie Della was born in 1880. She was followed by the last child Priscilla, born in 1882.

My mother never got to know her maternal great-grandfather as he died in 1902, before she was born. She told me that she recalled that he was spoken of in loving ways by her grandmother, and her great-aunts and -uncles and her own mother who was only eight years old when he died. She said that he was held in high regard by the surviving elders in the community. He was known in the community as "Wash," short for Washington, or as "Brother Wash." He was one of the founding members of the Mt. Olive Baptist Church established in Promise Land in 1884. I recall asking how she thought he may have looked. She said that she was told that he had a smooth brown complexion and was of small stature. My mother, however, had a vivid memory of her great-grandmother Rebecca. She recalled her physical appearance and her behavior. Rebecca Vanleer left quite an impression on her wide-eyed granddaughter. Mother recalled that Grandma Rebecca looked very much like a little ole white woman, who was quick and feisty. She spoke with an accent and instead of saying "I," she would use the word "der." Mother said that Grandma Rebecca reminded her of a bantam hen who was always ready to "flog" someone. She remembers hearing her say, "der gon fight you." This little lady must have been quite a spectacle for the eyes and mind of an impressionable preschooler. I believe that Rebecca, who would have been in her seventies, may have been exhibiting some signs of dementia. Rebecca Vanleer passed away in 1920. Little Essie was only four years old when she died.

Mother grew up knowing her great-aunts and -uncles except for her Uncle Dan, Aunt Panthera, and Aunt Milley. All of them had passed prior to or soon after her birth. Although they had passed on, they were remembered through family and community members' talk of them. They left behind property, spouses, and offspring. Through these sources Mother came to know them quite well. With affection, she recalled that those who remained on the farm lived on tracts of land that bordered the original homesite. Others moved elsewhere in the county, Nashville, or other surrounding areas in Tennessee and other states. She often spoke of the family gathering when Wash and Rebecca's offspring and descendants would return for visits. These gatherings included special church and school events, weddings, and funerals that would lure the large family back to the Promise Land Community. Mother continued to identify the old homes of her great-uncles and -aunts by their names until her demise. This practice helped me to become acquainted with most of these ancestors who I never had the pleasure of meeting.

The Vanleer Cemetery remains on the original property. This is where Wash and Rebecca and most of their children and extended family are interred. My parents and some of my siblings are also buried there and, if it is God's will, that is where I will also be laid to rest.

THE FIRST GENERATION OF WASH AND REBECCA'S DESCENDANTS

Lil Joe Vanleer (First Born Son)

Born in 1864, Lil Joe was the first child born to Wash and Rebecca. His birth occurred before his father had made the land purchase, which demonstrated that he and his family were indeed free to move forward independently. Joe grew up working on the farm alongside his father, creating a home and farm from a previously wooded area. This was undoubtedly quite a feat for a growing child. I can't imagine that he did not have much of a childhood as we know it today. When he became a man, his father gave him a sizable tract of land to farm on his own. He began courting a young woman from Cumberland Furnace. Her name was Delilah Brown. They later married on August 19, 1882, and settled on his farm. Like his father, Lil Joe was a successful farmer and both he and Delilah were well respected in the community. They welcomed their first son John Thomas into the family in 1883. Their second son, Ellege, arrived in 1886. It appears that all was going well until a horrible event occurred on the farm that shook up the entire Promise Land community and surrounding area.

It was an atrocious evil crime committed against the family. Perhaps it was motivated by envy of the success of Wash and his family as independent farmers and landowners. The incident took place on a cold winter night, when a white mob led by a man name Cyrus Mathis invaded Lil Joe's home.

The following account of the event was reported in the Clarksville Leaf Chronicle, February 19, 1893, under the heading, "Terrible Deeds Committed by Masked Men Near Charlotte":

> Mathis headed a crowd of boys to the residence of Joe Vanleer, an aged negro, outraged and beat his daughter, and then caught another woman who was staying at the place, outraging her also. The alarm was sounded soon after the men left the house and officers soon had Mathis and a young man named Elliott arrested, charged with taking a hand in meanness. They were carried to Charlotte and put in jail. Sunday the negroes flocked to the town from all directions, and it was thought at first the men would be lynched. Better counsel prevailed, however, and it is thought now that the law will be allowed to take its course. Other arrest will follow.

This story was told in the family through the years. However, it was told as if it was a secret not to be shared outside the confines of the immediate family. My mother was aware of it, and she told her children. I was actually astounded to find the newspaper account of this atrocity. There are some omissions from the newspaper account that are important to share. The men (not "boys") who invaded the residence were armed with rifles and shotguns. Lil Joe was twenty-nine years old at the time, however under the circumstances of being caught off guard in the middle of the night he may have appeared older and helpless. He was totally unprepared and unarmed. He was defenseless against the men as they raped ("outraged") his wife and his seventeen-year-old sister, Milley, who was sleeping over at his house. Also in the home were his two young sons. According to the story handed down, the whole family was traumatized by this event. Joe was angry, regretful, and chagrined that this had occurred under his watch and to his family. It greatly affected his wife and sister. They carried the hurt, humiliation, and scars of the violation for the rest of their lives. This may have been demonstrated by their behavior and choices that they made later in life. The extended family and community was a source of strength to help them cope and overcome to the fullest extent possible. Lil Joe, his father, and brothers became more vigilant in their coming and going. Although they were men of faith, they were known to be armed. As far as the "law taking its course," my mother said that she never heard if the men were ever prosecuted. To her knowledge there was no record or talk of any aftermath. This was a period in history when horrific crimes like these were flagrantly committed by white antagonists against Black lives throughout the South without retribution.

Lil Joe and Delilah demonstrated the resilience and fortitude that our ancestors are known to have had, as they moved on with their lives of farming and raising their family. Their sons helped on the farm and attended Promise Land School. I don't have much information on the youngest son, Ellege. However, John Thomas, whom my mother called "Uncle John" although he was the son of her great-uncle Joe, remained in Promise Land until he was a young adult. On December 26, 1905, at the age of twenty-one, John married a seventeen-year-old Bertie Bowen, a descendant of Nathan Bowen. The couple made their marital home with Lil Joe and Delilah. John continued to work on his father's farm. His mother Delilah passed away about a year after he and Bertie were married. She died in October 1906 at the age of forty-two, about twelve years after she had been assaulted and raped. According to family lore, she had no physical causes that attributed to her demise. It seems that after the assault, she attempted to carry on as wife and mother as she had been expected to do. Perhaps she believed that with her oldest son married and another adult woman in her home, she could now get away from it all and take her a well-deserved rest.

Delilah's death left her forty-one-year-old husband Joe residing in their home with his son and his son's new bride. On October 10, 1907, John Thomas and Bertie's first child, John Jr., was born. Their second child, Verle, was born almost a year later in 1908. A third child, Josephine, was born in 1910 and in 1914, Joseph, the fourth child was born. The little wood-frame house was quickly filling up. With his expanding family, John had some concerns about the safety and security on the farm. After all, he had been a child who witnessed the invasion of his father's home by a hate-filled, racist mob of intruders. Perhaps he had heard of other such incidents occurring around him. John had family and friends who were moving from Promise Land in large numbers to northern cities like Cleveland and Columbus, Ohio, as well as to Indianapolis and Detroit.

From the stories shared by friends of their success, he was inspired to consider giving up the farm and relocating. He shared these considerations with Bertie, who agreed that perhaps they could find a better life in the north. Together they convinced his father to uproot them and move to Cleveland, Ohio. His father probably accepted that he wasn't getting younger and that it would be difficult for him to run the farm alone. They decided to sell off goods, livestock, and tools to help fund the move. Other items like furniture, meat from the smokehouse, etc., they gave away to his grandmother and other family members. Before moving the whole family, John went to Cleveland and stayed with a former Promise Land resident while he looked for a job and a place for his family to stay. He found a job as a boiler room fireman. He also found an apartment near his place of employment for the family. In 1914, they moved to Cleveland, Ohio, which would become the home for Joe, John, Bertie, and the children for the rest of their lives.

John and Bertie had two more children after leaving Promise Land. They were Mary Elizabeth born in 1920 and Edward, born 1922. John had already started his employment before returning to Tennessee to bring the family back with him. He was able to maintain stable employment. He promptly found separate living arrangements for his father. His father, who was still under the age of fifty, also found sustainable employment. John and Bertie opened their home to relatives from Promise Land who sought to establish themselves in Cleveland. This included a teenage nephew, Hershell, whose mother had died before he had reached the age of majority. Sandy and Crawford Redden, brothers and the sons of John's Aunt Milley, also accepted John's invitation to utilize their home as a transitional springboard. After getting a foothold, the brothers also made Cleveland their permanent home.

Lil Joe Vanleer and his son John enjoyed a long-distance relationship with their family in Promise Land. Initially, they visited Promise Land almost annually. As years passed, their visits became more sporadic. His surviving siblings and their children reciprocated the visits. Other members of the community also felt welcome to visit the Vanleer family when they were in Cleveland. Lil Joe passed away of natural causes in Cleveland in 1936 at the age of seventy-four. He died a dignified and resilient man of faith. In Cleveland, he had found a church home for himself and his son's family to replace the one they had left in Promise Land. Despite the horrific incidents that he, his wife and young family endured nearly forty-three years before his death, he was able to live a reasonable long life with his mental faculties and physicality intact. I say long life, considering that average life expectancy Black men then was only fifty-nine years. His son, John who died in 1962 lived to the age of seventy-eight years old. Both John and his father were buried in Cleveland, Ohio.

Ellen Vanleer Majors Hannah and Daughter Anna

Ellen was the oldest girl born to Wash and Rebecca. She was known as "Sis" by her parents and siblings. To her nieces, nephews, and their children she was "Aunt Sis." She was an elderly woman, probably in her eighties, when I came to know her. She lived in the neighboring Hickman County, so we didn't see her often. However, she would come to visit my great-grandmother, her sister, Farmie on special occasions. As a child, I recognized that her thought processes had begun to fail her. During one of her visits, she was preparing her bath, when she came into the kitchen and got the butter from a tray on the table and proceeded to her bath area. Luckily, she was being assisted by another family member who caught her before she dropped the butter into the tub. In explaining her actions, she stated, "I thought that was soap." The kids got a big laugh from that. I feel blessed that I had the opportunity to have known this amazing woman born to formerly enslaved parents, even if it was for just a brief time. Her biography is a collection of my memories, especially stories from conversations from my elders; my mother's reminiscences; and from documents pertaining to the life of Aunt Sis.

Born shortly after the Civil War, Ellen Vanleer was born in the Cumberland Furnace just before her parents, Wash and Rebecca, like pioneers established their home in a previously unsettled area that would become known as Promise Land. Her father created a farm out of a vast forest. The chores required of a pioneer family were obviously great. However, Ellen grew up working with her family in the establishment of their farm. According to family history, she attended a home school in the community to learn to read and write. During her late teens, she took a job as a live-in domestic for a white family in Dickson. While in Dickson, she became acquainted with a young man named Drew Majors. After a brief courtship they were married with her parents' permission. Drew Majors took her to his home, which was on a farm in a community outside the Dickson city limits called Colesburg. On June 13, 1894, Ellen gave birth to a girl, who they named Anna. Anna's birth was followed within a reasonable timeframe by two sons in succession. They were named William and Paul. The family was sustained by their small farm, which they all pitched in to make a success. Ellen was an excellent homemaker. Her daughter modeled after her. At an early age she began to work alongside her mother. In addition to keeping house and helping with meal preparation, canning, and washing, Anna also helped her brothers and father with farm chores. This idyllic lifestyle changed greatly when Drew Majors passed away in 1907. His death left Ellen alone to raise three school-aged children. This loss may have resulted in Ellen giving up the farm and moving back to Dickson. After moving back to Dickson, Ellen resumed work as a cook and housekeeper in the homes of white families. She and her children settled in East Dickson in an area known as "Scofftown." My mother pointed out the location of their home to me numerous times. Apparently, family members would often visit and stay with Ellen at this address. Likewise, Ellen would visit her family in Promise Land.

Not long after relocating, Ellen's family suffered another tragic blow. The youngest son, Paul, died suddenly at the age of thirteen of an overwhelming infection. My mother was not born when this event happened, but she remembered it being discussed by her grandmother and aunts. Perhaps the impact of these losses helped draw Ellen closer to her family of origin. One thing for sure was that the family of origin had certainly dwindled significantly. By 1921, both Wash and Rebecca were deceased, and by 1926, five of their nine offspring had passed on.

My mother was five years old when her mother brought her from their home in Nashville to Promise Land to live with her grandparents, George and Farmie Bowen. She shared that she remembered her Aunt Sis coming to visit. She described her great-aunt Sis as being a stylish, middle-aged woman whose visits the whole family looked forward to. Mother was equally impressed by her older cousin Anna, who at that time was a young woman in her early twenties. Mother recalled hearing the grownups discuss that Sis was keeping company with a gentleman preacher, whose name was Rev. George Hannah. She remembered that her grandfather, George Bowen, invited Rev. Hannah to speak at the Mt. Olive African Methodist Episcopal Church in Promise Land. After that engagement, Rev. Hannah would often bring Ellen and Anna to visit. Rev. Hannah asked Ellen to marry him. They were married in Dickson on February 13, 1937. This was the second marriage for both. The couple is reported living in Dickson in the 1940 Census. Rev. Hannah died in 1942. Ellen lived independently for nearly a decade. During that time her surviving son, William Majors, also passed away. Anna had married years earlier and moved to Centerville, Tennessee, with her husband James Cathey. James Cathey was a widower, ten years older than Anna. He was the father of ten children, five girls and five boys. Anna happily assumed the role of instant mother when they married, and she moved to the farm.

As the years passed, Ellen's cognitive functioning declined, and she became less capable of self-care and independence. By this time Anna and James Cathey's children had grown up and moved out of the household. So, in 1946, Anna moved her eighty-year-old mother into the home which she shared with her aging husband and his eighty-seven-year-old mother. At fifty-four years old, Anna had become an in-home caregiver for her husband, her mother, and her mother-in-law. Her mother-in-law, Sylvia McCall, passed away shortly after Ellen moved into the home. Within two years of her mother-n-law's death, Anna's husband of fifteen years died. Then, on February 18, 1953, Anna's mother, Ellen Vanleer Majors Hannah died at the age of eighty-seven years old. She was returned to her family home in Promise Land for visitation, funeral at the Mt. Olive Baptist Church, and burial at the family cemetery in Promise Land.

Cousin Anna remained living alone at her home in Centerville for many years. I fondly remember visiting her on many occasions with my parents and siblings. It was always a pleasant visit; she would greet each of us with hugs and kisses. Her tiny house was always neat as a pin and so was she. I don't remember ever seeing her without being dressed in anything other than a freshly laundered print dress and starched white apron. The apron was significant to me, because it signaled that a deliciously prepared home cooked meal awaited us. This meal was cooked on her old wood-fired cookstove. And, it was not complete without iced tea and one of her delicious cobblers. She always managed to get all of us comfortably seated at her dining room table. It was usually at least eight of us and there we would linger long after the meal was finished.

As Cousin Anna aged, her stepdaughter, whose name was also Anna (to make a distinction she was called Anna Lou [Rodgers]), came to live with her. In 1974, the two of them moved to Anna Lou's home in Evansville, Indiana. Anna Lou had lived in Evansville for many years and there she had many family members, including a son, Jesse. Jesse, a young man, became quite an attentive and loving caregiver to his mother. Cousin

Anna died on December 4, 1999. She lived to be 105 years old. She left a host of grandchildren and great-grandchildren.

Isham Vanleer, Tennessee's Natural Born Negro Poet

Isham followed Ellen in birth order. He was born on the farm in 1869. Like his older siblings he had his work cut out from birth. Along with cultivating the farm, it appears that Isham took advantage of the meager education opportunities that were offered in Promise Land. By the time he was school age, literacy classes were being offered out of the home of Civil War veteran, Pvt. John Nesbitt and his wife, Ellen Clemmon Nesbitt. Miss Ellen had taken the initiative to teach young people and adults in the community to read and write. This was to facilitate acclimation to the new freedom. It was also the forerunner of the Promise Land School. Isham's literary skills and talents are evidence that he may have taken advantage of this opportunity.

It is not documented where or if Isham had any additional training; however, he became a prolific writer who proclaimed himself as "Isham C. Vanleer, Tennessee's Natural Born Negro Poet." My great-grandmother had a collection of his works, which passed down to my mother. It appears that his writings were published near the beginning of the twentieth century. All that I have from my great-grandmother's collection appears to have been copied from a book or periodical. The theme of the writings ranges from events that occurred during his life to hymn like sonnets. They include titles such as: "Titanic on Her Maiden Voyage on the Atlantic Ocean, April 14, 1912." This is his recapitulation of the fatal voyage of the Titanic. It contains fourteen verses that give accounts of the incident that he may have obtained from newspaper reports; Another example is "The N.C. & St. Louis Ry Wreck." This is a nine-verse poem/song about the tragic train derailment which happened in 1918 at Dutchman's Curve in Nashville, Tennessee. He has a more intimate and anguish-filled poem that he wrote which recounts details of the murder of his brother, Dan Vanleer. There is also a compelling hymnal composed by him entitled, "Inspired Thoughts of the Harvest Field." From the lyrics of this beautiful song, you will know that the author has a knowledge of farming. I could not help wondering if parts of the song were inspired by the evil deed that was perpetrated against his nephew's home in 1893.

In the research of Isham, I found a poem that was apparently submitted to a federal office. It was in the Washington, DC, Pension Correspondence and Case Files of Formerly Enslaved People, 1892–1922. This writing contains seventeen verses. There seems to be an attempt to blend historic with biblical occurrences. The following is a reprint of the original.

REVELATIONS OF THE WAR

(From the "National Capitol")

Think of this cruel war
With this slight illustration
Three years from the time declared
Abe Lincoln's proclamation.

In eighteen hundred and sixty-one
When Lincoln took his seal
As President for Uncle Sam
Did Booth cause his defeat.

Nineteen years from sixty-one
When Garfield was elected
Assassinated by Giteau,
How many were suspected.

This was the second effort made
The power to them was give
To deliver from under bondage
Like Moses did not live.

In eighteen hundred and ninety-seven
When McKinley took his station,
He was the third to carry out
Abe Lincoln's exultation.

Some will read and give a thought
With this consideration
How this government will be changed
Is beyond explanation.

Go, read the book of Moses,
What a fair representation
About the land that's promised
To the African generation.

Moses was the leader
God gave this information.
Abraham Lincoln this
In his dreaded visitation.

Aaron was next to Moses,
Short was his installation.
James A. Garfield was the same
All on this grand occasion.

Joshua was next commanded
With all of his persuasion—
Like Bill McKinley with this war
Will deal out consolation.

Forty years from sixty-one,
(Please watch this revelation)
Some will doubt, but surely find out
It's not imagination.

Forty years from the time
Of the emancipation
Uncle Sam will then decide
On the negro's emigration.

In nineteen hundred and one,
With little consultation,
Your president may be a king
Without hesitation.

United States will be surprise
To find obliteration,
And when this war is ended
She'll have her education.

Some good step will Congress take
In her future occupation,
To change some laws she does make
In her present legislation.

Equal rights will justice meet
And sign these obligations—
We are the purchase of his blood—
Have come through great tribulation.

Looking forward to that faith
With self-examination,
You can find this if you read
The plan of salvation.

ISHAM C. VANLEER
Tennessee's Natural Born Negro Poet

Isham's address is listed on some of his poems, which is an indication that he moved often during his relatively short life. He had at least three marriages. The first was at the age of eighteen, when he married a young woman who was from Coaling, a Charlotte community located north of Promise Land. Her name was Bettie Talley. They were married on November 23, 1877. His second marriage was in 1906 to Nettie Bosley of Cumberland Furnace. As a child I knew Miss Bosley as "Cousin Nette." I also knew her granddaughter, Juanita, who was the same age as my oldest sister. The two of them were friends. We knew that we were related, but we did not know how. As it appears that Cousin Nette's marriage to Isham dissolved, she had remarried when I knew her. Isham also moved on, and according to family and records, he worked as a laborer in Nashville. He also had several addresses in Nashville. Some of the addresses listed on some of his poems were 902 43rd Avenue North, 161 Lafayette Street, and 720 Gay Street. His last marriage was to Minnie McComic Neblett. They were married in the home of the bride, located in Hortense, which was like Promise Land, a Black settlement in Dickson County and established during the Reconstruction period. The marriage took place on August 18, 1912. Isham was living in Nashville when he died at the age of fifty-three of a heart attack. Funeral services were held for him at his home church, Mt. Olive AME Church in Promise Land. His remains are buried in the Vanleer Cemetery which is located on the land purchased by his father.

Panthera Vanleer Cunningham

Panthera was the second daughter and fourth child born to Wash and Rebecca. She was born in 1870. She was interchangeably known as "Pant" and "Panthie." My mother referred to her by both nicknames, probably because that is what she heard her mother and grandmother call her. Panthie was forty-two years old when she married Lev Cunningham, a local farmer and son of original Promise Land settlers Sol and Mandy Cunningham. He was ten years younger than Panthie. Panthie entered their marriage with three children aged eight months to twelve years old. Her children were the results of a long-term affair that she had with a man who was socially unavailable to her. He was a resident of the community who was already married. Her children included a son Hershel, a daughter Euvilous (the middle child), and the baby Wille B. She and her children were found in the 1900 Census, residing in the home of origin with her sister and brother-in-law, George and Farmie Bowen. After her marriage to Lev, the couple begin to clear the land that she had inherited from her father to build a home. It was located on an uncultivated, wooded area of the Vanleer's property and bordered near Lev's family farm. They built a small three-room wood-frame house. Although it was small it sufficed for the growing family. By 1917 three more children had been added to the family unit. They were two sons and a daughter, Richard, Mary Bea, and Beasley. Unfortunately, this flourishing household came to an abrupt halt. Sadly, Panthie passed away on February 27, 1919, at Vanderbilt Hospital in Nashville, where she was a patient being treated for intestinal obstruction. Peritonitis resulted from a surgery that she had undergone was listed as the cause of her death. She died less than two years after Beasley's birth.

Panthie's death created a major upheaval in the family structure. The children required separation in the aftermath of her departure. When the family gathered for her memorial services, in addition to grieving and planning her funeral, they were also tasked with planning placement of the children. Her husband and siblings decided that the older boys, Herchel who was seventeen years old, and Wille B. who was ten, would relocate from the community. Panthie's first cousin, John T. Vanleer, the oldest son of Little Joe, agreed to take them to live with him and his family in Cleveland, Ohio. Her sister, Nara, who resided in Promise Land at the time with her husband and three children, agreed to take ten-year-old Euvilous into their home. Five-year-old Richard was taken into the home of my great-grandparents, his Aunt Farmie and Uncle George. This was not a major adjustment for him as he was well accustomed to them as they lived near the Cunninghams, and he would be able to see his younger siblings often. His baby sister Mary Bea and Beasley would stay with their father.

The funeral was held at the Mt. Olive AME Church where she and Lev were members. The little one-room church overflowed. There were many friends and family members in the community and surrounding communities in attendance. In addition, the event drew the attendance of family members, friends, and acquaintances from nearby counties including Davidson, Hickman, and Montgomery, as well as from out of state. The funeral service was followed by her burial, which took place at her family's cemetery.

Nara Vanleer Nesbitt

Born in 1873, Nara was Wash and Rebecca's third daughter and fifth child. Like the other children she was raised on the farm. At the age of eighteen she married Johnnie Nesbitt, a young man who had also been raised in Promise Land, on September 20, 1891. Johnnie was the son of USCT veteran Arch Nesbitt and Tennessee Hickerson Nesbitt. Johnnie was twenty-one years old, and he grew up working on his father's farm. By the time he and Nara married, he had secured employment as a farm laborer at the Hickerson farm in Charlotte. This was the same farm where his mother, Tennessee Mahalia, had been enslaved before her emancipation. With a new bride, Johnnie accepted the opportunity to become a sharecropper on the Hickerson farm. He and Nara started their family soon after establishing their home. They were the parents of three children, Elizabeth born in 1892, Lilly born in 1894, and Johnnie McKinley born in 1897. Nara was content in her role as wife, mother, and homemaker. She was remembered by her family as being a great cook and housekeeper. She had inherited the skill of sewing from her mother and became a seamstress not just for her family but others in the extended family. Sometime around 1907 she became a widow. Johnnie passed away. The cause of his death is unknown to the writer. The date or the cause of his demise has not been revealed from my search of documents or from any oral family history. What is known is that Nara and the children moved from the Hickersons' farm to the home of her in-laws in Promise Land. Nara found work in Nashville as a live-in servant for a family who lived there. In the 1910 Census she is reported as residing in the home of the Riddle family who lived on West End Avenue in Nashville, where she is listed as the cook.

By the time the 1920 Census was issued, Nara had rented a home on 44th Avenue North in Nashville, where she was living with her children. She later purchased the home and resided there for the rest of her life. During her lifetime the home was always filled with her children, grandchildren, as well as other extended family members including nieces, nephews, and other visitors from the Promise Land community. Nara continued to support her family with work as a cook in the homes of private families. She also supplemented her income with work as a commercial seamstress. She had many faithful clients who kept her in business.

As her children grew up, they moved out on their own. Her son, John McKinley, went into the military in 1919 and served during World War I. After an honorable discharge he returned to Nashville and soon married. He established his own home in Nashville for himself and his family. Nara's daughters Elizabeth and Lilly both married. Like their brother, they established separate households, though for brief periods as their marriages were quickly dissolved and they would return to their mother's home. Elizabeth's husband left her a widow within a few years of their marriage. They did not have any children. After moving back into her mother's household, Elizabeth sadly passed away from kidney failure at the age of thirty-two. Lilly's marriage ended in divorce after welcoming two daughters into the unit. Her daughters, Jinara and Shirley, were quite young when they moved into their grandmother's home. In the late 1950s, Lilly relocated with her adult daughter Shirley, and Shirley's two children, to Detroit, Michigan. Jinara remained in the home alone until 1964 when she was institutionalized for mental health issues at Central State Hospital in Nashville. She remained at that hospital until her death in 1974. Her body was returned to the family cemetery for burial in Promise Land.

Nara passed away after a long illness at her beloved home on Friday evening, December 21, 1951, just two months after her sister Farmie Della's death. With a long residence in Nashville where she had cultivated relationships with her church, organizations, and a network of friends, clients, and associates, it was natural that her funeral would be held there and so it was. I remember the event of her death being a big topic of discussion among family and neighbors in Promise Land. I knew that she would be sorely missed by our family and extended family, as her home had served as a "must visit" by all the Promise Land community. It was decided that my younger siblings and I would not attend the funeral as my parents and older siblings would be traveling by car with my Aunt Mable and Uncle Peony. I was very disappointed but accepting of the decision, as I was still reeling from the death and services of my great-grandmother. Aunt Nara's funeral was held at the St. Luke AME Church in Nashville. She had been a member there since moving to Nashville nearly forty-five years earlier. Her remains were taken to the Vanleer Cemetery for interment.

Daniel Hays Vanleer (Dan)

Daniel Hayes Vanleer was the sixth child born to Wash and Rebecca. Born in 1874, he was also their third and last son. Like the other sons, Daniel was raised working on the farm and like many of the young men, he sought additional income by also working at the nearby Cumberland Furnace. When he was twenty-six years old, he married seventeen-year-old Sallie Edmondson, the daughter of Jefferson and Charlotte Bowen Edmondson of the Promise Land Community. They were married on December 20, 1900. The two settled in a house that Dan had built on a tract of land given him by his father. The house was located beneath the hill within walking distance from his parents' home.

On April 10, 1901, just four months and ten days after Dan and Sallie's nuptials, their bliss was shattered by a tragedy. Dan was fatally shot on the grounds of his workplace at the Cumberland Furnace. The family knew the story of this tragedy well. It was relived in discreet family conversations from one generation to the next. His brother Isham gave a very heartfelt and vivid recount of the tragedy in one of his poems entitled "The Death of Daniel Vanleer." In his narration of the fatal incident, Isham describes the scene, stating that Dan was ambushed and shot with the bullet piercing through his side. The recounting states that he fell immediately and landed prostrate on the ground. There were some who came near him and overheard his acknowledgment of the assailant. Isham wrote, "Tho' many friends stood aghast, Lord have mercy," was the last; "Tom Bowen has shot me." According to the poetic narrative, the assassin immediately absconded after the shooting. An account in *The Tennessean* dated April 12 reported that Vanleer was carrying a load of pig iron to put in a transport vessel on the grounds of the Warner furnace. Bowen had hidden inside the vessel. When Vanleer approached, Bowen took a single shot that "buried a squirrel load" into Vanleer's side, killing him instantly.

The paper further reported that there had been a previous altercation "some time ago" when Vanleer had "severely cut" Bowen, and at that time Bowen had said that he would kill Vanleer "at his first opportunity."

The news reported that Bowen turned himself in at the sheriff's office while officers were hunting for him. He waived the preliminary hearing and was taken into custody at the Charlotte Jail. A related story by a different newspaper reported in the headline nearly three months later, "Four Desperate Prisoners Escape from Charlotte Jail." The story reported that four men had escaped the jail on a Saturday afternoon June 24, 1901. Tom Bowen, according to the paper, was the only "colored" among the group who escaped. The charges for the four included murder, larceny, and assault with intent to kill. One of the escapees had been apprehended at the time of the report, however, "nothing had been heard" from the other three including Bowen.

This event was obviously devastating to the Vanleer and Bowen family. The anguish felt by Isham was very apparent in his writing. Death of a sibling is sure to draw distress, pain, and grief. When you add death by homicide, an extra layer of devastation is presented. When the homicide is perpetrated by a family member, the emotions brought to bear are exacerbated. Tom Bowen was the first cousin to Dan. Tom was nearly twenty years older than Dan. Dan had known him all of his life. Their families were close-knit and intertwined. They were also members of the same church in Promise Land. According to the family's spin, the dispute and altercation resulted from an alleged affair between Dan's wife and his cousin. At the time of the occurrence Tom Bowen was actually married and living with his wife and six children in Montgomery County, Tennessee. Despite the hurt and grief that it caused, the family was able to remain close-knit, and to live in peace and harmony. I am uncertain if Tom was ever apprehended by the law. I am aware that he returned to his family and apparently turned his life around. He became a very stable patriarch within his family and community. This will be elaborated on further when we explore the Bowen family saga.

Dan's bride, Sallie, continued to live in the home that he provided for her, and she lived there the rest of her life. I remember her well and recall her as being a very independent and self-reliant woman. Sallie moved on with her life following the death of Dan. She remarried a gentleman in the community whose name was John Suggs. They married in 1908 and had three children, a daughter who was named Hazel, followed by two sons, Emmitt and Leonard. By the time I was born, "Aunt Sallie," as she was known to me, was an elderly woman. Her sons were grown and married with young adult children of their own. Her daughter had died and left behind three young children who were raised by Aunt Sallie. Left were two sons, Robert Lee and Daniel, and a daughter Jean. Robert Lee and Daniel were grown and had moved out of her household. They would visit her often. I remember only Jean residing with Aunt Sallie. Jean was in high school, and I thought that she was absolutely gorgeous. I remember that she was the valedictorian of her graduating class. This achievement brought much pride to the community. After graduation, she moved to Nashville, married, and started a family. She was a charter member of the Promise Land Heritage Association and in 2010, she became a member of the PLHA Elder Circle. Jean passed away in 2016. Aunt Sallie lived to be ninety-nine years old. She died October 16, 1982, of a heart attack. She is buried in the Vanleer Cemetery.

Milley Vanleer and Husband Boss Redden

Milley was the fourth daughter and seventh child born into the Joe Washington Vanleer family. Like her siblings, Milley grew up on the farm. By the time she reached the age of seventeen, three of her older siblings were married. Her oldest brother, known as Little Joe, was married and lived near her father's farm. She would often stay at Little Joe's farm to assist her sister-in-law Delilah with work like canning and putting away meat during hog-killing season. She would also enjoy looking after their two young sons. It was during hog-killing season when a mob of white men invaded Joe's farm. This is when she and Delilah suffered the most vicious and horrendous assault to their bodies. They were violently raped by the intruders, which had a devastating effect on both of them. According to mother's report, Milley was small in stature. She was known to be quiet and soft-spoken. After the assault, she became even more withdrawn. She was afraid to venture far from her father's presence.

At the age of twenty-three she married a young man in the community whose name was William Plummer Redden. He was better known in the county as "Boss Redden." They were married on December 28, 1898. Boss's personality was the exact opposite of Milley's. He was large in stature, verbose, and outgoing. He was well acquainted with her father and met his approval to become her spouse. Perhaps his stature and personality made her feel safe and protected. After marrying, they lived briefly in the home of Boss's uncle and aunt, William and Priscilla Gilbert. The Gilberts were my paternal great-grandparents. They had raised Boss from the age of thirteen, when he had become orphaned by the death of both parents, Frank and Rachel Redden. During their stay in the Gilberts' household, their first child, Crawford, was born. Not long after Crawford's birth in 1900, the family moved into their own home. Their house was built on a plot of land given to Milley by her father, close to her parents' home. There had been a field where their house was built. So, the land was well cultivated with orchards of fruit tress including plum, peach, and apple trees. On their farm, they raised hogs for slaughter and had a mule for plowing. They shared a garden space and a smokehouse with her parents. There were more children who followed Crawford. Their son Sandy was born in 1901, daughter Pearlie was born in 1902, Mary in 1905, and son Percey in 1908. Milley and Boss Redden's household was enumerated at a total of seven in the 1910 US Census. In the midst of the expansion of her immediate family, Milley lost her father. Joe Washington Vanleer passed away in October 1902.

Even with the death of her father, Milley seemed to have found solace with her life on the farm surrounded by her aging mother, siblings, husband, and children. However, this all came to an end when she became ill with typhoid fever. After the family was quarantined, Milley died on October 18, 1916. She left behind her husband and five children. All of the children were under the age of eighteen. Then, all too soon after the death of Milley, the family unit was again shaken when twelve-year-old Mary became stricken by a malady that required her to be separated from the family and hospitalized in Nashville at Cottage Hospital on Cedar Street. She was treated at the hospital for inflammation of her appendix for nearly a month. Her health was never regained, and she passed away on October 27, 1917.

The family was undoubtedly shaken to the core by the loss of the wife and mother, followed in just over a year by the loss of a child and sibling. Boss demonstrated strength, faith, and resilience as he attempted to carry on in the role of single father and household head. He was an active participant in the community and well liked. He served as the associate pastor at St. John Methodist Church, one of the three churches in Promise Land. He was what the people in the community called a "jackleg preacher." This meant that he was not ordained or had not received any former training in the ministry. However, he took his job seriously and would fill in during the absence of the itinerant pastor assigned to the Dickson circuit. This duty was performed fairly often, especially during inclement or harsh weather. The mode of travel at that time was primarily horseback or horse and buggy. Sometimes severe rain and icy roads were not permissible to this mode of travel. It was during these occurrences that Boss would have to fill in for the preacher.

Throughout my life, I heard many humorous stories about Uncle Boss in the role of preacher. One of the stories was that he would often preach the same sermon. The theme of his sermon was "Little Children Love Ye One Another." It is told that once a young man approached him one Sunday following the closing of church services and loudly inquired of him, "Brother Boss, once again you have preached the same sermon. Do you know any other sermon to preach?" It was said that Boss responded to the insolent young man just as loudly has he had been spoken to. He said, "Son, are you doing what I preached?" The young man replied with a lowered volume to his voice, "Well, I guess maybe I don't, all the time." To that Brother Boss responded, "Then 'til you start doing what I preach, I will just keep preaching it."

Boss had also started to keep the company of a young woman in the community. Her name was Georgie Weakly Robertson. She was the daughter of early Promise Land settlers, Jerry and Mary Jane Robertson. This courtship was well accepted by Milley's sister, Farmie, and her husband, George Bowen. They were Boss's neighbors. It had also been revealed that Boss was actually the nephew of George Bowen. George's brother Tom had acknowledged that he was the biological father of Boss. When Boss announced that he and Georgie, who was known by the nickname "E," were getting married, it seemed that everyone was pleased. It was the consensus of the Vanleer family that the children needed someone to serve in the role of mother and Boss needed a companion to oversee the cooking and housekeeping in the home. They were married on May 4, 1918.

By the time I could remember, Uncle Boss and Aunt E were empty nesters. Their children had all grown up and moved away. The oldest son, Crawford, had left home long before I was born. His eventual home was Cleveland, Ohio. I remember that he would visit his father and stepmother. After his father had passed, he continued to come visit his stepmother and other relatives. Pearlie, the oldest daughter, left home before she reached the age of eighteen. She got married and lived briefly with her husband before leaving to stay in the home of her mother's sister, Nara. It was at Aunt Nara's home when she succumbed after several months to acute tuberculosis. She was twenty years old when she died on February

22, 1925. Her brother Percy also moved to Nashville. Percy lived in Nashville prior to enlisting in the army where he served during WWII. After his honorable discharge he returned to Nashville. He got married and had a child who he named Pearlie, in honor of his sister. I recall Percy visiting Uncle Boss and Aunt E. It seems that he always came alone and would stay a couple of days. As a young adult, I recall visiting his adult daughter, Pearlie, at her home in Nashville with my parents. Like his brother Crawford, Sandy also settled in Cleveland, Ohio. I don't remember ever meeting him, but I heard family members speak of him. Sandy passed away at the age of seventy-seven, in a long-term care nursing facility in Cleveland in 1978. He was never married.

As a child I fondly remember Uncle Boss and Aunt E living next door to my great-grandmother. I was free to independently go to their house and visit with them. I enjoyed exploring the pictures on the credenza in the parlor and asking Aunt E to name the people whose images were staring back at me. She would patiently answer my inquiries although she had done so many times before. I also remember that they had lots of cats that I enjoyed playing with. Uncle Boss even had a little door on hinges, next to the back door. This door allowed the cats to freely enter and exit the house at their will. Uncle Boss was usually busy with gardening or visiting others in the community. There was a family story of Uncle Boss finding several jars at different times in his garden filled to the brim with silver dollars and other coins. It was believed that the coins were buried on the property by Great-Grandpa Wash Vanleer. I noted in reading the original deed when he purchased his property that he made a cash down payment of $200. In the document there was no mention of a loan or bank involvement in the transaction. It is very possible that my great-grandfather never used a bank. Burying and hiding his money was his way of securing his financial resources.

As a child with the knowledge of this family lore, my brother and I would often spend hours digging in the old garden site to explore our chances of unearthing some hidden treasures.

Another contribution made to the community by Aunt E and Uncle Boss was that their home was used as a boarding house for teachers at the Promise Land School. In the history of the school, some of the teachers actually lived in the community, but there were others who came from other communities or from Nashville. From the pictures on the credenza, I know for sure at least four teachers had been boarders in the Redden

Home. They were Miss Ross, Mr. Brown, Mr. Dixon, and my former teacher Miss Ollie Huddleston. It is believed that Miss Ross came from another Dickson County community, while Mr. Brown and Mr. Dixon were from Nashville. Miss Huddleston lived in Dickson. She was assigned to Promise Land School in 1945 and served as teacher until 1957 when the school was consolidated with Cedar Grove School in Charlotte, the nearest segregated school in the county. Miss Huddleston would usually arrive at the Reddens' home on Sunday evening. On Friday, she would be picked up and transported back to her home.

The Reddens' home was situated on an unpaved narrow road, about a quarter of a mile long, between Highway 48 North and Clarksville Road (now Promise Land Road). It was likely fashioned by wagons and pedestrian traffic. As community residents acquired automobiles and began to drive along the road it naturally broadened. This short stretch of road was called "The Lane." Along The Lane were several homes including the Reddens' and my great-grandmother's. At the end of the lane on Clarksville Road, was a bank of mailboxes for the residents. I remember that Uncle Boss would pick up the mail belonging to the elders and deliver it to them. He was known to keep that little lane hot. Therefore, it was not surprising that in the 1980s when Dickson County Council decided to assign names to the rural roads that this small stretch was given the name Redden Crossing in his memory. Both Uncle Boss and Aunt E were well appreciated and respected by members of the community. People in the community were greatly saddened when he passed away due to a fatal heart attack in July 1952. Aunt E continued to live alone for several years in the home that they had shared, until she became too frail to continue living on her own. Her brother, Baxter Robertson, who also lived in Promise Land, built an extra room for her in the home that he shared with his wife and my aunt, Ruby. Aunt E was moved in with them and lived there until her death in February 1963. Her death was due to natural infirmities of aging. Both she and Uncle Boss were buried in the Vanleer Cemetery.

7
FAITH AND RESILIENCE

PRISCILLA VANLEER GREER JACKSON

PRISCILLA WAS THE SIXTH DAUGHTER and last child born to Wash and Rebecca. Priscilla was born on January 12, 1882. Wash was thirty-eight years old, and Rebecca was thirty-five years old when she came into the world. It appears that her childhood was abbreviated by the choices that she made. Those may have been greatly shaped by family events. These events may have led to her carrying a persona that did not match her chronological age. The family lore passed down to my mother and from her to me is that as a young girl, Priscilla was at the Nesbitt Store in Promise Land when she met a young man, whose name was Sam Greer. Eighteen-year-old Sam Greer was originally from Bedford County, Tennessee. He worked as a teamster for a merchandise supplier in Nashville. He had been assigned to deliver supplies and products to merchants in the Charlotte, Promise Land, and Cumberland Furnace areas when he met Priscilla. Priscilla was about twelve years old then. Perhaps being the youngest of five older sisters, three of whom were married, Priscilla had acquired some of their behaviors and mannerisms that made her appear more mature. There was something about her that attracted Sam Greer to pursue a relationship with her. Perhaps she saw in him something that made her feel safe and secure. The invasion of her brother Joe Jr.'s home had happened recently and likely loomed large over her thinking. Perhaps the thought of moving to a place like Nashville, where Sam was currently living, appeared safer than her home in Promise Land. Whatever the reason, she was captured by the young man's advances and his interest was reciprocated. He was in the Promise Land / Charlotte vicinity for a brief period of a few days. During that period, she was convinced to leave her family and accompany Sam to Nashville. Priscilla's parents objected to Sam's offer and forbade Priscilla to go with him. Despite this, Priscilla left home to explore a life with Sam. Her decision was probably very hard for her father to accept. Wash coped with it by wiping his hands clean of her. He vowed to her and the rest of the family that she would not be welcome back into his home if she were to leave.

A 1900 US Census report found Sam and Priscilla living together as husband and wife in Ward 16 of Nashville. They had a three-year-old son, George, who is included as a household member in the census report. Also in the household was Lula Moore, a sixty-year-old woman who is listed as a boarder. The census further reported that Sam, aged twenty-five, and Priscilla, aged nineteen, as renters of their home on King Street. They were reported to have married in 1894. Sam's occupation is reported as a "teamster."

According to my mother, Priscilla remained estranged from her family of origin during her marriage to Sam. However, their union was characterized by poverty, tragedy, alcoholism, and abuse. Together, Sam and Priscilla had five children. Priscilla was fifteen years old when their first child was born and was thirty-one years old when the last child was born in May 1913. Five years after George's birth, Priscilla gave birth to her only girl, Samuella. Five years later, she gave birth to a son, Lewis. During the period of these births, the family was struggling. Sam had started to drink excessively and was abusive to Priscilla. Just months after Lewis's birth on March 18, 1907, he was declared dead on August 7,1907, after a three day stay at Hubbard Hospital. The cause of death was listed as "inanition," which means malnourished. This tragedy was followed by the death of his older sister, Samuella, on July 30, 1907. Bearing the loss of two children had to have been difficult for the two young parents who were already facing difficulties. However, they remained together and managed to have two more children, Homer, born January 15, 1910, and Sam Henry, born May 10, 1913.

By the early 1920s Priscilla apparently had had enough of the abuse and impoverishment that she was experiencing with Sam. By this time, she had reconnected with her family, especially her sister Nara who had relocated to Nashville. Being with Nara enabled her to reconcile with her other surviving siblings. Her father had died within ten years of her leaving. She had also lost at least two siblings before 1920. Her mother Rebecca passed away in 1920. Perhaps reconnecting with her family of orientation enabled and empowered her to walk away from her union with her husband. She also left behind her three sons, who ranged in age from twenty-three years to seven. At the time of her leaving the older sons had begun to emulate their father's penchant for alcohol.

Initially, Priscilla found work as a cook in private homes. She found housing in a rooming house on Cedar Street (now Charlotte Ave.). At some point she accepted an invitation from her cousin, John Vanleer, the son of her Uncle Joe, to join him in Cleveland, Ohio. She accepted John's invitation and relocated to Ohio. Soon after moving to Ohio, she met a man whose name was James Jackson. Jackson was a fifty-one-year-old widower originally from Paducah, Kentucky. He was employed as a cigarmaker. She started keeping company with Mr. Jackson, who soon proposed marriage to her. Priscilla married James Jackson on Armistice Day 1925. She was thirty-nine years old when they married. Unfortunately, their marriage was short-lived. After a few short years of marriage, it appears that Priscilla left James Jackson and returned to Tennessee. There was no documented evidence or family oral history regarding the cause of this separation. Nor is there any indication that there was a divorce. After separating from Mr. Jackson, Priscilla continued to use his last name.

The 1930 Census reports her living in Nashville. She was forty-four years old and was residing as a tenant in the home of a coworker. The coworker's name was Maude Jordan. Priscilla and Maude worked for the Davidson County School System. She was a cook for a school lunchroom and Maude was a school janitor. My mother said that during the 1930s and '40s, she remembers that her great-aunt Priscilla frequently came to Promise Land to visit her older sister, Farmie Della, Mother's grandmother. Priscilla would come for special events such as the Mt. Olive AME Church homecoming and the annual Charlotte Picnic. On these occasions, her other out-of-town aunts, uncles, and other extended family would come home. She said that on holidays such as Christmas and Thanksgiving, her grandmother would go to a great extent to prepare for her sisters Ellen, Nara, and Priscilla's visits.

The reclamation with her family of origin enabled Priscilla to reconcile to some extent with her first husband. Perhaps recognizing that she had her family's love and support, she gained the strength to confront Sam. This reconciliation allowed her to openly visit with her sons.

Although Priscilla did not bring her sons with her when she visited Promise Land, she would often share updates about them with her sisters Ellen and Farmie Della. Living in Nashville, her sister Nara had reestablished a close bond with Priscilla and she was familiar with Sam and his sons. Nara shared with other family members that Sam's drinking had increased over time. Despite that, he had a close and loving bond with his sons. Priscilla appeared to maintain a physical distance from Sam by selecting the west side of Nashville as her chosen place of residence.

Sam and the three sons remained in the same section of Nashville where he and Priscilla had originally established their marital home. This location was in the vicinity of Bass Street, which was the neighborhood of the first Nashville Black settlement post emancipation. It was near a United States Army fortification built during the Civil War known as Fort Negley. Many of the original settlers in this community along with members of the US Colored Troops were forced to build the fort. Over the years, Fort Negley had fallen into ruins. In recent years, the fort has received revitalization and is today a celebrated park that has been preserved as a monument to the USCT. The neighborhood that included Bass and surrounding streets has been erased by the construction of Interstate Highway 65.

After the death of Aunt Priscilla and her sister Nara, our family lost contact with Sam Greer and their sons. Research on Sam Greer revealed that their oldest son George passed away on July 10, 1955, at the age of fifty-seven. At the time of his death, he lived on Woods Street in Nashville. He was reported to be a widower, who was employed as a truck driver who hauled produce. He died alone at home, which required a police investigation with a coroner's report. The report revealed that his death resulted from natural causes without "foul play." He was pronounced dead at Hubbard Hospital. George's brother Homer Greer died on January 1, 1964, at Hubbard Hospital where he was hospitalized for carcinoma of the esophagus. He was fifty-four years old. He was reported as divorced and residing at 634 Bass Street in Nashville. The Greer's youngest son, Sam Henry, died at the age of twenty-nine on June 14, 1942. He was unmarried and employed as a porter at a beer tavern at the time of his death. He was a victim of homicide with stab wounds to the chest. Outliving five offspring and Priscilla, Sam succumbed to death on August 2, 1964, just eight months after his son, Homer's death. Sam lived to be seventy-nine years old. He died while under care at Hubbard Hospital for thrombophlebitis and cellulitis of the left leg. The cause of death was cardio infarction, which was secondary to the other reported diagnoses. The death certificate reported that he was employed as a laborer at a junk yard. His address was listed the same as his son Homer's. All of Priscilla's children and her first husband were buried at Mt. Ararat Cemetery in Nashville.

There were several interesting findings on the death certificates of Sam and the Greer offspring. Sam and Priscilla are listed as parents on the death certificate of each child. On Sam's death certificate (1964) he is listed as "widowed," and Priscilla is reported as his deceased wife. All members of the unit including Priscilla received their final care at Hubbard Hospital. I attribute this consistency in the reports to the person or persons who supplied the information. Sam provided the social information on the certificates for the children, Lewis and Samuella. On the certificates of Sam, George, and Homer, the person who provided the social information of each deceased was a man identified as "Dennis Caruthers." Usually, the person called upon to provide this kind of information is a relative or close friend. It appears that Dennis Caruthers had a long-term relationship with Sam and his family and was very likely a relative to Sam. The name Caruthers was familiar to me. I recall as a child, we had relatives by that name who lived in Centerville, Tennessee. I remember that my mother referred to them as Cousin Tyke and Cousin Jessie Caruthers. The two of them passed away in the early 1960s. After their deaths, we seemed to have had no other connection to this family. I believe that they were related to Aunt Priscilla, but just how I was unsure until seeing the death certificates. Lennis Caruthers's address was listed as the same as Sam's. I am convinced that the Caruthers were relatives of Sam Greer. This further ensures that Priscilla had an enduring relationship with Sam.

Priscilla was living independently at a home which she owned, located at 1634 Jackson Street in North Nashville. She was working as a housekeeper for a private family when she was diagnosed with pancreatic cancer with metastasis. She was hospitalized at Hubbard Hospital for six weeks before succumbing to death on November 11, 1949. Her death certificate reported her as "married," which is evidence that she never divorced James Jackson.

Her body was brought back to Promise Land for memorial services including visitations and funeral services. W.C. McGavock Funeral Home of Nashville oversaw her final arrangements. The undertakers brought her remains to the home where she was born, the home of her deceased parents. However, at the time of her death, my widowed great-grandmother Farmie Della was the owner of the home. Priscilla's remains were placed in the new room that my Uncle Peony had constructed and added to the home. Her body was laid in state overnight, so that family and friends could visit her corpse and fellowship with the family. This was called "the wake." We now call it "the visitation." There was lots of food brought to the house, and many visitors and family members came in and out of the house during this bereavement period. I was three years old at the time. It was exciting and a little scary. I remember my father lifting me up in front of the casket so that I could see her. It was the first dead person that I had ever encountered. It was an unforgettable experience. The next day her funeral was held at the Mount Olive AME Church. She was buried after the funeral at the Vanleer Cemetery in Promise Land.

FARMIE DELLA VANLEER BOWEN

The last daughter of Wash and Rebecca Vanleer to be profiled is my great-grandmother, Farmie Della. She was the fifth daughter born to the Vanleers. Farmie was born February 2, 1880. She was only fifteen years old when she married George Washington Bowen, a twenty-seven-year-old farmer and son of early Promise Land settlers Nathan and Lucy Carr Bowen. Farmie was the second of Wash and Rebecca's daughters to marry. The first to marry was their youngest daughter Priscilla, who left home at the age of twelve, with a young man who was passing through the community and was unknown to her family. She relocated with him to Nashville without her parents' blessings or consent. About a year later, on May 5, 1895, Farmie Della married a man who was twelve years older. The difference was that she married a man who grew up in Promise Land; they were members of the same church and their families shared common bonds. So, the marriage between Farmie and George Bowen was completely sanctioned and blessed by their families. Wash and Rebecca consented to the couple moving into their home. On the deaths of Wash and Rebecca, their daughter Farmie and her husband George became the owners of the original homestead. It was the place of birth of all their children and remained in the family until it was destroyed by fire in December 1967. The story of the Bowen family will continue as the story of Nathan and Lucy Carr Bowen unfolds.

NATHAN AND LUCY CARR BOWEN

Records reveal that Nathan Bowen was born into slavery about 1832 in Hickman County, Tennessee. The story handed down through the generations was that his mother was an enslaved woman named Rebecca, who was born about 1810. His father was unknown by the early ancestors; however, recent DNA results link his biological father as one of the sons of his slave holders, Allen and Nancy Ford Bowen. We are fairly certain that before his emancipation he was enslaved on the farm in Charlotte, Tennessee, owned by Rebecca Bowen, widow of Allen H. Bowen. The 1860 US Federal Census – Slave Schedules show that Rebecca Bowen was the owner of fifteen enslaved people. One was a man whose age was twenty-seven years old, which would have been about the age of Nathan. Rebecca Bowen's farm was near the farm of slaveholder, Meakin Carr. Carr owned a young woman who matched the age of Lucy, the young woman with whom Nathan would establish a relationship/marital bond. Nathan and Lucy had begun procreation of their family prior to emancipation. There were three children on the 1860 Slave Schedule with Lucy who matched the gender and ages of children that Lucy and Nathan shared.

Nathan and Lucy were both about thirty-two years old when they were emancipated from slavery. They established a home together and lived as husband and wife. We have no civil record of their marriage; however, it was completely accepted as a bonded relationship by them, their family, friends, and acquaintances. A document found through the Freedman's Bureau records suggest that a labor contract was established on January 1, 1866, shortly after their emancipation. The contract is between the family of Nathan Bowen and B. W. Nicks, a businessman and farmer. Nicks and his sons owned a blacksmith shop in Charlotte, District 6. The contract was for one year beginning at the date of signing and ending December 31, 1866. In the contract Nathan and his family would be housed on Nicks's property. Both Nathan and Lucy would be paid $15 a month to provide labor on the farm and blacksmith shop. Nathan was to serve as a helper in the shop. He along with his sons Richard and Dillard were to work as farm laborers. They would receive clothing under the contract. Lucy would be required to cook, provide laundry services, and do housework. Lucy and the other children did not receive clothing under the contract, but they did receive rations. Should Nathan raise an independent crop on the farm, he was to pay one-third of the value of his crop to Nicks. At the end of the contract year, Nicks was to pay Nathan one hundred dollars. Perhaps with this earning Nathan was able to save toward the purchase of land for his own farm. In 1870 he purchased ten acres of land in the Promise Land settlement.

Nathan and Lucy's family continued to expand after liberation. Their oldest child, daughter Hulda, was eighteen years old by the time of her emancipation. She was betrothed to a free man of color whose name was Willis Buck Easley. Easley lived in Hickman County. During the resettlement, she left her parents and joined her soon-to-be spouse. With Nathan and Lucy in the establishment of their new abode were their sons, Richard, Dillard, Thomas, and James. Their older sons were all teenagers or at least preadolescent youth, with ages ranging from eight to sixteen years. Between 1860 to 1870 six more children were added to the family, four girls and two boys. They had twins, Richard and Charlotte, born in 1861, followed by Bettie Missouri in 1862, George in 1864, and Caroline in 1869. Morris, who was also known as Marsh, was born in 1870.

Like other newly freed families, Nathan and his wife and children established their home in the rural area north of Charlotte that would become known as Promise Land. Although the land he settled was owned by someone else, it had not been inhabited in many years and showed no signs of cultivation. It was a stony overgrown forestry located on the crest of a hill. It was located just off the Clarksville Stage Road, which is now called Promise Land Road and intersects adjacent to the Redden Crossing Road. The current road on which the property is located is Gill Road. At the time of the Bowens settling there, there were no roads. It was just wilderness that required much work in clearing in order for them to build their simply constructed, small wood-frame house. Having older children to share the workload was a blessing. It was a very difficult undertaking. It was fortunate that the settlers helped each other in making the transition. I remember the site as a vacant overgrown lot long after Nathan Bowen's house had been torn down and others who had lived around him had vacated the premises. I remember that as kids, my siblings and I found many arrowheads, suggesting that indigenous Americans had once occupied the area. In the mid-1950s, Levi and Robert Britt, the grandson of Nathan's son James, cleared the area and had begun to construct a frame for a home that was never finished. It was later torn down. The only thing remaining on the ten acres that Nathan had once owned is the inactive/abandoned Bowen Cemetery.

As the Bowen family were in pursuit of acclimating to life as freed people, a tragic incident occurred that would shake up the community and threaten the core of the family's equilibrium. Residing not far from the Bowens was another family. They lived in the hollow just below the Bowen's place. The father of the family was a man whose name was Bob

Collier. Collier was known to be boisterous, intimidating, and frequently inebriated. In a drunken state, he would often physically attack his wife and children. Members of his family would run to the Bowens' home for shelter and protection from him. Nathan confronted Bob Collier on one occasion when Collier's wife had sought Nathan's help. At that time Nathan gave Collier a warning. He told him that if he heard again of Collier assaulting his wife or children, he would take it upon himself to deal with him. It was a late evening near the end of March 1870, Nathan and his family had gone to bed, when he was awakened by his dogs barking. Next, he heard the voice of Bob Collier, loudly cursing and threatening to kill him. By Collier's voice and the ranting, Nathan detected that he was drinking or intoxicated. Nathan yelled to him to get away from his house. However, Collier continued to threaten and hurl insults at Nathan. Nathan warned him that if he did not leave, he would shoot him. Collier responded to Nathan's retort by throwing a rock that broke out a window. Nathan made sure his wife and children were sheltered from harm. He then got his shotgun and went to the door. Collier who continued swearing, was standing in the path that led directly to the door of Nathan's home; he was holding something in his hand. Nathan, holding his gun in a defensive manner, shouted another warning to Collier to leave the premises. Instead, Collier aggressively charged him. It was at that point that Nathan pulled the trigger of the shotgun. Collier was knocked down by the blast and was fatally wounded. The shouting by the two men had drawn the attention of nearby neighbors. They came to the site to see the cause of the disturbance. Nathan checked to see if his family was unharmed and attempted to comfort them. His older sons begged him to let them come outside with him. He firmly told them to stay inside and look after their mother and smaller children. Others who were there examined Collier and determined that he was dead. One of the spectators covered his body with a coat while another onlooker got the sheriff. When the authorities arrived, Collier was taken away by a horse-driven ambulance. Nathan was placed under arrest for murder and was taken to the jail in Charlotte where he awaited a trial.

Nathan was taken into custody on March 21, 1870. His trial was held during the month of June at the Dickson County Courthouse located just across the street from the jail. His wife, older sons, and friends from the settlement attended the trial when possible. On June 30, Nathan was convicted of second-degree murder and sentenced to ten years in the Tennessee State Penitentiary. This was a difficult time for his family and community. Not only was his family grief-stricken by his sentencing, but the victim's family was also mourning the loss. Collier left behind a young wife and four young daughters. Both the Collier and Bowen families were impoverished. Their farms were among the poorest of the village. At the time of Nathan's sentencing, the growing season was just beginning. Fortunately, he had sons who would be able to see that the crops were properly cared for. His older boys would be responsible for taking care of the hogs and the two mules, and maintaining and harvesting the crops. They received help from neighbors including the Nesbitt, Vanleer, Hall, and other families in the village. In addition to caring for three small children under the age of six, Nathan's wife Lucy was in the fifth month of pregnancy with their ninth child.

Like the hardship faced by the Bowen family, the Colliers' plight was even greater. The thirty-four-year-old widow was taking care of her infirm, elderly mother and four young daughters whose ages were from three to eight years old. Their possessions were much less than the Bowens. The people led by the two organized churches in the community assisted the family as much as possible. They shared canned vegetables and fruit, as well as fresh fruit from orchards, garden vegetables, meat from their smokehouses, and clothing with the family. Although the family was terrified of Bob Collier, they loved him, and his absence created a void.

Nathan's family was unable to visit him. Travel outside of the county and the settlement was rare and far in between because less than a handful of the settlers owned horses and buggies. However, most of his children were literate and were able to correspond with him by mail. Many believed that he had been wrongfully convicted. They believed that he was condemned for defending his home and family for which he had a right to do. Apparently, the talk got around to the appropriate people in the county because by the fifth year of his incarceration a petition for his pardon was filed, along with a letter to Governor James D. Porter, a Democrat who served the State of Tennessee from 1875 to 1879. The handwritten letter was composed by William McCreary, a white farmer who lived in District 6, the same as the new settlement. The letter written on June 19, 1875, contained the following:

> Gov. James D. Porter,
> Nashville Governor: Instructed by Gen. Cheatham to furnish the name of a convict for pardon; I respectfully present:
> Nathan Bowen, Dickson County murder, 10 years from June 30th 1870.

It is due Governor! That you should know the reasons why this man is selected. He is middle aged, has a wife and children, who regularly correspond with him, and having yet 5 years to serve, a pardon will be of great benefit to him and them.

We came up here with one, and his conduct has been good, has done his work faithfully, and I do not believe I have spoken 20 words to him on any subject in 4½ years. He is a quiet, sensible, and obedient negro.

From Mr. Darwin Pucket a citizen of Dickson County, I learned that the negro killed was a desperado, a terror to the county; as Ced Perkins was to Davidson County, and that the citizens were glad to get rid of him; that he went to Bowen's home, a difficulty occurred & during the affray Bowen shot him.

Very Respectfully Yours,
WW McCreary[1]

The letter was addressed to James D. Porter, the twenty-second governor to serve Tennessee. Born in Paris, Tennessee, and the son of a physician, Porter was a lawyer who graduated from the University of Nashville. He was an advocate for education, and it was under his administration that Meharry Medical College was founded. It was during the first of two terms served by him that Nathan Bowen was pardoned. McCreary referenced the names of several others in his petition including "General Cheatham." He was referring to Benjamin Franklin Cheatham, a Confederate major general who was born into a prominent family in Nashville. His mother was a descendant of General James Robertson, a founder of Nashville and "father" of Middle Tennessee, who came from Virginia. Cheatham County, a neighboring county east of Dickson, was named in his honor. He was an unsuccessful candidate for the United States House of Representatives in 1872. However, it appears that McCreary thought that his name carried enough weight to garner the governor's attention. This along with Nathan's prison record, standing in his community, relationship with family and friends, and the circumstances that surrounded the shooting all contributed to the governor's favorable response to the petition for his exoneration. Nathan received a full pardon on June 19, 1875, and he was released home from prison.

After his release, Nathan returned to his family and community. According to stories handed down, this was a joyous event. Family, friends, and neighbors gathered and celebrated with a feast at his home. Upon his return, Nathan found that his household had evolved from what it was before his conviction. His older sons had grown into young men. Tom the oldest had moved out and was living on his own as a sharecropper in neighboring Montgomery County north of Promise Land and Dickson County. This move put Tom within proximity of a young lady with whom he was keeping company. Dillard, James, and Richard remained in the home but there were signs that they too would soon be leaving. Nathan had become acquainted with Morris, a new son, who was born after his incarceration. Morris was five years old. There was also another new addition to the household. It was his two-year-old granddaughter, whose name was Comfort. Comfort was alleged to have been the daughter of thirteen-year-old Richard. Comfort's mother, Josephine Snowden, was an orphan who was only twelve years old when Comfort was born. After Comfort was born, she was placed in the care of Richard and his mother. Josephine, who was being raised by elderly guardians, arranged for her to live with their son in Nashville. Josephine had been in the care of W. B. and Sadie Weakley, an elderly couple who were among the early settlers in Promise Land. The Weakleys believed that due to their advancing age it was best to put Josephine in the care of their son Isaac and his wife who lived in Nashville.

Adjusting to the new family dynamics was just one of several hurdles that Nathan had to contend. His absence required him to reclaim his role identification as head of household, husband, and father. Recognizing God's grace in his plight, he became more fervent in his faith and encouraged his family to follow his lead. He was affiliated with a group of worshippers organized under the Mt. Olive African Methodist Episcopal Church. At that time, they did not have a building for worship, so services were held in the various homes of the members. It would not be until 1884 before the members moved into a church building that had been erected on the property of Lias Jackson. The building belonged to the Baptist congregation. Mt. Olive AME would share tenancy and hold services on the second and fourth Sundays. The Baptist congregation would hold services on the first, third, and fifth Sundays. Nathan delighted himself in these services and when the building was opened, he would attend every Sunday. The community was close-knit. The friendship and kinship bonds were strong. Although his family had done well managing and maintaining the small farm, Nathan's skills and know-how were much needed. He enjoyed his life as a farmer, especially farming his own land. He was also an avid hunter and relished hunting with his sons and neighbors John Nesbitt, Wash Vanleer, Sol Cunningham, and others. Hunting was not just sport for these men. The game that they caught was to feed their families. They were also generous in sharing their bounty with the widows and elderly residents in the community.

As a former convict, Nathan had been disenfranchised of his rights. In the process of re-establishing himself, he knew that having these rights restored was important. Seven years after his pardon, Nathan requested and received full restoration of his citizenship. He appeared in Dickson County Circuit Court on July 21, 1882, on behalf of himself. The court record revealed that the restoration status was determined by the full pardon that Nathan had received in 1875; his life and conduct since the pardon; his maintaining residence in Dickson County; and the neighbors reports of good character, i.e., demonstrating honesty, respectability, and veracity. The document further reported, "His status with all rights and privileges are restored including to vote, give evidence, and all the rights and privileges of a citizen of the state declared and powers of this court extends."[2]

I am sure that the acquisition of this document was very meaningful to a man who had received confirmation of his liberty not once but three times during his life. The emancipation from slavery, the governor's pardon from imprisonment, and to have his full citizenship restored after being convicted of a crime was a major feat for Nathan. His faith in God with refection on these blessings were likely the influences that led Nathan to become a minister of the gospel. He became an African Methodist Episcopal minister and served as pastor at Mt. Olive AME Church. Some of his sons and other descendants would follow in his footsteps in the ministry of the gospel.

Near the end of the 1880s, as Nathan was approaching the end of his life's journey, two impactful events occurred. The first was the death of his beloved Lucy, his life partner and mother of his children. Lucy passed away about 1887. There is no record of the exact date of her death and what is known is based on oral history. At the time of Lucy's demise, she and Nathan were empty nesters. Most of their children were married or at least living on their own. Even the grandchild, Comfort, had moved with her parents, Richard and Josephine, who had married in 1876. Apparently, Nathan didn't like being alone. On January 5, 1888, he married his widowed fifty-three-year-old neighbor, Lucinda Hall. Lucinda Hall was the mother of five adult children and three grandchildren. Lucinda had a blended family when they married, and like other descendants of early settlers, a few remained as residents of the Promise Land until their deaths.

Those who moved away continued to maintain a bond with the community. To this day Lucinda still has descendants who among the handful who actually still reside in the community. Unfortunately, Nathan's marriage to Lucinda was short-lived. He passed away at their home in 1890. According to my mother he died of "old age." He was only fifty-eight years old, which would be considered young by today's standard. Nathan and his first wife, Lucy, are buried at the Bowen Cemetery in Promise Land. According to my mother the last burial in this cemetery was in the 1930s. Nathan's second wife Lucinda lived to be eighty-two years old. She died in 1914.

HULDA BOWEN EASLEY

Nathan and Lucy's oldest daughter was Hulda, born in 1841. She was born into slavery, and it was not until she was a twenty-four-year-old adult that she would be emancipated. The selection of her unusual name caused me to ponder if this was a suggestion of her parents' faith. The name comes from the name "Huldah," who was a Hebrew prophetess found in the Bible (2 Kings 22: 14–20 and 2 Chronicles 34:22–28). This is one of several instances where I found that my ancestors selected biblical names for their children. I found this especially true with Nathan Bowen and my father's grandfather William Gilbert, in the naming of their children. As we have found in the review of her father's life, he became a man of faith which seem to have been a multigenerational calling.

From all accounts it seems that Hulda settled in District 2 of Hickman County, Tennessee, after slavery. By 1866, she had married Willis Easley, who had been a free man of color prior to emancipation. She had also given birth to their first son, Isaac. The family resided in Centerville, Tennessee, where her husband is listed as a farmer in the 1870 Census. Hulda and Willis Easley had four sons: Isaac, Nelson, William Thomas, and Elijah. Their oldest son Isaac became well-known and an influential minister of the gospel. He was pastor of the Edmondson Chapel Baptist Church in Brentwood, Tennessee, located in Williamson County. His grandson Rev. Thomas Henry Easley followed in his footsteps and became the pastor of the Brentwood church. Thomas Henry Easley graduated the Baptist Theological Seminary in Nashville. Edmondson Chapel was relocated to Antioch, Tennessee, where it stands today. Rev. Thomas Easley's final pastoral assignment was with New Hope Baptist Church at 1310 Hawkins Street in Nashville. He was elected moderator of the Nashville District

Association that served forty-five member churches. He served the association for twenty-nine years. During this tenure the association purchased a home for widows and orphans and a 160-acre farm that employed individuals who had difficulty finding employment elsewhere. Rev. Thomas Easley died in 1954 at the age of fifty-six years.

Hulda lived to see her sons become young men; however she departed her life on earth after only forty-six years. She passed away on Christmas Day 1901 after a lengthy hospital stay. The cause of her death was reported to be heart disease with a manifestation of paralysis of the heart and limbs. She was buried at Greenwood Cemetery in Nashville. Her husband, Willis Easley, lived to the age of eighty-three years before he succumbed to death in 1930. He had enjoyed a long life as a farmer until his death at the home that he and Hulda had shared in Centerville, Tennessee.

TOM BOWEN

Tom or Thomas was born March 14, 1855. Like his sister, Hulda, he was born before emancipation from slavey. He was a boy of ten years old when he first experienced freedom. A year after emancipation, his name along with the names of his brothers, Dillard and Richard, and their mother Lucy, were included on a sharecropping labor agreement. The agreement was entered on January 1, 1866, between his father Nathan and businessman/farmer B. W. Nicks. By 1874, his father had purchased land in Promise Land for his family. Tom was about twenty years old when this land was purchased. He moved onto the property with his parents and siblings. He was likely an asset to his parents in helping to get the land cleared, building a house, and establishing the small farm. Also, during this time, Tom had fathered a child with a married woman who lived the in community. The child's name was William P. Redden (nicknamed Boss). It is likely Tom kept this indiscretion from the custodial father of Boss and revealed it only after both parents had died, leaving Boss an orphan at the age of twelve. Boss and his younger brother Ed were raised by their uncle and aunt, William and Priscilla Redden Gilbert.

Tom lived in Nathan and Lucy Bowen's household until he was a young man. As a young man, he became an African Methodist Episcopal Church circuit pastor. His first preaching experience was at the Mt. Olive AME Church in Promise Land, the same church where his father had served as pastor. He was later assigned a church in Montgomery County's Civil District 15, in an area known as Field Spring. It was there he met and married a young lady, whose name was Cecilia Daily. They married about 1880. Their first child together was a girl named Haga, born in December 1881. She was followed by brother Joe, born January 1885; then William, born August 1887; Arnett Wendall, born August 1890; Daily, born August 1892; and a sister Veanna, born 1899. The last child born to Tom and Cecilia was a son, whom they named Greeley Horace Bowen. Greeley was born in September 1904.

Although Tom was married with a family and a minister of the gospel, it did not stop his dalliances and impudence. One such incident led to a crime that almost destroyed the Bowen and Vanleer families. It was the murder of his cousin Daniel Hayes Vanleer. This story is covered in the prior story of Joe Washington Vanleer's family. This tragic outcome of a romantic entanglement demonstrated the strength, resilience, and magnanimous spirit that existed between the two families. The same characteristics were demonstrated in Tom's family of procreation. Despite the legal and moral consequences that Tom faced, he was able to mend the hurt and disappointment he had caused his family. His wife, to whom he had been married for twenty-one years, gave him absolution. They remained husband and wife for another twenty-seven years, welcoming the birth of three additional children. Tom died at the age of seventy-three years old in June 1928. He was buried in Steel Springs. His wife Cecilia lived to be seventy-eight years old. She passed away in 1943. The couple were able to live to see the fruit of their determination to stay united and raise their family together. Their children grew up in a home and community where faith in God permeated. Their youngest son, Greeley Horace Bowen, was a shining example that was set by his family.

GREELEY HORACE BOWEN

Greeley was the youngest of Tom and Cecelia's children. He was born and lived in Mongomery County, Tennessee, all of his life. He married Christine Hopkins on December 25, 1923. They were the parents of five daughters: Mildred, born 1925; Flora, born 1926; Eva, born 1929; Mary, born 1930 (died in infancy); Christine, born 1932; and Helen, born 1935. His mother lived with the family until her death in 1943. His only surviving daughter Flora, who is currently ninety-seven years old, describes her father as a "farmer and preacher." Although he owned and maintained a farm most of his adult life, in later years he worked in a foundry and a tobacco factory in the city of Clarksville. Flora remembers their home, where her father was a caring man who guided the family with love and faith in God. They would begin each day with prayer. The Lord's Prayer was prayed in unison at breakfast and at dinner a more extended prayer was offered for the family. The whole family would be present for all meals when possible. The family did many things as a group, especially so with the farming chores. She said that her mother would work with her father with the crops during the day and would return to the house in time to prepare a full meal for the family.

Flora remembers that her father and mother encouraged her and her sisters to study and aim high. All three of the older daughters—Mildred, Flora, and Eva—graduated valedictorians at Burt High School in Clarksville. The other two, Christine and Helen, graduated as honor students. After graduating high school, Mildred enrolled at Tennessee A&I State College, known now as Tennessee State University (TSU), where she majored in elementary education. A year later, her sister Flora joined her at A&I, as it was called then. Flora said that she was counseled by Mildred to not major in elementary education. She took her sister's advice and majored in history with a minor in sociology. Prior to enrolling his daughters in school, their father spoke with the college's dean of housing and secured off-campus housing for them. He also found each of them jobs as nannies for families whom he selected as suitable employers for his daughters. This allowed his daughters to have a small income to cover some of the expenses associated with their education. Having part-time jobs did not interfere with the primary goals of Mildred and Flora. They continued the study habits that they had grown accustomed to. They participated in extracurricular activities offered through the college. In discussing dating while in college, Flora shared with me that as a student she dated a young man who later in life became a well-known journalist and American diplomat.

That young man was Carl Rowan. In 1961, he served the administration of John F. Kennedy, first as deputy assistant secretary of state for public affairs and later ambassador of Finland. Under President Lyndon Johnson, he was named director of the US Information Agency, a position that gave him a seat on the National Security Council. He left the government in 1965 and started his syndicated newspaper column, which appeared in one hundred newspapers. He wrote his last column a few days before his death on September 23, 2000. Needless to say, I was very impressed by my cousin's dating partner at TSU. As a graduate of TSU myself, I am equally impressed by my fellow alumni Mr. Carl Rowan.

Returning to the subject of the education and achievements of Greeley Bowen's daughters, it is important to include that the younger set of daughters, including Eva as well as Christine and Helen, followed the paths of their older sisters. They also enrolled at Tennessee A&I. According to Flora, things were a little different for them. Their father was more economically stable than he was when she and Mildred were in school. Therefore, a part-time job was optional for them. They lived in nearby off-campus housing. Eva took a part-time job at a pharmacy near campus. The youngest two of the daughters also had the option to drop out of school and pursue another path. That option was marriage. The younger siblings found love and then marriage while pursuing their college degrees. They postponed their education. However, they returned later and obtained their degrees. Eva and Helen also became educators and Christine became a social worker. Meanwhile, both Mildred and Flora had successfully started their careers as educators. Mildred began her career as a teacher at the segregated Burt High School, her former alma mater. After the first few years there, she married a young man that she had been dating. She later moved with her husband and their sons to Chicago, Illinois. Mildred continued to work in her chosen profession, while raising her family. However, Flora returned to Montgomery County where she worked as an elementary school teacher. During this time, she also married, had two children, and earned two master's degrees. She served at several schools, elementary and junior high, in Montgomery County. She worked in various capacities, including teacher, guidance counselor, and principal, but her tenure in Montgomery County, Tennessee, was temporarily interrupted when she and the children joined her husband and their father in Germany, where he was serving a United States military assignment. During the time in Germany, Flora was appointed to teach at the Amerg American School of Germany. When she returned to the US, she would continue to teach in the Montgomery County school system. She retired after serving as an educator in the county for forty years. In 1998, the library at the Rossview Middle School was named the "Flora Richbourg Library" in her honor.

While in Germany, Flora was able to connect with her sister, Eva, who was also married to a US soldier stationed there. Eva was a math teacher who taught at Burt High School in Clarksville and in Germany. She also gave birth to a little girl while in Germany. When the family returned to the United States, Eva resumed her teaching career in Clarksville. Unfortunately, Eva passed away at the age of thirty-five years old, leaving behind her husband and their nine-year-old daughter. Flora believes that Eva may have had sickle cell anemia, which could have been a contributor to her early demise. Eva displayed symptoms of sickle cell disease, which included episodic pain crises and bouts with respiratory problems. At the time of her death, she had been experiencing joint pain and she had been diagnosed with pneumonia. She died in the early 1960s prior to widely known sickle cell testing and diagnosis in the United States.

It was interesting to learn this because based on the early unexplained deaths of family members, I had suspected that sickle cell disease may have been prevalent in the Bowen family line. Sickle cell disease is a genetic disease that includes a variety of hemoglobinopathies (e.g., sickle cell anemia, sickle thalassemia, sickle C-trait, etc.). Prior to the establishment of the Comprehensive Sickle Cell Disease Center throughout the United States in 1972, there was little information about this malady. Many people affected by it went undiagnosed.

The successes and determination of Greeley Bowen's offspring are a demonstration of his influence on their development. He was not just a devoted husband, father, and household leader. He was also a faith leader. Rev. Greeley was called into the ministry in 1931. His first assignment was the African Methodist Episcopal District of Sulfur Spring, Tennessee, the largest congregation within his charge. These were all small, rural, outlying Clarksville communities. He was later assigned to the district that included Mt. Olive AME Church in Promise Land. His family of origin and the community were pleased to have him return home. My mother held her Cousin Greeley in high esteem. She remembered well his pastorship in Promise Land. She said that he expressed his athletic prowess when preaching. She described him leaping from side to side in the pulpit when filled with the spirit. His cousin Jesse Bowen was converted during one of Rev. Greeley's sermons at Mt. Olive. During his tenure at Mt. Olive, he helped to organize a benevolent organization to aid families in the community. According to Flora, when he was serving in the district that included Round Pond AME Church, he actively headed another benevolent auxiliary known as the Sons of Union and Daughters of Zion. While serving in another district, he spearheaded the 13 District Voting Alliance, whose mission was to advocate and encourage voting of African Americans. He was a caring and compassionate pastor, who was well liked by the many congregations that the served. He served many in both rural and urban areas. At the end of his ministerial journey, he was assigned to churches in Nashville. His journey came to an end on April 11, 1973, when he and his wife, Christine, were involved in a tragic automobile accident. The Bowens were two of seven people who were killed in a collision that happened on a highway near Springfield, Tennessee. With them that evening were Rev. Dorset B. Willams Sr. and his wife, who were also killed, and Carrie Keesee Morris. Rev. Williams was driving as they traveled home from a district meeting that had been held in Gallatin, Tennessee. The two ministers had participated in the services that evening. Rev. and Mrs. Greeley H. Bowen had a double funeral at their home church, Martin Chapel AME Church in Montgomery County. They were also laid to rest in the Martin Chapel Cemetery.

Being assigned to a church in Promise Land allowed Rev. Greeley to reconnect with his family and community of origin. This was not the case with his older siblings, who were born and raised in Montgomery County. This estrangement resulted in a disconnect with Promise Land. We will see this pattern occur repeatedly with families who separated or moved away from the community before the second or third generation.

8
COMMUNITY BUILDING AND GREAT MIGRATIONS

NATHAN'S FIRST GENERATION CONTINUES

ONLY A HANDFUL OF NATHAN BOWEN'S children remained close to the soil in Promise Land. Others left the area within the first generation. That is what happened with his sons Dillard, James, Richard, and Morris, and his daughters Hulda, Bettie, and Caroline. They did not wander very far; in that they settled in neighboring communities or counties. This resettlement created enough distance to prevent their family of origin from developing a close association, familiarity, and bonding with their procreated families. Lack of automobile transportation precluded mobility, so the families did not see each other often. While Tom also settled in a community in Montgomery County, Tennessee, it closely bordered Dickson County. He could easily visit family and friends in Cumberland Furnace and Promise Land by horseback. He was one of the early paid laborers at the Cumberland Furnace, and he lived in his parents' home beyond the age of twenty-one. These factors allowed him to establish himself as an adult in the community. Therefore, he had the opportunity to develop a network that strengthened his ties to the community, while circumstances may have been different for his siblings who married earlier. Reasons such as early marriages to persons who lived in other parts of Dickson County or in other counties altogether may have contributed to the estrangement from the Promise Land community. Employment opportunities were another reason for relocating, as well as other social circumstances that drew the Bowens and other first-generation offspring from the settlement community. The commonality which seemed to have helped them remain in the community of origin was that the people who they married were also bred in the Promise Land community. This includes Nathan's son George, who married the daughter of Joe Washington Vanleer, and his daughter, Charlotte, who married the son of Jefferson Edmondson. Like Bowen, both Edmondson and Vanleer were original settlers in the Promise Land community. Both George and Charlotte along with their spouses remained in Promise Land and engendered multiple generations of descendants who were born and raised in the community. Although many of the descendants migrated elsewhere or have passed away, many of their offspring are aware of their ties to the Promise Land community.

Dillard, Richard, James, Morris, Bettie, and Caroline became the first descendants of Nathan and Lucy Bowen who moved away from the community, while George and Charlotte stayed.

Dillard followed Tom in leaving the household established in Promise Land by his parents. It is very likely that he had moved before his father was released from prison. Records reveal that he lived in Cumberland Furnace and was employed at the furnace as a teamster. Marrying several times, his first wife was Amelia (Mellie) Knight of Cumberland Furnace. The 1880 Census reports that he and Mellie lived in Cumberland Furnace and were the parents of two sons, Robert born in 1873 and Willie born in 1879. In 1889, Mellie gave birth to their daughter Della. After Della's birth I was unable to find any further information on Amelia. It did appear that Dillard had moved on with his life. Furnace work and farm labor were his primary occupations. The skills he gained from working at the furnace enabled him to find work at a charcoal plant at the Tennessee Corporation in Hickman County. Perhaps living between the two towns contributed to the dissolution of his marital relationships. A marriage certificate dated September 20, 1898, reveals that he married Phyllis Hopson of Cumberland Furnace. In addition to Mellie and Phyllis, he was in a relationship with another woman whose name was Susan Vanleer Elreage. Susan was the mother of his son Leander (Lee) Bowen, born January 25, 1895. Only a few years later, the 1900 Census reports him living again in Cumberland Furnace with his wife Phyllis. He is listed as forty-eight years old, and Phyllis is thirty-four. The children listed in the household with them are Della, his daughter to him and first wife Mellie. Della was sixteen years old at the time the 1900 Census was taken. The other children in the household were eleven-year-old Thomas, four-year-old Leander, and eleven-month-old Clive; and the stepchildren, thirteen-year-old Courtney Hopson and six-year-old Lily Hopson, as well as Phyllis's seventy-three-year-old mother. Not in the household at the time of this census were Dillard and Phyllis' sons, Charlie, who was born in 1900, James, born in 1903, and Bosley, born in 1908. Dillard continued to live and work at the furnace until his death. He maintained close ties to the Promise Land community through relationships and his ties to the St. John Methodist Church. He died at his home in 1928 after a long illness. He was buried in the Bowen Family Cemetery in Promise Land. His legacy remains through his descendants who are scattered throughout Dickson and Hickman Counties, and in the state of Ohio, particularly in Columbus where a large number of his second generation settled.

Wrigley, Tennessee, in Hickman County became an attraction for young men who were familiar with the ironworks industry at Cumberland Furnace. Dillard's sons, Charlie, James, Bosley, and Lee settled in Wrigley, Tennessee, where they worked at the iron and coal furnace. The iron and coal furnace morphed into the Tennessee Products, a corporation which held mining operations throughout Middle Tennessee. They had plants in Lewis, Wayne, Hamiliton, and Hickman Counties. The one in Hickman County was the former Warner Blast Furnace owned by Edwin Warner and his sons James and Percy Warner. The furnace closed in the 1890s. The site was acquired by the Bon Air & Iron Corp in the 1900s under Tennessee Products. In 1917, James Cummins took over the business and brought in investors like William Wrigley, who was the owner of the Chicago Cubs and the Wrigley's Chewing Gum Company. The primary products at the time of Cummins were iron and charcoal mining. The plant flourished into a full-scale community. In 1919, the company town was named Wrigley, in honor of William Wrigley.

Wrigley was a huge attraction to the first and second generation of former slaves in Dickson County. It provided a change of geographic scenery without having to travel too far. With the new plant in operation, it boasted company living accommodations; the employees were paid in scrip; and there was a company store. Because of the connection to a professional baseball league, the company invested enthusiastically in an amateur baseball team. They had a baseball field in proximity to the plant. The team had hand-me-down uniforms from the major leagues, and they competed against teams from plants in other Tennessee counties. The baseball amenities catered primarily to the white plant workers. But it provided great entertainment and peripheral involvement for the Black employees. Wrigley had a sizable and growing Black population. They lived separately from the white plant workers. The white workers lived in the valley near the plant and the Black families lived on a hill up from the plant. The 1930 Census listed the area address a "Negro Hill." In the Negro Hill area was a combined church and school building for the Black residents. They also had their own facility for dancing and social gatherings. It is easy to understand the attraction and migration of residents from the Promise Land and Cumberland Furnace communities to Wrigley.

By the mid-1960s much of the plant had discontinued operations. By this time the mining of resources and disposal of waste had taken its toll on the environment. In 1989, because of contaminated debris and soil from the facility operations, the area was put on the Superfund Program's National Priorities List for cleaning up some of the nation's most contaminated areas. The population in the Wrigley community plummeted greatly after the closing of the plant. In 2010 there was only 281 people residing in the community.

As a teenager, I remember Wrigley as a hot spot with two juke joints and the Sunday afternoon baseball games. It was then that I became acquainted with my relatives, particularly Bowen and Vanleer descendants residing there. My mother and relatives of her generation were able to recall the past of the once vibrant community of Wrigley. It was during these times of hanging out in Wrigley that my mother let me know right away that I had kinfolk living there. Through a relative from Wrigley, I was recently put in touch with a cousin, Juanita Bowen Harris. Ninety-two-year-old Juanita is the daughter of Dillard's son Lee Bowen.

Juanita shared with me that her mother, Hattie Lathan, married her father Lee Bowen in 1920. They had five children, of which Juanita was the youngest. Her father was a World War I veteran who worked at the furnace plant as a molder. Her mother died when Juanita was a baby. After her mother's death, Juanita and some of her siblings were sent to live one of her mother's sisters in Clarksville, Tennessee. She remembers in 1941, her Uncle Bosley, who lived in Cleveland, Ohio, coming to her aunt's house with the news that her father, Lee, had been shot at the plant and was taken to a hospital in Nashville. Lee did not survive the injuries. He died at Hubbard Hospital on September 26, 1941, with uremia secondary to a gunshot wound. Juanita said that she never knew the exact reason that her father was shot. All that she knew was that it happened because of a "personal dispute." To her knowledge no one was ever charged with his murder.

When asked about her memories of Wrigley, she recalled that her maternal grandparents, John and Tish Lathan, lived down the hill, near the plant in a "little log cabin." She knew them as Grandpa John and Mama Tish. She also remembers visiting her father in Wrigley and him taking her for a walk down the hill to the company store. The store was a large building with an open area for merchandise. Her father bought her a large cookie. He then took her over to the ledger. The ledger was a large book attached to a rope attached to a table. In the ledger, her father recorded the "due bill." Located over from the ledger, against the wall were a row of offices "for the men who ran the plant." She said in the valley where the plant or furnace was located, the homes had electrical power. Up the hill where her father lived, there was no electricity. She remembered one December evening, she and her sister were going to the church to a Christmas program. It had gotten dark as they walked. There were no streetlights. As they walked, they heard a noise that sounded like something coming toward them. They became frightened and ran back home.

Juanita said some of her father's brothers relocated from Wrigley to Columbus, Ohio, and some of her siblings had followed them. At about the age of nine years old, she and her sister Willie Mae joined the rest of the family in Ohio. Her paternal grandmother, Phyliss, relocated with her children in Wrigley after her husband Dillard died. She later followed her children when they migrated to Columbus. The family settled in an area of Columbus known as American Addition. Platted in 1898, American Addition became a haven for Black families migrating from the South. Many families migrating from the Promise Land and Cumberland Furnace communities made their homes in this rural area located approximately 3.5 miles from the Columbus Central Business District. I recall Mr. Hubert Thompson, who was a former Cumberland Furnace resident and who had family who had moved to Columbus, commenting after a visit to the American Addition section. He said, "I saw so many of my folks there, that I thought for a minute that I was at Stokes Store." Stokes Store was a purveyor in the Cumberland Furnace that now serves as the Cumberland Furnace Community Center. By 1934, there were 120 households in the American Addition community. Juanita described it as a community that very much resembled the rural community that she had left in Hickman County, Tennessee. There were homes without indoor plumbing and electricity. People raised hogs and chickens as well as cultivated gardens. The City of Columbus annexed the community in 1959. The annexation brought about improvement in the community. Juanita grew up in American Addition, married, and raised her children in this community where she still resides today. Less than half a mile from the American Addition was the Buckeye Malleable Iron and Coupler Company where they made farm implements and couplers for railroad cars. By 1900 the manufacturers found that there was a need for stronger coupling assemblies, which led to using steel and a name change to Buckeye Steel Castings. It is pretty certain that the proximity to a familiar employment source was an attraction for the Middle Tennessee migrants.

Richard Bowen

It is likely that Richard, who was called Dick, followed his brother Dillard as the next offspring to leave the nest. It seems that he may have moved out on his own before his father was released from prison. He was a mere child of fifteen, when he married his child bride, Josephine Snowden, who was the same age. They were married on April 18, 1876. Their daughter, Comfort, was four years old when they married. Dick was working at the Cumberland Furnace as a teamster, where he drove a team of mules hauling lumber and supplies to and from the furnace. The couple established their home near the furnace, where they sharecropped and provided domestic services in exchange for lodging. The couple's age and status as formerly enslaved people had an obvious impact on their marriage sustainability and their roles as parents. It affected the stability of their marital and family foundation. In just twenty-three years, the couple became the parents of seven children. The children in birth order were Comfort (1872), James Thomas (1877), Richard Early (1884), Martha (1886), Bertie (1888), Missouri (1894), and Scofield (1895). The 1880 Census reports the family living in Promise Land District 8. At that time only Comfort and James Thomas were born. It was interesting to find that Richard's age is listed on the census as "28" years old and his wife's age was listed as "20." I wonder if this was a deliberate strategy by Dick to create an appearance of being older. Perhaps it was advantageous for him to advance his age for certain situations. These situations may have included things like applying for a job or seeking housing. Employers or landlords tended then, and as they do now, to equate reliability and dependability with equal maturity.

Dick and his sister Charlotte were twins, which meant that their birthdate would have been the same. They were born during slavery; there was no record of their actual birthdate. The year of birth was estimated to be 1861.

A review of the young couple's family life, including parenthood, demonstrates that they faced many challenges and difficulties. In the 1910 Census it was reported that Josephine had experienced ten pregnancies, however, at the time, she had only six surviving children. There may have been some miscarriages, and we know that there was the death of at least one child. Their first child, Comfort, was born when Josephine was only twelve years old. Unfortunately, Comfort did not survive to the age of ten. As noted earlier, she was still alive at the time the 1880 Census was taken. Stories and discussion of her short lifespan were handed down through the generations. The cause of her death is not known to me. Comfort is among several Bowen youth who died in childhood. There may have been one common genetic factor that contributed to many of these deaths. That factor was a hemoglobinopathy known as sickle cell disease which was discussed in a previous chapter regarding the death of one of Greeley Bowen's daughters. Just as it does today, adolescent pregnancy and delivery comes with its own set of high-risk factors for the mother as well as the child. Adolescent mothers (aged ten to nineteen years) face greater risks of eclampsia, puerperal endometritis, and systemic infections than women aged twenty to twenty-four years. Babies of adolescent mothers face higher risk of low birth weight, preterm birth, and severe neonatal conditions. Socioeconomic and environmental conditions posed even greater threats to maternal and child health during the Reconstruction period. Josephine's social history as an orphan from early childhood, being raised by possibly a nonrelated elderly couple in Promise Land, and then sent off to live with the couple's adult son in Nashville, were all likely to have resulted in psychosocial trauma for her. If she and Dick had the option of making the decision to marry at such a young age, it was probably a difficult one for them to make. On the other hand, they may have seen marriage as a way to escape their dilemma. It gave them the opportunity to raise their own child and allowed them autonomy to be independent of their parents and guardians. As first-generation youth born to parents who had to navigate and adjust to the newness of freedom themselves, Dick and Josephine may have lacked the tools, including psychosocial, economic, and environmental resources, required to maximize their potential to be effective parents and partners to each other. With the stress of losing a child to death, along with being struggling immature parents, one can only imagine the impact that it could have had on their psychic well-being and relationship.

They were two young kids who had stepped into adult roles that they may not have been quite prepared to handle. They were bridging a period in history where, less than a generation before them, an intact Black family had no value. In the system of slavery, members of Black families could be separated at the will of their owner. They were chattel. Family members could be sold, leased, or bartered at any time by their enslaver. Likewise, the age appropriateness for sexual activity for the enslaved people had a different standard than for the majority race. Enslaved male and female fertility regardless of age was a valued commodity for slaveowners. Procreation during the early development of enslaved individuals was encouraged and fostered by their owners. Young Dick and Josephine were now faced with the responsibility of acclimating to a new value system for Black families. These were values that would benefit them. It was a challenging adjustment that required on-the-job training for them.

It is not certain how long Dick and Josephine's marriage lasted. The last official record that placed them as an intact unit is the 1880 Census. The only children reported in that census were Comfort and James. The other five children were born later, between 1884 to 1895. It is evident that Dick was still a part of the family unit until at least 1895, when Scoffield, the last child, was born.

In June 1907, Josephine married an elderly widowed gentleman from the community whose name was William Hutton. Hutton was a well-established farmer and minister with adult children who also lived in the community. He served as the pastor at the Methodist Episcopal Church in the community. In the 1910 Census, living in the household with Rev. William Hutton and Josephine, was the pastor's eighteen-year-old son Braden. Braden served as one of the musicians who participated in the 1913 Emancipation Day celebration that took place in the community. *The Nashville Globe* reported his father as one of the event's speakers. Also, included in the household are Josephine's children, Missouri, who was sixteen years old, and Schofield who was fourteen. Hutton's eighty-nine-year-old mother was also a member of the household.

By the time of the 1910 Census, Dick and Josephine's oldest child, Comfort, had died in 1882 at the age of ten. Their son James Thomas was at least thirty-years old, married and living with his own family of procreation. Records revealed that that their other children had moved from the household at early ages. In the 1900 Census report, their twelve-year-old daughter, Bertie, is found to be living in the household of William and Prucilla Gilbert's household. When I discovered this several years ago, my mother was still alive. I asked her to tell me who was Bertie Bowen and why she would have been living in the home of my paternal great-grandparents. My mother, who was not born at the time of this census report, said she didn't know exactly why Bertie was living with the Gilberts. However, she remembered her "Cousin Bertie." Mother explained that Bertie was one of her great-uncle Richard's children. She further explained that it was not unusual for families to take children who lived in the community into their own homes to assist them. It was an informal arrangement usually with only the verbal consent of one biological parent. Mother said that the Gilberts's daughter, Frances (Aunt Toad), was like a "social worker" known to bring "stray children" who were having troubles into her home to help them. What Mother was saying was that this was the community's way of providing a safety net for at-risk children. I would hear a similar story later from an elderly gentleman who told me that "Aunt Toad" took him in when he left his parent's home. In 1905, Bertie married John Thomas Vanleer, of the community. John Thomas was the grandson of Joe Washington Vanleer. Bertie settled with John Thomas on his farm, and they started their family. They remained in Promise Land until the family moved to Cleveland, Ohio, sometime before 1920. She enjoyed twenty-four years of marriage to John Thomas Vanleer. Unfortunately, she passed away at the young age of forty-one. Like Bertie, some of her siblings followed her pattern of venturing away from their home of origin to find alternative living arrangements.

From family oral history, it is said that Martha, who was two years older than Bertie, found work as a live-in domestic for a white family in Dickson when she was twelve years old. The head of the household where she found employment was the manager of a retail store in Dickson. In about 1909, Martha's employee accepted the offer to relocate to Omaha and manage a store there. Martha, who was unmarried and about twenty-three years old, along with her three young children, accompanied her employer to Nebraska. According to family history, Martha became ill less than a year after relocating to Nebraska. She arranged to send the three children back by train to Tennessee, to be cared for by her younger sister Missouri who was still living in the home of her mother and stepfather in Promise Land. The oldest child, Jesse, who was seven years old at the time, was charged with caring for his younger siblings, Lesley Otis and

Lucy. They arrived safely in the care of their aunt. Sometime after the children had returned to Promise Land, they would learn that their mother had died. They were naturally saddened by the loss of their mother, but they were equally distressed over the loss of an infant brother whom their mother had given birth to just before they were sent to Tennessee. Their brother had been named Cleophus. The children knew very little details of Martha's death and the placement of Cleophus.

When Jesse grew up, he married my father's younger sister, Hattie Gilbert. He didn't know it then, but he would become one of my most admired uncles. A handsome, bespectacled man who carried himself with dignity and authority, Uncle Jesse was a man of few words unless he was speaking in the pulpit. In family and social gatherings, he would seldom take part in the joking and boisterous behavior that was customary by so many in the family. When something was said or done that would draw laughter from others, you would find him stifling his laughter by lowing his head and releasing a barely audible chuckle. As a young college student, I remember having long and insightful conversations with my Uncle Jesse. During my undergraduate study at Tennessee State University, Uncle Jesse would pick me up at my dormitory so that I might ride home to church with him and Aunt Hattie. Uncle Jesse, had been assigned as pastor of St. John United Methodist Church in Promise Land and two other churches in the Dickson County Parrish. I remember having a very deep and insightful conversation with him on one of these trips. He told me some things about his childhood. He shared with me his experience of traveling back to Tennessee from Omaha, with only his younger brother and sister. Uncle Jesse was only seven years old and was told that he was to watch out for his siblings. His mother had just given birth to a baby whose name was Cleophus. His mother had become ill after giving birth. He said that they were being sent back home to his grandmother by train, to be cared for by his Aunt Missouri. His grandmother and aunt were there to meet him. Soon after their return to Promise Land, he learned that their mother had died. He never heard what happened to his little brother Cleophus. He said that he was sure that his aunt and the other adults knew more about his mother's death and the aftermath in Omaha than what was shared with him and his siblings. He remembered that his grandmother went to Omaha following the death. When she returned, he would walk in on conversations between adults that would stop as long as he was in the room or within earshot. He never thought of asking questions for fear that it would be considered improper for a child to question adults. He said that he withdrew and busied himself looking after his brother and sister. He also took a job as a field hand on a nearby farm. By the time he was twelve years old, he was offered the opportunity to live on the farm where he worked. He accepted the offer and since then he has been on his own.

The farm where Jesse lived and worked was in proximity to Promise Land. This enabled him to remain in contact with his grandmother Josephine Snowden, his Aunt Missouri, and his younger siblings. He was also enrolled at the Promise Land School and attended St. John Methodist, his grandmother's church. As a young adult he moved to Nashville where he worked and advanced his education. In 1921, he married Hattie Gilbert. They made their home in Promise Land, where their three daughters Ruth, Jewell, and Robbie were born. When their daughters were in elementary school, the family moved to Nashville. In Nashville, the family united with Gordon Memorial Methodist Church. At Gordon, Jesse was made a licensed, local preacher, assistant pastor, and class leader. He furthered his divinity training at Fisk University, Scarritt College, and Philander Smith College in Arkansas. In 1931 he became an ordained Methodist Episcopal minister under the Tennessee Conference and was assigned as pastor of the Murfreesboro Circuit. He also served other parishes during his tenure, including Dickson Parish of which his home church, St. John in Promise Land, was a member. At the time of his death, May 11, 1971, Rev. Bowen was serving the Springfield Parish.

In 1935, Rev. Bowen instituted an annual homecoming day at Promise Land. This annual event would occur on the first Sunday in the month of June. Whatever church that was pastored by Rev. Bowen at the time of the annual event would accompany him to Promise Land for a full day of worship services. Often the visiting church would be transported to Promise Land by a chartered bus. The worship services would be punctuated by a "basket dinner." This was a huge event celebrated by the community as well as churches from neighboring communities. Households in the community and visiting churches would pack baskets for their individual families with enough to share with visitors. The dinners would be spread out on the grounds of the church, with an open invitation to whoever wished to join the basket host. Elements of this event are still a part of the programming for the Promise Land Annual Festival, hosted by the Promise Land Heritage Association. During the Bowen family reunion in 1998, Rev. Bowen's daughter Jewell proposed that for the 2000 reunion, the family would celebrate the new millennium by inviting families with roots in Promise Land to gather at the site with dinner baskets to be shared with all in attendance. Unfortunately, Jewell passed away in 1999, the year before the event occurred. 2000 marked the first Promise Land Festival, a public event that is held annually. In memory of the St. John Methodist's annual homecoming day started in 1936, the PLHA instituted worship services with a luncheon at the Promise Land Historic Site on the First Sunday in June following the festival. This event is usually attended by the organization's Board and members, community descendants, and special invited guests.

Charlotte Bowen Edmondson

Born in October 1861, Charlotte was Richard (Dick) Bowen's twin. She grew up on the Bowen Farm in Promise Land. At the age of twenty-four, she married Jefferson Edmondson Jr., the son of early Promise Land settlers Jeff Edmondson (1826) and Charlotte Gilbert Vanleer (born 1835). Jeff Sr.'s wife Charlotte was the sister to my great-grandfather, William Gilbert. They were the parents of the following offspring: Lucy Edmondson Carter (born about 1851), Jeff Edmondson Jr. (born 1852), Joe Edmondson (born 1853), Benjamin Edmondson (born 1853), John Edmondson Sr. (born 1866), James "Jim" Edmondson (born 1866) and William Edmondson (born 1874).

Their fourth son, John, would marry Susan Vanleer, daughter of USCT veteran Edward Vanleer. John and Susan were the parents of my mother's stepfather, Leslie Edmondson. John's brother, James, "Jim," was my father's stepfather.

Jeff Jr. married a woman whose name was Charlotte, the same as his mother's name. His wife was the daughter of Nathan Bowen. They were the parents of seven children, whose names and date of birth are as follows: Sallie Edmondson (Vanleer, Garrett, and Suggs), born 1888; Jettie Edmondson, born 1992; Cluster Edmondson Robertson, born 1896; Elva C. Edmondson, born 1896; Rosie G. Edmondson, born 1901; Willie Edmondson, born 1902; and Ethel C. Edmondson, born 1906.

The Edmondson family begat a large proportion of the families who lived in the Promise Land and Cumberland Furnace communities and has generated a large proportion of the surviving descendants.

In the 1990 Bowen family reunion journal, my mother wrote of her remembrance of her great-aunt Charlotte, she wrote:

Aunt Charlotte (nicknamed "Puss") was Uncle Richard's twin. She was a very quiet person who would often be found humming or singing to herself. One of her favorite songs was "Sit Down Servant." She was so kind to all of us children in the community. She would give the girls pretty scraps of material that she had saved for quilt pieces. We would use the scraps to make doll dresses. She was a large robust woman, who wore her hair neatly wrapped with a scarf that reminded me of the picture of Aunt Jemima. I remember seeing her walking to the Nesbitt Spring to wash. She would have to walk across an old foot log, all the time balancing a large bundle of clothes wrapped in a white sheet on top of her head. She was like a mother to her many grandchildren, nieces, nephews, and friends. They all called her "Mimmy." When she passed away, I remember standing on the front porch to see her wooden coffin carried to the Bowen Graveyard on USCT Veteran, Mr. Landy Williams's wood wagon. It was a very cold day and it was a sad yet frightening experience to some of us watching. I was on the porch with some of her grandchildren, the children of her daughter, Cluster Robertson. They were Calvin, Pete, Lucy, Myrtle, and Louise. It was the first time that most of us had seen a wooden coffin.[1]

George Washington Bowen

My great-grandfather George Washington Bowen was the seventh child born to Nathan and Lucy Carr. He was born in April 1868. He learned early to farm from his older brothers, as he was a small child when his father was incarcerated for murder. With his older brothers he took care of the homefront during his father's absence. He was fond of the opportunity to study and took pride in his literacy abilities. In 1886 he took the exam offered by the Dickson County Education System to become a primary school teacher. He passed the examination and was assigned to teach at a school for the children of sharecroppers at the Cannady Farms located north of Promise Land near Cumberland Furnace. A few years later he was assigned to a "colored school" in the Mt. Zion community in Charlotte. As a schoolmaster he was nicknamed "Doc Bowen." On May 20, 1895, at the age of twenty-seven years old he married my great-grandmother Farmie Della Vanleer, the daughter of Joe Washington and Rebecca Vanleer. After marrying Farmie, he moved into the home of her parents. Though he was frail and sick, Farmie's father welcomed George into the family. Joe Washington Vanleer and George belonged to the same church and were very fond of each other. At the time of the marriage, Joe's sons were deceased or had moved away. He had no sons available to run the farm. Joe passed away within five years of George and Farmie' s marriage. George assumed the role of the patriarch and oversaw complete control of the farm and household. Farmie, who was ten years younger than George, was a very active woman. She quickly assumed the role of matriarch of the home, as her mother was showing signs of dementia and required supervision. Both Farmie and George were members of the Mt. Olive AME Church in Promise Land. The couple were considered leaders in the church. Farmie was said to be a prayer warrior and known for her soul-stirring prayers. George gained a reputation as a sought-after orator by churches in nearby communities, and for leading "Dr. Watts" hymns.[2] He also served as Sunday School superintendent.

As a young woman, Farmie had developed an interest in natural remedies and herbs. She had learned to identify plants that could be used for medicinal and nutritional purposes. This was a skill that she had learned from her mother. I remember as a child going to the woods with her to forage for wild plants including mushrooms, garlic, sage, ginseng, poke salad, etc. She always had home remedies for colds, insect bites, upset stomach, headaches, or any other related ailments. In addition to being a practicing herbalist, my grandmother was a licensed midwife who practiced under the supervision of Lemuel Loggins, MD, of Charlotte. She delivered the babies of the residents of the community who gave birth at home during the period of 1915 to 1949. These deliveries included her own grandchildren and great-grandchildren.

In addition to farming, teaching, and public speaking, George enjoyed hunting with his friends. On a hunting adventure with his friend and colleague who taught at Promise Land School, Ernest Nesbitt, George suffered a near casualty when Ernest's gun was accidentally discharged and shattered his left leg. The leg was so badly injured that it had to be amputated. Doctors later fitted him with a wooden peg prothesis. With that he gained a new nickname. He became known as "Peg." He wore this wooden prothesis until his death. Peg may have been prone to physical mishaps. On another occasion, a finger on his left hand was accidentally amputated on some type of farm machinery. Both the leg and finger were buried in the grave of his father, Nathan, at the Bowen Cemetery. After the loss of the leg, George gave up teaching so that he could devote more time to tending his farm. He had inherited complete control of the farm after his father's death. There were no more brothers-in-law around to assist him. In order to recover the income lost from teaching, he took on working outside his farm to assist a white farmer named Lincoln Miller who lived nearby. He and George had always maintained a good relationship on their neighboring farms. My mother said that one day they had a violent dispute. She was nearby playing with some other kids when she heard her grandfather shouting at the "top of his voice at that white man." Her grandfather, who appeared furious, had picked up a stone and was threatening the man. She overheard him say, "Mr. Miller, I want you to know that I was born free! I am not your slave! . . . I'll give up my crop here on your farm. Just pay me what you owe me!" George dropped the brick and turned to walk away. Miller quickly followed behind him pleading, "Wait Peg, wait Peg, let's talk this over." George replied, "No, there is nothing to talk over." George continued back to his home. Sometime later Miller carried the money he owed George to his home and paid him. They reconciled their differences, but George never worked for Miller again. Years later when George died, Lincoln Miller stood at the head of George's grave with a bouquet of red roses and placed them on the grave.

George and Farmie had seven children. They were Mary (Molly), Georgia, Essie, Myrtle, Carrie C., Asa C. (Snook), and Mabel. Their fifth child, Carrie C., contracted tuberculosis and died at the age of sixteen. Their only son, Asa C., who was known by his nickname Snook, was born with a developmental disability, which severely delayed his mental capacity. He functioned on the level of a child. He was cared for in the home by his parents and siblings until 1944 when his widowed mother could no longer manage his care due to her own failing health. In 1943, she had him placed in a state mental facility in Nashville, where he died within a year at the age of twenty-nine years old. The other adult children had already moved out of the home and were establishing their own independent lives. That is, all except Mabel, who stayed at the home with her mother and others who moved in and out of the household during Farmie's remaining years on earth. The household was very fluid with the coming and going of the occupants.

The oldest child Mary, who was called Molly, was the first to leave. She moved around 1915 and was soon followed by her sisters Myrtle, Essie, and Georgia. All of them moved to Nashville to live temporarily with their mother's sister Nara Nesbitt. At the age of eighteen, Molly gave birth to my mother, Essie Vanleer Gilbert.

9
MISS ESSIE'S HOUSE

IT IS IMPORTANT to point out that my mother's middle name is a given name. It is the same as her grandmother's maiden name. However, her grandmother wanted her to have her last name. Therefore, as a child growing up, my mother was referred to as "Van" or "Vanleer" by her maternal family. She loved being called by this name. My mother was born at Hubbard Hospital. Grandmother reported that my mother's father was a young man from the Promise Land community, whose name was Hersey Kirkman. Both she and Hersey lived in Nashville and had been keeping company with each other prior to leaving Promise Land. Hersey Kirkman's mother, who was widowed and had remarried, and her offspring always accepted my mother as her grandchild. My grandmother also had another suitor who was in the military. His name was Lesley Edmondson. When Lesley Edmondson was discharged from the US Army in 1917 and returned home, she resumed her relationship with him. They married shortly after his return.

During her romantic entanglement, my grandmother had brought my mother to Promise Land to live temporarily with her parents. While in Promise Land, my mother established a close bond with her maternal grandparents and her paternal grandmother, Lizzie Kirkman Nesbitt, who also lived in the community. When my mother was four years old, her mother and stepfather announced that they were moving to Omaha, Nebraska, and they wanted to take her with them. Lesley had served abroad during WWI. This experience gave him a desire for a life beyond Promise Land and any other part of Tennessee. My grandmother was anxious to share this adventure with him. However, my mother said that she adamantly opposed the notion of her having to leave those whom she had grown to love in Promise Land. She said that she cried and made a big fuss to express her opposition. She did not want to leave her grandparents on either side. She had grown remarkably close to her biological father's mother, who she called "Gramma Lizzie." Gramma Lizzie owned a grocery store next door to St. John Church. It seemed that she had an endless supply of candy to give her granddaughter. Mother said that she also could not bear the thought of leaving her young aunt and playmate, Mabel, who was only two years older than her. Her grandfather George stepped in and proclaimed that if she did not wish to go, no one could force her to do so. That was the final word on the matter. Mother said at that moment her grandfather, whom she called "Pappy," made her so happy he became her lifelong hero.

My mother was able to be raised by her grandparents while her mother and stepfather went off to "explore their fortune" (my mother's words). From our conversations, I am sure that she missed her mother much more than she verbally expressed. However, she was born in a loving close-knit household. She also felt loved and protected by extended family and friends in the community. She shared stories of her early life experiences with her grandmother whom she, her cousins, and later her own children called "Mymie," and her grandfather whom the household called Pappy. She remembered that at night the whole household would gather for prayer with Mymie and Pappy. She marveled that despite having only one "good leg," Pappy would kneel on his good leg and pray the most fervent prayers for the household. She also recalled how she would climb into his lap, and he would read to her or have her read to him. He also taught her math and would have her solve arithmetic problems that required her to use her adding, subtracting, dividing, and multiplication skills. He would engage her, Mabel, and other children in the household in spelling bees and finding countries and continents on the globe. The globe was a prize possession in the home and not to be used without supervision. As she told her story, I recognized where she received some of her parenting skills, as she would subject my siblings and I to similar impromptu educational sessions. I always felt intimidated and nervous with these academic sessions. I thought it was like playing school. As I grew older, I developed a different perspective of the role of education in the home.

Mother enjoyed a very special childhood herself. She admired her grandparents and loved living with them. She was not the only child in the home. Living there were also her Aunt Mabel and two cousins, Richard, her Great-Aunt Pantie's son, and Toby, her Aunt Georgia's son. All of the children were within the same age range. This is an example of the generosity and love that her grandparents showed for their children. Although there were other children in the household, my mother was very aware that she held a special place in the hearts of her grandparents. She loved that she was interchangeably called "Vanleer" or "Van" by everyone in the household and her friends. The exceptional status that she received in her home gave her confidence and security outside the home and in the community. Encouraged by her grandfather, she became an active participant in the arts, including performing and public speaking. When she was in the sixth grade, the teacher at Promise Land School resigned. At the beginning of the new school year, the county had not sent a new teacher to the school. Van took the initiative to go to the school superintendent's office located on the square in Charlotte and request a teacher. Mr. Luther, the school superintendent, was amazed by this eleven-year-old girl taking the initiative to come to his office and demand instruction. He was so impressed by her that he invited her to go to the nearby store for a "cold drink." She accepted his invitation, enroute, the superintendent stopped by the offices of "other important men" to introduce her and tell them why she had come to visit him. He promised her that he would definitely send a teacher within weeks. Within a few weeks, Mother said that she heard the dogs ferociously barking one afternoon. She and her cousins went to investigate why they were barking. They encountered a stranger, who was well dressed and spoke in a commanding voice. He spoke to the children and introduced himself as "Mr. Brown," the new teacher who had been assigned to Promise Land School. He was looking for the house where he had been told that he would find lodging. Mother said that she was so excited to get this news. However, this wasn't the case for her cousins Richard and Toby. It meant that their long holiday would soon come to an end. They were, however, delighted to show Mr. Brown to Uncle Boss and Aunt E's house, located next door to them. This was the house where the new teacher would find accommodations.

A very sad period in my mother's life was when her grandfather became ill and was diagnosed with tuberculosis. He was bedbound at home for several months before he recovered. During this time, she remembered the neighbors coming to assist with farming chores including caring for the livestock and raising crops, as well as cutting timber on the property for firewood. He recovered and was able to return to farming. Unfortunately, several months later, he became violently ill while working in the field. He started coughing, which caused regurgitation of blood. From the field he took the wagon wheel–created dirt road called The Lane to his home. It was the route that my mother and the other children traveled to and from school. This road is now called the Redden Crossing Road, which is about a quarter of a mile long from the Promise Land Road, passing Vanleer's farm to Highway 48. On the way home from school that afternoon with her housemates, Mabel, Richard, and Toby, Mother said that Cousin Emma, who lived at the corner of The Lane, stopped them to tell them that their grandfather had taken ill in the field but had made it home. With that news, my mother said she and Mabel started running ahead of Richard and Toby, who were only four years and could not keep up. They ran as fast as they could; along the lane near the house they saw evidence of his hemorrhaging, what looked like bloody vomit. This only increased their anxiety. On the porch there was another small pool of blood on the ground. When they got inside, it seemed like chaos. Snook was having a hysterical fit, thrashing, and crying inconsolably. He was a big fourteen-year-old who behaved like a child. Aunt Sallie, Mymie's sister-in-law and neighbor, was there trying to console him and keep him from hurting himself. A neighbor, Mr. Will Langford, came in with a pot of water and headed toward the sick room. Mother said that she and Mabel bolted into the room right behind him. Aunt Sallie called them back, but Mymie overheard and said, "Let them come back." Mabel and Van found Pappy on the bed in his room, which adjoined the sitting room where the others were. The room was separated only by a doorway covered by wine-colored taffeta curtains. In the room with Pappy was Mymie and Uncle Boss, their nephew. They had cleaned him up and had put him in the bed. Pappy was dressed in a large off-white flannel shirt and covered with a quilt that Mymie had been working on just a few days prior. The bloody clothes that he had been wearing were lying on the floor in a heap covering his old dirt-clogged work brogans at the foot of the bed. Mother said she ran to his side. To her his face seemed to glow, there was a stubble of his graying beard. His eyes were closed. She ran to his side and threw herself at him with her face against his. She felt the warmth of his face, but there was no breathing. She cried with her tears drenching his face. Her grandmother gently pulled her away, saying "he's gone baby." My mother's beloved "Pappy" had died on his bed on May 20, 1929. He was only sixty-three years old. I often heard my mother retell the story of this event. George Bowen was buried in the Vanleer Cemetery, where a plot next to his grave remained vacant for years, waiting for his dear Farmie Della to join him. The Vanleer Cemetery was on the family farm in close proximity to the family home. My siblings and I would often visit the cemetery when we were kids. It was near Uncle Boss's hog pen. Near the hog pen, there was a path lined by fruit and nut trees on each side that led to the graveyard. We would go watch Uncle Boss slop the hogs and would sometimes wander off to survey the delectable bounty provided by God in the orchard. In the summer we would find peaches and plums. In the fall we would raid the pear, apples, walnut, and hickory trees.

The orchard led to the graveyard. Located at the front of the graveyard was the most prominent stone that marked the grave of Joe Washington Vanleer. Next to his grave was Rebecca, his wife. The graves of their offspring, their spouses, and relatives were ordered by the date of their deaths. There were few manufactured tombstones. However, most of the graves had a large rock at the head and a smaller rock at what was designated the foot. Next to the large rock would be a marker with identifying information with the name and dates of birth and death. The ink on some of the markers had faded, signifying that the death had occurred many years past. Some of the graves were much fresher than others. This was indicated by the lucidity of the identifying information, as well as the color intensity of the ribbons and plastic flowers. We would always visit the graves of those who had recently died. On Decoration Day (Memorial Day), Mother would go with us to decorate the graves. Our beloved Mymie, Pappy, and dear sweet Aunt Mabel were all there when we were kids.

Farmie lived a long full life after George's death. She was now head of her household. Her children and grandchildren kept her busy with their comings and goings. The Bowen offspring were fruitful. Molly and her husband were living in Omaha, Nebraska. In Omaha, they had increased the family. Born to them were two daughters, Robbie Mae and Sarah, and a son Staney. All were born before 1925. Georgia, the oldest of the children was unmarried and lived in the home of her employer in Nashville. She had one child whose real name was Oris Lee but was called "Toby." Toby had been in the care of his grandmother from birth. The third offspring, Essie, continued to live in Nashville. Long before her father's death, she had met and married a man named James Miller. They had a son whose name was Robert Lee, who was born in 1914. Myrtle had joined her older sister, Molly, and was residing in Omaha. There she met a young man there named Willie Battle. Willie had migrated to Omaha from North Carolina. He and Myrtle married and started raising a family.

On June 4, 1933, seventeen-year-old Essie "Van" married my father, Robert Gilbert. My mother had finished Promise Land School and never went on to complete high school. The nearest high school for Black students was in Dickson, ten miles away, and the only way she could attend would have required living in a boarding home, which Mymie was unable to afford. My grandmother was pressuring my mother to join her and the rest of the family in Omaha. Mother was just as opposed then to moving to Omaha as she had been when she was four years old. The only difference was that her "Pappy" was no longer there to advocate for her. My father, who was ten years older than my mother, was a handsome, hardworking, caring man and a very devoted suitor to mother. My father was the primary provider for his own mother and younger siblings. He had proposed marriage to Mother. These qualities aided my mother's decision to accept his proposal. In time she would confide to me that at the time of his proposal, she didn't love him. She believed that she could "grow to love him." After marrying him she moved into his home, which he shared with his mother and younger brothers. Having a bird's eye view of their marriage for more than fifty plus years, I admit that I never had any doubt of my mother's love for my father, nor his love for her. She worshipped and adored him. He was her king who catered to her every need, and she, his queen.

About eight years after my parents married, Mabel, the youngest daughter of George and Farmie, also got married. She married my father's half brother, Wesley C. Edmondson. Wesley was better known as "Peony," a name that had been with him all his life. The story behind his name was that when he was born the peonies were in bloom. His mother thought that his appearance rivaled the peonies, so she nicknamed him Peony. His actual name was Wesley Clara (named after his maternal aunt, Clara). Formally he would use only his initials "W. C.," I think I understand that he chose not to be called Clara. At the time of their marriage, Peony had just been discharged for his service during WWII. Farmie was delighted with Peony and Mabel's marriage. He was a good son-in-law who took on some of the masculine responsibilities around the house. Peony was an extraordinary carpenter who worked for the celebrated Black architect, Moses McKissack III, of McKissack and McKissack in Nashville.

Soon after moving into the home, Peony began to remodel the house to expand the accommodations. He converted the old wood-frame house with three rooms on the lower level and two large rooms upstairs into an updated red brick siding six-room house with shingled roof. The upstairs was made into a utility and storage area. He removed the stairs that led to a room that had served as the kitchen and dining area. That room was converted into a large dining room. He closed in the back porch and made it into a kitchen. He added new two bedrooms downstairs. Although Mother, Richard, and Toby had grown up and were no longer in the home, their absence didn't make it more spacious. Aunt Georgia, Toby's mother, had given birth to a little girl . . . who was now living in the home. Her name was Mabel in honor of her aunt who had become her guardian. In order to minimize confusion in the name, little Mabel was called "Tootsie." Tootsie wasn't the youngest child in the household for long.

In 1940, Tootsie's mother Georgia gave birth to another little girl, whose name was Carrie Pearl. Carrie was also placed in her Aunt Mabel's care. Aunt Georgia appeared to have suffered from some type of developmental disability. She was functional but irresponsible. Unmarried, she worked as a domestic in Nashville. Near the time of delivery of each pregnancy, she would come home so that her mother could assist her with the delivery. Without adequate resources and support to raise the children, she would leave them in the care of her mother. Despite leaving the children with her mother and sister to raise, Georgia was a devoted and loving parent. She would visit her children, often bringing them gifts. I remember at Christmas, she would come and stay for an extended period, and she would have gifts for everyone, including me. Carrie was Aunt Georgia's last child. When the children were old enough to venture out on their own, all of them headed to Nashville to be with their mother for a while until they established themselves.

The Bowen household was very dynamic when it came to the occupants. It seems that as Aunt Mabel and Uncle Peony were settling into being a married couple who were caring for Mymie and their nieces, Tootsie, and Carrie, another change was on the horizon. Aunt Mabel's older sister, Essie, had been divorced from her husband James Miller for several years. Their son Robert Lee was grown and was serving in the US Navy when Aunt Essie was stricken with a debilitating neurological illness that affected her ability to ambulate and manage self-care. Mymie insisted that Aunt Essie move back into her home so that she could care for her. I was about three years old at the time. My great-grandmother seems to have been doing a good job taking care of her sick daughter, and my mother would go there each day to help out. Due to having preschool-aged children, my mother's availability to help was limited. Then Mymie got sick herself and required bedrest. Aunt Mabel worked as a maid in the home of a Dickson bank president who lived in Cumberland Furnace. She was given a leave of absence from work to take care of her mother and aunt. Aunt Essie's son Robert Lee had been discharged from the Navy, was married, and lived in the San Francisco Bay Area. He and Aunt Mabel decided that in order to ease her load as caregiver, it would be best for his mother to come and live with him. Aunt Mabel accompanied Aunt Essie to California by plane. My mother stayed with Mymie and oversaw the household during Aunt Mabel's absence. When Aunt Mabel returned, she found that Mymie's health had continued to decline. Family and neighbors came to sit with her around the clock.

My great-grandmother did not recover from this illness. At the age of seventy-one, she passed away in her home on October 1, 1951. The cause of death was hypertensive cardiac disease and renal failure. She was survived by two siblings, Nara and Ellen, and four children: Georgia, Molly, Essie, Myrtle, and Mabel. Mabel oversaw all arrangements for her funeral and burial. The evening before her funeral and burial, a wake was held in her home where she lay in state, in the new room that her son-in-law had added to her home. The next day her funeral was held at St. John Methodist Church. She was buried after the funeral service at the Vanleer Cemetery.

It seems like after Mymie died, Aunt Mabel's household drastically changed. It resembled a nuclear family with only her, Uncle Peony, and their niece Carrie living there. Carrie was school aged, and they raised her as their child. They called her "Pussycat" and she was treated like a princess. Aunt Mabel and Uncle Peony also continued to upgrade their home with modern electrical appliances, new furniture, a telephone, and the first television in the community. From my perspective, I equated them to the people I saw on television, *Ozzie and Harriet*, *The Life of Riley*, et cetera. I was impressed by Uncle Peony's 1951 black Ford, which he kept sparklingly shined and that Aunt Mabel drove. She was the only Black woman in the community who drove a car. Needless to say, our family practically lived there with them. The whole family would be at their house on Friday nights to watch the *Cavalcade of Sports*, which was the boxing matches "brought to you by Gilette." My sister Della and Carrie were in the same grade and enjoyed each other's company. So, she was allowed to live with them. The rest of us were frequent visitors at my aunt and uncle's home whenever we were allowed.

All of us were devastated when Aunt Mabel was diagnosed with colon cancer. She was so active, bubbly, and full of life, and at the age of forty she was given this terminal diagnosis. This diagnosis came when there were major transitions on the horizon for our family. My sister Beverly was graduating from high school in the spring of 1956, and she would be moving to Nebraska with our grandmother to attend the University of Omaha. Mother would learn that she was pregnant with her eighth child. These events would unfold as Aunt Mabel would undergo treatment and subsequently succumb to cancer.

Beverly was a highly active senior who was looking forward to graduation. Along the way, she was selected as the homecoming queen, and no one could have demonstrated their pride in her achievement more than Aunt Mabel. Aunt Mabel took her shopping for the homecoming pageant in Nashville and purchased her gown at Cain-Sloan department store, a prominent shop in the city. The homecoming pageant and parade was a major event for our family. Everyone in the immediate family attended except for our oldest Bobbye Jane, who had moved to St. Louis, Missouri, with our father's brother, Jewel Gilbert. When Bobbye finished Promise Land School, there was no reliable source of transportation for her to attend the segregated high school in Dickson. As a solution to this problem our uncle and his wife agreed to have her live with them. The rest of us including Aunt Mabel, Uncle Peony, our pastor, Rev. Marcellus, and his family attended the homecoming events.

During the beginning of her senior year, Beverly learned that Mother was pregnant. That did not sit well with her at all. She shared with me after I was older just how angry it made her. Her issue was that she was sixteen years old and would be graduating from high school. She believed that it was embarrassing for her to welcome a new sibling at that age. She got over this concern and became a source of support to our mother. She would look after me and my younger sister Linda, when Mother had a doctor's appointment or had to look after Aunt Mabel. She would also come home from school and make dinner for the family. Despite taking on more responsibilities at home, it did not affect her schoolwork. She graduated as valedictorian of her class. By the time of her graduation, Aunt Mabel had started to show signs of illness. She had lost a significant amount of weight and was taking frequent naps during the day. Around the second week of July that year, she was admitted to Vanderbilt Hospital. Within days of her admission, Mother went into labor and Dad took her to Memorial Hospital in Clarksville. Our baby sister Rita was born on July 15, 1956, and my mother was discharged about two weeks after her birth. Aunt Mabel came home about the same time but was readmitted to Vanderbilt within a few days due to an acute medical problem. During the brief time she was at home, Mother took the baby and moved into Aunt Mabel's house to be with her. After Aunt Mabel went back to the hospital, Mother requested us to bring all the newborn's essentials to her. She wanted to be there for her beloved aunt when she returned home. Unfortunately, Aunt Mabel never returned home. She passed away at the hospital on August 8, 1956. Her funeral and burial arrangements followed the pattern of her mother, who had preceded her in death just five years earlier.

During the time of Aunt Mabel's death and funeral, the two households were bursting at the seams with extended family and guests. Some stayed at Aunt Mabel's house, while others stayed at our home. Our grandparents along with mother's siblings, Aunt Robbie, Aunt Sarah, and Uncle Stanley had come. Mother's cousin Richard Jenkins, with whom she had grown up, his wife known as Cousin Pimps, and their children were also there. All these guests had to be boarded. At that time when Black people traveled, many of the hotels and motels would not provide lodging for Black families. We made pallets on the floors at each home for the children to sleep. The beds were reserved for adults. Mother did not give up the bedroom at Aunt Mabel's house. She had claimed it for herself, her husband, and baby Rita. She stayed put, but willingly gave up their bed at her own home to the out-of-town guests. When it came time for family to return to their homes there was much sadness with their departures. Mother's parents and siblings were the last to leave. This was especially difficult for us, because Beverly was leaving with them. She would be enrolling in college and would not be returning to Tennessee for quite a while. I remember that she cried so hard. So did the rest of us. When were able to pull away from each other, she got into the car with her waiting travelers. It was reminiscent of years earlier, when our sister Bobbye left with our Uncle Jewel to live in St. Louis. This was a scene that would be repeated each summer when she returned home for a short visit and when the time came for her to return to St. Louis.

When Beverly left, only six children remained with our parents. Left behind were the baby Rita, Linda, who was seven years old, Billy who was twelve years old, Della who was sixteen, Joe was seventeen, and I myself, ten years old at the time. Most of us continued to stay at Aunt Mabel's house where mother was staying. Our father would come to Aunt Mabel's house after work and have dinner. Sometimes he would stay all night; other times he would come back to our house to stay with the children and check on things. One day Mother announced at dinner that she wanted the whole family to move into Aunt Mabel's house, which was our "new home." Uncle Peony was staying in Nashville with his brother, and it brought him closer to his job. He had talked with Mother and Dad about moving into the house that he had shared with Aunt Mabel. He had planned to look for a place in Nashville. Carrie, his and Aunt Mabel's sixteen-year-old niece, had asked him what she would do. He told her that she should stay with her cousin Van (my mother) and her children at the house where she had always lived. When Uncle Peony told Mother of his thoughts, she was very pleased because this was the home that she had grown up in and she and Dad had already assured Carrie that they would raise her along with their children. My siblings Billy, Linda, and I were students at Promise Land School. Billy was in the sixth grade, and this would be his last year at the school. There was talk that Promise Land School would close when his class of twelve students transferred into Junior High at Hampton. The few remaining students left would be bused to nearby segregated Cedar Grove School in the city of Charlotte. This consolidation of Promise Land School became a reality in the new school year of 1957. Della, Carrie, and Joe were students at Hampton High School in Dickson. Della and Carrie were sophomores, and Joe was a junior.

We received a letter each week from Beverly. She told us how she missed being with us and inquired about everyone in the community. Her letters were upbeat and humorous. I would read them over and over. Although she acknowledged that she missed us, she was making a go of her situation. She had met her cousins, Aunt Robbie's and Aunt Sarah's children. Aunt Robbie had a son and a daughter, and Aunt Sarah had two sons, all of whom were younger than Beverly. Aunt Robbie's daughter, Twinkie, was about the same age as Rita. She used Twinkie's development as a scale for predicting Rita's growth and development. She liked the university, successfully auditioned for the university choir, and was looking forward to performing with them. While there, she also pledged to become a neophyte of Alpha Kappa Alpha. She would not be able to pledge into the actual sorority until her second year of college. Although the school was predominantly white, she seemed to have had little difficulty adapting into the setting. Grandmother worked hard to help her acclimate to her new environment. Grannie held a party in her honor to introduce Beverly to peers at the church where she and Grandfather attended. At this event she met an endearing friend she would have for life. It was Charline Gibson, the wife of major league baseball player Bob Gibson.

For most of the family, life seemed to have moved on. But, as a child, I could detect Mother's sadness and despair. She spent a lot of time sleeping. She took care of Rita but did little else. Often, Della and Carrie would cook dinner for the family when they came home from school. They would groom Linda and me for school most days. Other days we would do our best at doing for ourselves. Billy and I had chores, like washing and hanging out the clothes on the clothesline; this included diapers. I remember this being a difficult job in the winter when it was cold. The old wringer washing machine was outside the house. Sometimes Mother would help us. Taking the laundry down after it had dried was our job. Della and Carrie would fold and iron the laundry. Billy and I would help prepare the laundry for ironing by sprinkling them and rolling them up. Joe was responsible for keeping a fire going in the two stoves in the house. He would chop the wood and bring the wood inside the house so that Mother could keep the fire stoked during the day.

Dad would have the fire nice and fueled when we got up each morning and left for school. Dad, who left early for work, would most of the time make breakfast for us before he departed. Dad worked as a construction laborer. It was outside work. I remember waking up to rain and I hoped that it would be consistent so that he would not be able to go to work. Then he would be there to make a big breakfast with the eggs fried just the way I liked them. He could also tie my shoes laces so that they would stay laced. When I tied them, they would keep coming untied. Little did I know then that when he missed a day at work, he did not get paid. Mother had several physical complaints that accounted for her staying in bed. She also had frequent visits to the doctor. I remember walking into the kitchen one day and finding Mother standing at the sink, quietly sobbing. When I asked her why she was crying, she replied "I miss Mymie and Mabel and I miss Bell." Bell was Beverly's nickname.

In the spring of 1957 my father's brother, Theo Edmondson, died suddenly of a heart attack while sleeping. This was a major shock to the family. Beverly was more than distressed when she received the notice. Even more alarming for her was her inability to come and be with family and extended family, because she dearly loved her Uncle Theo. She had been a member of the singing group Theo Edmondson and the Promise Land Singers, which he formed when she was a teenager. She had grown up with and shared a close bond with her cousins(his daughters) who were also in the group. Beverly was unable to come home and mourn with the family and attend his funeral.

As summer approached that year, Beverly notified us in a letter that she would be coming home to stay. She said that she missed us so much being away from home. She especially missed being with Rita, whom she had barely got to know before leaving. She told us that she had decided to transfer to Tennessee State University. She also had a plan of how she would support herself. Through her high school principal, Larry Pendergrass, she had been introduced to the owner of the Kuhn's Five and Dime Store in Dickson, Jack Kuhn. Jack Kuhn and his wife Lois were seeking a live-in nanny for their three children at their home in Belle Meade, an upscale section in Nashville. They offered the job to Beverly, and she had accepted it. In August 1957, Beverly returned home to the delight of her family. Beverly settled in without a hitch. She moved in with the Kuhns and enrolled at TSU. Majoring in business administration at TSU, she carried a full course load as well as fulfilled her scholarship as a work-study student in the office of the department head. It was not long before Beverly was joined at TSU by her siblings, Joe and Della.

Joe graduated from Hampton High School in May 1958. He left home soon after graduating and moved to Nashville to live with Uncle Peony and his new wife, Aunt Ressie. Joe soon found work at a Nashville restaurant. That fall, he enrolled at TSU. Both Della and Carrie graduated from high school in 1959. Della followed in Beverly's footsteps. She was the homecoming queen and class valedictorian. She received a scholarship that paid for her tuition at TSU. Beverly helped her find a job as a live-in nanny for a family who lived near the Kuhns. She became the nanny for a preadolescent girl. Like Beverly, she enrolled full time at TSU and commuted from Belle Meade to campus. Della majored in elementary education, which was a career that she had set as a goal from elementary school. Cousin Carrie moved to Nashville to live with her older sister, Mabel, after graduating high school. She enrolled in cosmetology school. After completing her training, she relocated to Omaha to live with our grandmother.

Left at home with our parents were Billy, Linda, Rita, and myself. Mother seemed to have recovered from her emotional slump and was rallying in her role as mother, homemaker, and wife. From my point of view, things were going well on the home front. By the time I entered high school, Beverly had graduated college, moved back home, and accepted a job as a teacher at Hampton High School. As a high school freshman, I was delighted to have my older sister as my shorthand and typing teacher. Beverly was a great teacher who was well liked by her students. She was kind, sensitive, and respectful of the her charges. I had always found her to be charming, witty, and wise. She was a good dresser, who pranced around the school in high-heeled shoes. I was so proud of her and so were my siblings and parents. We loved having her at home. She had a little green 1955 Ford we called the "Green Gander." We enjoyed commuting to school and traveling to events with her. Not only did we commute to school each day, but we attended all the school athletic games at home and away. I recall riding along in the Gander with the radio blasting on WVOL, while grooving to the latest tunes by Marvin Gaye, James Brown, or whoever the DJ was spinning that particular morning. Beverly would say, "Watch me make the Gander dance." By manipulating the steering controls, gears, brakes, and accelerator, she would make the car launch forward, bounce, and keep time to the music. I just remember laughing a lot and having so much fun. Although we were enjoying ourselves with our older sister back at home with us, we did not shirk our academic responsibilities. Our parents, especially Mother, had taught us to be goal oriented. Preparation to meet those goals came naturally for us. Having Beverly at home was a boost to the whole family.

We were faced with many challenges as a family, like in the summer of 1960, when Mother was admitted to the hospital for gall bladder surgery. While she was hospitalized other medical problems surfaced. These problems resulted in a much longer hospital stay than we had expected. Della was on break from school and the family for whom she worked were on vacation. After discussion, it was decided that Della would not return to school or work during the fall semester. She would stay home with Rita, who was not yet in school. The plan was that she would return for the winter semester. Dad, Billy, and I were there to assist in the home. Beverly was working full time and taking courses toward her master's degree at the time. Joe had left college and was serving in the Air Force. Mother had multiple surgeries and was hospitalized for nearly three months. When she returned home after a few weeks of convalescence she was able to resume homemaking responsibilities. Della was thrilled that she was able to resume her education.

Mother shared with me years later the emotional upheaval she experienced following the birth of her last child and now the death of her beloved aunt, best friend, and confidant Mabel had really taken a toll on her mental health. She told me that when my baby sister was born, and then soon after she lost whom she considered her "lifeline" Mabel, she felt like she wanted to die. Added to these major life changes, both her oldest children, Bobbye and Beverly, were away in other states. She felt she had no one to confide in. I suspect that there were unresolved issues of early separation from her mother contributing to her emotional turmoil. However, she never acknowledged that. She said that her body reacted to her thoughts and feelings. She believed that the grief and despair led to her physical illness. She acknowledged that although my father showed her love and affection, she didn't believe that he could understand her emotional pain and grief. She revealed that her strength to hold on actually came from her faith in God, but without my father and her kids in her life, she didn't think that she would have made it.

I am grateful for the opportunity to have had my mother as a daily companion after my retirement and my ultimate return home to care for her. After graduating high school in 1964, I left home for college and from there I set out on a career path. This path took me away from my family home for nearly forty years. Retiring in 2003, I decided to return home to care for Mother who was an aging widow, living alone at that time. I established a home next door to her. She soon moved into my home with me. This allowed us to have many long and in-depth conversations. I wish that we had known what she was going through then and had gotten her the mental health counseling that she needed. It may have spared her from the physical and emotional pain and discomfort that she endured. Despite withstanding this difficult life episode, Mother emerged like the phoenix, rising from the ashes.

Perhaps her having to withstand the crisis she faced then was God's way of preparing her for other challenges that she would face throughout the rest of her life. She showed strength and endurance at the age of sixty-eight years old when her spouse of fifty-one years passed away in April 1984. She was alone with him when he passed away. He left her with beautiful memories that she often shared in conversations with others. Her resilience after his death was remarkable. A month before Dad died, my brother Billy and his wife Ingrid lost nineteen-month-old son Clay to meningitis. Clay's illness and death was totally unexpected and a shock to the family. During the deaths of Clay and Dad, my oldest sister, Bobbye, had been diagnosed with terminal breast cancer, which she had managed for a little over eleven years.

It was Bobbye's desire to die in Tennessee with her mother and sister Beverly. In January 1986 it was arranged for her to be flown from her home in New Jersey to Nashville accompanied by Mother and Beverly. A ground ambulance met them at the airport and transported Bobbye to their home. On a sunny warm day in February 1986, Bobbye passed away sitting at the window in the dining room just as she had asked God to allow. Mother was there with her just as she had wanted to be. After Bobbye's death, mother's remaining children rallied around her. She helped her daughter Beverly, who was engaged, plan her wedding. Beverly was marrying a fellow educator and longtime suitor, Hyburnia Williams. Mother oversaw the wedding that took place on July 2, 1989, at St. John United Methodist Church (UMC) in Promise Land. It was a beautiful wedding and the first I ever recall occurring in the church. Mother also took time to visit her other children who lived in Columbus, Ohio, Westchester County, New York, and Maryland. On her eighty-fifth birthday her children hosted a birthday party for her in Maryland entitled "Amazing Mother." She was called on so many times to demonstrate her amazing abilities.

On September 23, 2003, once again her strength and fortitude were called upon when her baby Rita died suddenly of heart and lung disease. That was really tough for my mother. But again, we as her children had to be her strength with the grace of God. A memorial service was held for Rita in Maryland with her family and friends there. Her body was then flown to Tennessee for funeral services and burial in the Vanleer Cemetery. It was shortly after Rita's death that I moved to Tennessee. I had no idea how therapeutic this transition would be for me. It was wonderful that I could be here with Mother to help her through the grief process, but I found that being here was what I also needed.

Despite all that my mother went through, she had many good things to happen in her life and much to have been grateful for. She enjoyed an active and involved life when Dad was alive and after his death. When Dad was living, Mother volunteered as a Gray Lady at the local hospital, she also volunteered at the Help Center a community resource facility in Dickson. They were both active members of the St. John UMC but participated with other churches in the community and organizations like the Dickson Democrats. Mother was a member of Methodist Women Organization, the Union Choir, and the Federation of Black Women. After Dad's death, she became active in the Dickson County Historical Society and began her work to preserve the Promise Land Community. She was a charter member of the Promise Land Community Club and organized the first Promise Land reunion with the help of local nieces Robbie Bowen and Jewel Bennett, Cousin Tamar Primm, daughter Beverly Williams, and others. Mother traveled and spent extended time with her children living in other cities. She accompanied me on my first trip to visit and meet family in Nebraska in 1986. In doing so, we developed a stronger relationship with her siblings and their children. This resulted in organizing and hosting the first Bowen family reunion in Promise Land the following year. Under her leadership, Promise Land received a Tennessee State Marker recognizing the historical significance of the community. The Dickson County Road Commissioner Jasper McEwen presented her with a certification for her assistance in getting the Promise Land Road paved. Much of her work laid the groundwork for the current efforts of the Promise Land Heritage Association. Our family and community have benefited greatly from her work to document and share our history. I am so grateful to God, because she was a praying woman who believed and trusted him. He blessed her with a long life of 101 years.

In reviewing my mother's life, one of the major losses that she experienced was the loss of her ancestral home. In December 1966, the nearly hundred-year-old home, built by Joe Washington Vanleer, burned down to the ground due to faulty electrical wiring. Dad was coming home from work when he saw that a section of the house was ablaze. He rushed in and rescued Mother who was about to prepare dinner. The house was a total loss. I was a student living in the dorm at TSU at the time. Billy was serving in Vietnam. Della had graduated TSU and was living in New York City, and Joe had been discharged from the Air Force and was living in San Francisco. Beverly, Linda, and Rita came home from school to discover the loss. The family temporarily moved in with Dad's sister, Aunt Ruby. Aunt Ruby, who also lived in Promise Land, had recently become a widow and lived alone. Family, friends, and neighbors quickly came to our aid, offering whatever assistance possible to help us restore equilibrium. Beverly, Mother, and Dad explored the insurance benefits and looked into the possibility of renting a home. Beverly started almost immediately looking into having a new home built. When she found that she could get the loan and had found a builder, she and our parents decided not to rebuild at the old home location. They decided to build on another parcel of Joe Washington Vanleer's original land purchase. At that time the parcel belonged to the heirs of his oldest son, Lil Joe. It was built along State Highway 48 North. This made the commute to the new home more accessible.

The new home was finished in July 1967 and the family moved in. Mother, Dad, Beverly, Linda, and Rita were the primary dwellers, but it quickly became a treasured domicile for all of us. Beverly was gracious and always made it a welcome center not just to her siblings, but to all extended family members and friends. The home had always been the source of many great family gatherings, hosting holiday events, reunions, and parties. We were fortunate that the whole family and extended family was intact for these gatherings.

Since those early years of the new home, we have lost many family members including our father's sister Ruth Robertson (Aunt Ruby), November 1973; his brothers, Peony Edmondson, October 1974; Jewel Gilbert, February 1982. Our beloved father Robert Gilbert himself passed away April 18, 1984; and his sister, Hattie Bowen died December 1984. Our sister, Bobbye Jane Gilbert Beasly, passed away on February 18, 1986; our dear sweet baby Rita Gilbert, September 23, 2003; our dear mother, Essie Gilbert, May 19, 2017, and our beloved Beverly Gilbert Williams, February 6, 2020.

Beverly married a wonderful man, Hyburnia Williams on July 2, 1982. Like Beverly, Hyburnia was an educator for the Montgomery School System in Clarksville, Tennessee. After marriage, Beverly moved to Clarksville with her husband, thus, leaving the home to our mother.

THE STORY OF WILLIAM AND PRISCILLA REDDEN GILBERT

William Gilbert was my paternal grandfather. Born into slavery about 1826 on a large gristmill farm located on Barton's Creek near Cumberland Furnace, he was owned by a man who also carried the name William Gilbert. His biological father, who was born about 1800, also carried the same moniker as their enslaver. His grandfather, grandmother Violet Gilbert Vanleer, and their children were purchased by ironmaster Anthony Wayne Vanleer around 1827 for enslavement at the Cumberland Furnace. William "Will" was retained on the Gilbert Plantation until emancipation. He had other siblings born after the sale to Vanleer. In all there were six children born to William Sr. and Violet Gilbert. The children were: Fannie Gilbert Clemmons born 1823 and died 1893; Susan Gilbert Vanleer

Knight born 1824 and died 1895; Prince Gilbert Vanleer Kirkman born 1827 and died 1914; Charlotte "Puss" Vanleer born 1835; Dinah Vanleer Bronson born 1839; and my great-grandfather. For notation, many of the formerly enslaved people carried the name of the enslaver into freedom. Others adopted new names.

To distinguish between names of my father's great-grandfather and grandfather, I will refer to the senior Gilbert as "William" and his son as "Will." At the age of twenty-four, Will married Priscilla Redden in 1850. Priscilla was fourteen years old. She was also enslaved on a farm in Barton's Creek. Her father was Frank Reddon, and her mother was unknown to her. Priscilla and Will had four sons before the emancipation. Their oldest son was Mark Jacob, who was born about 1854. Mark was my dad's father. The other sons born to Will and Priscilla were John and Jeremiah. After emancipation, the couple settled with their three sons in an area that would become Promise Land. A record of deed reveals that William "Will" Gilbert paid $358.54 cents as a down payment for a tract as "parcel of land" to W. H. Hooper. It was not recorded in this document how many acres of land were in this purchase, however, the document stated that Gilbert was to pay an additional $168 dollars "and bearing interest" in twelve months of signing. This additional note was to serve as a "lien on the land conveyed." It is interesting that although Gilbert is identified as the payee and debt holder of the land purchased, his wife was named as the person to whom the land was conveyed. The date of this transaction was January 9, 1878. A related document dated December 4, 1912, concerning the same land transfer, shows that the amount of acreage transferred was fifty-nine and a half acres.

After emancipation, a daughter whose name was Fannie was born to Will and Priscilla in 1874. Her nickname was "Toad." She was known as "Aunt Toad" to my dad and to his siblings. The 1870 Census lists all three sons the Gilbert's household. However, in the 1880 Census, the sons John and Jeremiah are not included. In 1880, they would have been young adults; recognizing this, I also looked for them as residents in other households, but was unsuccessful. My dad never mentioned having uncles. Although John and Jeremiah were unaccounted for after 1870, Priscilla and Will's household did expand. Their household grew to include Priscilla's deceased brother Charles and his wife Rachel's sons. Both Charles and Rachel had died young and left behind two sons, eight-year-old William Plummer and his five-year-old brother Ed Redden, who were raised by the Gilberts. In addition to the two Redden boys, their son Mark had fathered a child named Maggie in 1882. Mark was not married to Maggie's mother, but he brought her to his parents' home, so that they could help him raise her.

I never knew my paternal grandfather, Mark Gilbert. He was eleven years old when he became emancipated from slavery, and I have often wondered what this new freedom meant to a child his age. I am sure it was a struggle for him as his parents worked toward acclimating to independence. Mark was on the threshold of childhood and adulthood. He was the oldest of Will and Priscilla's children. I imagine him bearing a great responsibility in helping his family adjust from slavery to freedom.

There was a period when his family was bound by a work contract to a white farmer before they were able to purchase the land to settle in Promise Land. I imagine that my dad, although he was only five years old when his father died, took on many characteristics and traits of his father. My dad was a go getter. He was a hardworking, resourceful man, who was well liked for his personality, charm, and ingenuity. I have always thought of Mark being the same way. He worked with his father in building and establishing the family farm. At the age of thirty-one years old, records show that in 1885 he was appointed by the US War Department to work as a civilian at the Upper Nashville Island, Cumberland River on a Naval ship according to the Register of Civil, Military and Naval Service, 1863–1959.[1] His job title is not reported, nor is his length of service reported. By 1888 he was reported to be working at the Cumberland Ironworks at Bear Creek in Stewart County, Tennessee. This county borders Dickson County. It is there where Mark met his wife to be, Josie Armstrong. Both were employed at the furnace, Mark as a laborer and Josie as an employee who brought water to the men working in the ironworks. Mark proposed marriage to Josie and, although she was sixteen years old at the time, she accepted his proposal. Mark was thirty-four years of age at the time of their marriage on July 1, 1889. His bride was seventeen years old. They were married at the courthouse in Charlotte. Will Gilbert's childhood friend, USCT veteran John Nesbitt posted $1200 bond for their marriage. Marriage bond payment was a practice that was especially common in Southern states through the first half of the nineteenth century. It was a pledge or guarantee given to the court by the intended groom and bondsman to affirm that there was no moral or legal reason why the couple could not be married and also the groom would not change his mind. If for any reason the marriage could not move forward, the bond money would be forfeited.

My paternal grandmother Josie died in 1945, the year before my birth.

If I asked anyone who knew of her to tell me about her, one of the first things that they would tell me was how attractive she was. So, I imagine that Mark believed that he had quite a prized possession when he married her. Josie was born a little more than ten years after slavery. However, her family on both sides represented several generations of enslavement. In a review of an 1859 Slave Record for the Cumberland Ironworks of Stewart County Tennessee, I found her maternal grandparents as well as her mother and father listed. Her grandparents were Ed and Charlotte Blair. Her father James (Little River) Armstrong was born about 1820 and her mother Harriet Blair born 1844 are also listed on the schedule. Not listed on the register were her paternal grandparents, Bill "Bushman" Buck Rivers who was born about 1800, and Emmaline Rivers. Bill was more commonly known by his Native American name, Buck Rivers. Emmaline, who had African ancestry, was born about the same time as Buck. Both were enslaved during part of their lives. Buck died in 1896 and was buried at Indian Mound in Stewart County. I don't have any information regarding Emmaline's death.[2]

Jim Armstrong, Josie's father, was enslaved as a blacksmith at the Cumberland Ironworks. In 1864, at the age of forty-four, he enlisted with the USCT of the Union army. He was assigned to the Kentucky Volunteer Mounted Infantry Regiment. He also served as a blacksmith during his military service. After military service, Armstrong was released as a free man. He returned to Stewart County and continued his trade as a paid blacksmith at the Cumberland Ironworks. He and Harriet were the parents to fifteen children. They were born from 1859 to 1890. Including my grandmother, I was familiar with the names of at least ten of their children. Some of the offspring settled in surrounding areas of Promise Land, including Cumberland Furnace and Nashville. After becoming a widow, my great-Grandma Harriet moved to Promise Land to live with my Grandma Josie. She ultimately moved to St. Louis, Missouri, to live with her son William who lived there. She lived out the rest of her life in St. Louis, where she died in 1934 at the age of ninety. As a child I remember our dad taking us annually to visit cousins in Erin, Stewart County, Tennessee.

At the time that Mark and Josie married, the settlement that his parents Will and Priscilla had created was growing and overflowing. Their own children had grown up and branched out on their own, and so had others who they had welcomed into their home. Their young nephew, Eddie Redden had built a house on the tract of land that he had inherited from the Gilberts. He had a wife, children, and a nice sized farm. This was the same for the Gilberts daughter, Toad. Toad married a man whose name was Bob Hampton. Although they did not have children of their own, Toad was known to take in children from the community who had been left to care for themselves. Mark's daughter, Maggie, grew up quickly. She married a man named Edward Bartee who had no ties to the community. They had three children together, which included a set of twins, before he left his family. I never heard any discussion of where he went or why. Maggie continued to live with her children in the home of her grandparents. Extended family, like Will's sister, Charlotte (Puss) and her husband Jeff Edmondson made their home in the vicinity of the Gilberts. This growing Promise Land sub community became known as Gilbert Town. Gilbert Town became a popular gathering place for the community's young people, as well as the youth in nearby Cumberland Furnace. Musical talents and skills ran in the Gilbert and Edmondson family. There were homegrown singers, musicians, and dancers who attracted others from outside their compound to party.

By the time that Mark and Josie started their family, his daughter Maggie and cousin Ed had both grown up, married, and started families as well their children were close in age and grew up together. They were close-knit and formed a natural play group. Mark and Josie's children included their oldest, William Jewel, followed by Ruby who they called "Sister," Hattie "Baby Sis," and my dad. Maggie or "Sis Mag" as she was known by my dad and his siblings, had three children, who included a set of twins, Bill D. and Ollie Mae and Mattie their oldest. Ed's children were Christie, Charley, Joe, Mae Jane, and Hattie Redden. As a child I had the opportunity to observe the bond that continued to exist between these surviving individuals in their adulthood. Following their parents these offspring were the second generation of the Gilbert Town Crew. My mother said her grandparents would not permit her to attend the gatherings in Gilbert Town. She said that the community's pious adults referred to the crew as "Rounders," which meant rebel rousers or good timers. My dad told me about the fun that they had at their gatherings. There would always be good food, stories being told, music, and dancing. Among their inner circle were some of the best singers and dancers around. My dad's brother, Jewel, was a singer, songwriter, and banjo player. I remember as a child, he would bring his banjo to the family gatherings. One of my favorite songs that he would sing was one that he had written called "My Ole Mule."

This song style was country and humorous. The lyrics were:

My ole mule has got the devil in him.
Darned ole fool has got the devil in him.

O my ole mule has got the devil in him
Devil in that honkey honkey, donkey donkey.

Road him to the graveyard.
The night was black as jet.
That ole fool laid in the middle of the road
I guess he's out there yet.[3]

As an adult Uncle Jewel became a member of a high society orchestra in St. Louis. He played in this orchestra until his death. His sister, Ruby, was a piano player. Later in life she would be the piano player for St. John Methodist Church. All of them could sing in harmony. As adults they would sing as a quartet. My uncles, O.C. and Theodore, were sought-after soloists in their adult years. Uncle Theodore was the organizer and director of a popular gospel ensemble in the 1950s called "Theo Edmondson and the Promise Land Singers." The ensemble comprised his two daughters, Bernice (the pianist) and Wilma, his niece/my sister Beverly, and Mary, who would later become his daughter-in-law. The youngest of the brothers, Tom, played guitar as a young man and as an adult. I remember in 1957, Cousin Bubba invited Uncle Tom and his band to play for a dance at Promise Land School. Uncle Tom's band was called "Tom Cat and His Kittens." It was my first dance, and everything was astounding to me.

Among his peers, my dad was the comic relief. He kept people laughing. He also played a few notes on the piano. I remember him playing and singing a tune at family gatherings called "Who's Been Here Since I Been Gone." I was told by some of those who remembered my dad and his cousin Hattie Redden Robertson dancing together. They said that the two of them would turn the parties out when they would "cut-a-rug" on the bare ground under the moonlit night in Gilbert Town.

I can't say that the artistic talents came from a single side of the family, although I believe that a great deal came from the maternal side of the family. Grandma Josie was known to have a beautiful voice. At least that is what I heard from some of the elders in the community. She would lead songs at St. John during worship service. I know that there was one particular song that my dad called "Mama's Song." The song was "What a Friend We Have in Jesus." My dad loved that song and loved hearing it sang. He said that every time he heard it, it would remind him of his mother and provoke him to tears. There is a member of Grandma Josie's family of origin who has received national and international acclaim for his musical and graphic artistic talents. His name is Howard Armstrong. Howard Armstrong was the son of Grandma Josie's brother, Rev. Thomas Armstrong. Rev. Armstrong moved from Stewart County for work at a Cumberland Ironworks Steel Mill in East Tennessee. Rev. Armstrong, the father of nine children, raised his family in LaFollette, Tennessee. He was a musician who made handmade string instruments for his five sons and taught them to play the instruments. All five of the sons sang as a quintet and accompanied themselves with the handmade instruments.

His son Howard, who would later adopt the stage name "Louie Bluie" was a standout among his brothers. He played fiddle, mandolin, and guitar. He attended Tennessee State Normal College as an art student studying graphic art and design, while playing cello in the symphony orchestra as well as fiddle in a jazz band. He would later travel the country with a band led by Blind Roland Martin. He also traveled throughout the world as a musician and was fluent in seven languages. A recipient of the National Heritage Fellowship Award in 1990, and the Tennessee Governor's Award in the Arts in 2003. Howard is recognized annually for his works at the "Louie Bluie Festival" held each year in LaFollette. Howard Armstrong died July 30, 2003, in Boston, Massachusetts. I think it is safe to say that much of the artistic skills and talents displayed by the Gilbert and Edmondson offspring may have come from their mother.

As the family entered into the twentieth century, Grandpa Mark and Grandma Josie lived in a small house with their four children just across the path from his sister Toad's house. My dad, born July 22, 1905, was the last child born to them. Mark was fifty-one years old at the time of my dad's birth. He was working for himself as a farmer at that time, as he had been diagnosed with asthma. Asthma caused him shortness of breath and decreased his strength. Farming was difficult for him, and he would sometimes have to go to bed to regain his physical strength. His cousin Jim Edmondson had lost his wife, Sylvia, leaving him alone to raise three children, two daughters and a son. His children ranged in age from late teens to preadolescence.

When Jim fell on hard times and was unable to work, he asked his cousin Mark if he and his children could move in with him and Josie.

Jim, being a man in his early forties and able bodied, led Mark to believe that he would be of help to him on the farm. In addition, he had always perceived Jim as a good person whom he trusted. So, he agreed to allow him and his children to move into his home. His decision increased the household numbers and also shattered the equilibrium of the family.

When the 1910 Census was taken, the report found Mark, at the age of fifty-four, was the household head of twelve people. The household included his thirty-seven-year-old wife Josie, their four children, his cousin Jim, and Jim's children eighteen-year-old Nissie, fifteen-year-old Sylvonia, and nine-year-old Burdine. There were two other children listed in the household as Mark's children. The two children were two-year-old Theodore and nine-month-old Peony. The problem was that Mark was not the father of the youngest two children. They had been fathered by his cousin Jim. It was evident that he had been betrayed by his wife and his cousin. Their indiscretion had obviously caused discontent, disappointment, and unhappiness for Mark. Probably feeling hurt, dejected, and embarrassed, Mark left his family and moved to Nashville into a boarding home. On December 7, 1911, Mark was found lying unconscious at Fatherland and 11th Street in East Nashville,. He died shortly after being discovered at about 7 a.m. His body was taken by ambulance to a morgue at 422 Cedar Street (now Martin Luther King Jr. Blvd), where he was pronounced dead as a result of mitral insufficiency, secondary to asthma. The informant who provided the social information for the death certificate apparently did not know Mark. Consequently, much of the information was left blank. However, his occupation was reported as "laborer." Based on the time that he was found, he was likely on his way to a job he had found to support himself. After receiving notification of his death, his wife and his mother identified his body and made funeral arrangements for him. His funeral was held at the St. John Methodist Church where Mark and his family were members, and he was buried in the family cemetery in Gilbert Town.

Mark's family continued to live in their home at Gilbert Town. Jim Edmondson and his children also continued to live with Josie and the children. Mark's sister Toad was very outspoken about her displeasure with Jim and Josie's betrayal of her brother and with their living arrangement. On March 24, 1912, Jim and Josie were married at the Charlotte courthouse. Their marriage did not satisfy Toad's contention. In December 1912, Toad's mother Priscilla took legal action to ensure that the majority of the property purchased by her husband Will would stay in their immediate family. She signed a deed conveying fifty-nine and three-quarters acres of the property to her daughter. The handwritten clause in the deed read as follows: In consideration of "the love and affection that I have for my daughter Fannie (Toad) Hampton and in consideration for her caring and waiting on me and looking after my wants and arranging for my comfort." This was the reason Priscella deeded the property to her only surviving child. The deed excluded five and a half acres, which was to go to Mark Gilbert's heirs and five and a half acres to her nephew Ed Redden.

Recognizing that she was the principal property owner in Gilbert Town, Toad was emboldened to continue her wrath and animosity toward Josie and Jim. Her actions ultimately resulted in them leaving their home in Gilbert Town. Around 1920, the family moved to central Promise Land. Jim's cousin John Wesley Edmondson, a carpenter, built a house for them that was located just off State Highway 48 North. At that time, all of Jim's first set of children were adults and living on their own. Josie's stepchildren, Nessie, Sylvonia, and Burdine all had moved to other states. Only four of Josie's biological children remained at home with them. They included my dad, who was the oldest, as well as his brothers, Peony, James, and Tom.

Josie lived in this home until her death. Her husband Jim died in 1932. But I don't think that she ever lived alone. She shared her home initially with her sons. However, the children who lived in Promise Land or nearby would be in and out of the home. I am not sure if her daughter's married before her sons, but both daughters had married in December 1921. Hattie married Jesse Bowen, of the community, on December 4, 1921. Ruby married Baxter Robertson who was also a young man from Promise Land, on December 25, 1921. Theodore married Lizzie Vanleer, a young woman from the community. O. C. married the teacher at Promise Land School. Her name was Amy Knott, from Montgomery County, Tennessee. After marriage, O. C. and Amy made their home in a neighboring rural Montgomery County community. Amy left the Dickson County School System and accepted employment as a teacher with the Montgomery County school district. Josie's oldest son, William Jewel, married a young lady from the community whose name was Willa Mae Edmondson. This marriage did not last very long. Willa Mae moved to Indianapolis, Indiana, and by the end of the 1930s, Jewel had moved to St. Louis, Missouri, where he joined his namesake and his mother's brother, William Armstrong. In St. Louis he met and married his second wife, Mary Tyler from

Mississippi. St. Louis became their home for life. Both Jewel and Mary passed away in the 1980s.

My dad took on the role as breadwinner for his mother after her second husband died. Eventually he married my mother on June 4, 1933. He remained in the household with his mother when his first child, Bobbye Jane, was born November 23, 1935. By the time his second child Beverly, was born in 1937, he had moved to another house in Promise Land. His brother Tom had married Dorothy Jackson of Promise Land and they had moved to Nashville. James also remained in the home after he had married Bettye Ruth Collier, and they also started their family in the home with Grandma Josie. Peony was the last to marry. He enlisted in the US Army and served during WWII. After discharge, he married my Aunt Mabel. It is apparent that Grandma's home was dynamic, alive, and the inhabitants ever-changing. I think that her surroundings spoke to her vibrance. She had members of her family of origin nearby to give support and love. After her father died, her mother Harriet Armstrong came to live with her for a while. She also had her sister Ella Vassar Bell, and Ella's children, daughters Clara, known affectionally as "Tump," and Bea, and son Mack who lived nearby in Cumberland Furnace. They would visit her often. Her sister Clara, who her daughter was named after, married a man from Promise Land. His name was Wesley Hall. They were all part of her immediate family constellation who were locally available to her: her brother Robert and his wife, Mynie Armstrong, lived in Cumberland Furnace. Her sister-in-law, Mynie was a teacher at Promise Land School from 1914 to 1921, before they moved to Cleveland, Ohio. Many of her family joined the Great Migration north before her death or soon after. Her stepchildren were among those who migrated but were yet so endeared to her they returned to visit her often and remained in the family network. Grandma Josie lived a full and what appears to have been a happy life. She spent the rest of her life at her house on the highway. She never attempted to claim her property in Gilbert Town, neither did any of her children. Aunt Toad passed away just three years before Grandma. I am not sure if they ever mended fences. It was never discussed in family gatherings or in any other setting that I know of. Aunt Toad was spoken of in a loving way by her nieces and nephews. My dad would admonish us at times when he thought our behavior was selfish, saying: "You are acting like Aunt Toad." I surmise that he may have been repeating a characterization ascribed to her by his mother. Yet it was not overt animosity toward her.

Grandma's stepson Burdine moved to Indianapolis in the late 1930s. His sisters moved to Columbus, Ohio, before their father died. They would return home for visits occasionally. Burdine would however, return to Promise Land almost annually until his death. He would come usually for the Charlotte Picnic and sometimes for the annual homecoming day, better known as the First Sunday in June. He shared a close relationship with his siblings and they were likewise endeared to him. Among the siblings, I never heard them refer to any of the twelve as "half" or "step." They were just brothers and sisters. Like his siblings, he was a gifted vocalist. I will always remember the brothers getting together to harmonize. It would be spontaneous. It could be during a gathering in the homes or at the church. If most of the brothers were in attendance, it was a guarantee that they would sing. Uncle Burdine seemed to have been taller than the others. One of his legs was longer than the other. The affected leg was bowed from the knee down, seemingly to accommodate the shorter one. He would wear a woven straw sailor hat that added to his height. He was known to be affectionate, always freely giving hugs and kisses. But most noticeable about him was his jovial personality and comedic charm.

My dad's siblings enjoyed getting together as a group. I imagine that it was reminiscent of and a carryover from their childhood and youth in Gilbert Town. I was happy to get a glimpse and be a part of these gatherings. Especially following annual events our families would gather at one of the homes, outside in the yard. There would be food, music, dancing, lots of jokes, and storytelling. The adults would encourage the young people to compete against each other in dancing. They would throw coins at us as we danced. We would be trying to pick up the coins from the grass while trying to keep time with the music. That was a real challenge for me, because I was never one of the best dancers. My cousin Mickey, who was the same age as me, would really put on a show during these competitions. He would stand on his head, do the split, and dance like he had ants in his pants. It was not just the dancing that they encouraged. They also had us express ourselves in other ways. We would sing, join in the story and joke telling. The children were invited and welcomed to be among the adults. The older children were asked about themselves, such as "I hear you graduated this year, what do you plan to do next"? Open-ended inquiries were made, allowing the youth to speak without feeling limited. If any of the young people had graduated high school, college, or any type of achievement prior to the gathering, they could expect an onslaught of gifts and accolades. The kinfolk were very liberal with encouragement and recognition for achievements. The inclusion, kindness, and support shown toward us was evidence of their expectation and hope for us.

Their support and devotion were not just limited to the gatherings. We could count on a positive response from our extended family each time assistance was requested. When I went off to college in Nashville, I felt comfortable knowing that I could call on my extended family there for help if ever needed. At the time I left home, I had three uncles and aunts as well as cousins who lived near the campus.

Uncle Peony had remarried after Aunt Mabel died. His new wife, Aunt Ressie, quickly adjusted to our family. I was often invited to their home for a meal or to stay overnight. Aunt Ressie would take me shopping or to the beauty shop. I could see her pride when she introduced me to her friends or family. She claimed that my mannerism and hair style reminded her of Jackie Kennedy. So, in introducing me she would say jokingly, "This is Miss Jackie Kennedy." When I was doing an internship at the VA Hospital, I was assigned to make a home visit to a veteran. I asked Uncle Tom, who lived near the campus, if he would provide transportation for me. He seemed pleased that I asked. He transported me to the client's home and waited until I had completed the visit, then took me back to campus. I had countless meals at my Aunt Hattie and Uncle Jesse's home. Their home was like my home away from home. It wasn't just the family in Nashville, but my family in Promise Land made me feel special also. My Uncle James, who was always like a big brother, would greet me when I returned home, which was quite often, as though I had been away for years. He was so special to me. I thought I would die when he passed away in my junior year of college. He died in his sleep of a heart attack. He was in his mid-forties. At home I also had my family of origin, my Aunt Ruby and Uncle Baxter Robertson, Aunt Lizzie Edmondson, Cousin Hattie Robertson, Cousin Tamar, and William Primm and others. We still had a village in Promise Land. These people helped to keep me grounded. I was just as concerned that I would not disappoint them as I was with my parents. Therefore, I was careful to be on my best behavior.

Having family and extended family always made me feel inclusive and valued. It fostered creativity and confidence. I am certain that my siblings and cousins experienced similar feelings. The exposure and experience of growing up in a close-knit family and community shaped who we became as adults, just as our parents' background influenced the paths that they took in life. To be raised in a community like Promise Land gives so much credence to the African proverb, "It takes a village to raise a child."

Promise Land provided me with a safe, healthy, nurturing, environment in which to strive. My family, extended family, neighbors, teachers, and preachers gave me the security and confidence to develop and flourish. Through this experience I have been able to realize my hopes and dreams. From this blessing, hopefully, I have, and will continue to touch others, just as I have been touched by my early environment and life experience.

EPILOGUE

COUNTED AMONG THE LIVING AND NOT THE DEAD

MOST TOWNS ESTABLISHED BY AFRICAN AMERICAN communities during the Civil War and Reconstruction no longer exist. While many of the sites where they were established still bear their names—such as Black John Hollow, Turnbull, Dry Hollow, and Hendricks in Dickson County and others bearing colorful names like Sugar Flats and Needmore in Wilson County or Africanna Town, Boiling Springs, and Vinegar Hill in Montgomery County—few of the descendants of the original residents still call these areas home. Promise Land is one of the exceptions in Middle Tennessee. Its residents survived the state's quick dismantling of Reconstruction and the terror of legal and extralegal tactics deployed to prevent access to the promises of democracy. They endured efforts to establish racial discrimination under a new guise called Jim Crow and, for the next half century, only enjoyed partial inclusion in American society.

Many communities fell victim to the Great Migration where between six and seven million African Americans left the South for northern and western cities. While some Promise Land residents embraced the economic opportunities offered by Cleveland, Columbus, Detroit, and Indianapolis, Promise Land managed to maintain a remnant of its original population, one that remained committed to celebrating the community's history and collective memory. The number of African Americans living in Dickson County has experienced only a modest increase from the early days of emancipation to the present. In 1870, there were 1,677 freed persons in the county representing 18 percent of the population. A little more than 150 years later, there are 2,155 African Americans living in Dickson County, and they represent only 4 percent of its residents.[1]

Despite the departure of African Americans and the subsequent disintegration of the Reconstruction communities they established, Middle Tennessee has been a part of a new movement colloquially called the "New Great Migration" which has brought many Northern African Americans back to the South. Interestingly, a report from the Brookings Institute reveals that this new migration does not consist of the elderly, stating that the new emigrants have been "disproportionately young and well educated."[2] This Homecoming has drawn many families—some of whom are separated from slavery by only two generations—back home. Conversations with descendants reveal that although many left for northern and western climes seeking better opportunities their hearts were never far from their homes in Promise Land.

Dr. Sokoto Fulani's memories of the space demonstrate that in addition to tobacco, corn, and other crops, the soil cultivated a fierce sense of independence among its residents. Fulani traced this spirit to the first settlers who in "1870 coming out of slavery . . . established themselves as landowners." According to Fulani, they emerged from enslavement with "a mentality that says we are humans, and we are free, and we do not work for the people, we work for ourselves and we do for ourselves."[3] This independence led to his family leaving Promise Land seeking a better life in Ohio in 1952, but despite finding economic and social success in the Buckeye state, the hollow where they lived in Promise Land—a space that did not have electricity when they left—remained their spiritual and physical home. Fulani credits the survival of Promise Land with the determination of James Arthur Edmondson and many of the matriarchs of the Edmondson, Gilbert, Primm, and Collier families who refused to allow the history and memory of the community to perish. These efforts coalesced on the first weekend in June, a historically sacred day for Promise Land and its descendants, one where the joy and aspirations of the founders intersected the hope and pride of the present while inspiring a determination to work for the future.

The church and school, the most prominent institutions from the era of Jim Crow, are lasting monuments from that period and still unify the descendants to this day. One resident recalled that during the early to mid-twentieth century, the mile and a half long dirt road leading to the church and school would produce more dust than usual during the first days of what was the reunion weekend, causing her to despair about the amount of dust that settled on her patent leather shoes. Once the dust cleared, however, she recalled seeing the mothers and the women of the community preparing "what would be called basket dinners" composed of BBQ chicken, rolls, macaroni and cheese, and chicken and dumplings. For much of its history, Promise Land exported much of the culture, love, and joy it fostered among the descendants of its original founders at these meetings and spread them across the globe.

This gathering—now known as the Promise Land Festival—still serves the purpose of bringing former residents home and being a space where they can reflect about the days of their youth, but the church, school, community center, the bench that bears the name of Essie Vanleer Gilbert, the Vanleer and Nesbitt cemeteries, and the earth that connects these sites are at once transformed into one of the most engaging instructional spaces about African American history and culture in Middle Tennessee. If needed, one could teach a course on the entire African American experience in the United States based upon the history Promise Land. But the joy visitors experience in Promise Land is something the most skilled teacher could not replicate in the classroom.

Today Promise Land still draws its descendants back during the first weekend in June, but now friends, family, students, and people with an interest in its history also heed the call of this land to experience the ethos and spirit of the place. During its settlement and for most of its early history, its residents viewed the land as a promise bestowed upon them by a benevolent creator. As the nineteenth and early twentieth centuries progressed, Promise Land came to represent the hope and aspirations of a people who negotiated the boundaries placed in front of them as a result of Jim Crow. In the twenty-first century, it invites the world to visit and fellowship with its descendants. Promise Land stands as a new testament to the determination of families and a community to not let their history and memories perish.

NOTES

PREFACE

1. 1850 US Census, Slave Schedule, Davidson County, TN.
2. 1860 US Census, Population Schedules, Dickson County.
3. C. Perry Patterson, *The Negro in Tennessee, 1790–1865*. University of Texas Bulletin, no. 2205 (Austin: University of Texas, 1922; repr., New York: Negro Universities Press, 1968), 155.
4. *National Era*, December 18, 1856.
5. Frederick Douglass, *Narrative of the Life of Frederick Douglass Written by Himself*, ed. David Blight (Boston: Bedford St. Martins, 1993), 80–82.
6. *Nashville Union and American*, December 18, 1859.
7. Constitution of the Confederate States of America, Article 1, Section 9, 1861.
8. "An Address to the People of the Free States by the President of the Southern Confederacy," *Richmond Examiner*, January 5, 1863.

CHAPTER 4

1. Public Acts of the State of Tennessee, Passed at the Extra Session of the Thirty-Third General Assembly, April 1861 (Nashville: J.O. Griffith & Co, Public Printers, Union and American Office), 49, 50.
2. Abraham Lincoln, "Letter in Reply to Horace Greeley on Slavery and the Union—The Restoration of the Union the Paramount Object," The American Presidency Project, accessed May 6, 2025, https://www.presidency.ucsb.edu/documents/letter-reply-horace-greeley-slavery-and-the-union-the-restoration-the-union-the-paramount.
3. "Rebel Congress on Negro Soldiers," *Nashville Daily Union*, September 2, 1862.
4. Emancipation Proclamation, January 1, 1863.

5. Dudley Taylor Cornish, *The Sable Arm: Negro Troops in the Union Army, 1861–1865* (New York: W.W. Norton, 1966), 288–89.
6. "Negro Insubordination," *Nashville Union and American*, December 11, 1856.
7. "An Address to the People of the Free States."
8. *Christian Recorder*, June 10, 1865.
9. Acts of the State of Tennessee Passed at the First Session of the Thirty-Fifth General Assembly for the Years 1867–68 (Nashville: S.C. Mercer, 1868), 366.
10. The plaque placed on Jones's office by members of the Ku Klux Klan cites the December 24, 1865, date as the date the group was organized, while Elaine Parson's most recent work argues that the six men created the group during the summer of 1866. See Elaine Frantz Parson, *Ku Klux: The Birth of the Ku Klux Klan during Reconstruction* (Chapel Hill: University of North Carolina Press, 2015).
11. Quoted from an affidavit filed with the Department of Army regarding John Nesbitt's application for disability.
12. Testimony of Daniel Grimes, *Bill and Patsy Grimes v. John Blacksmith*, October 1917–May 31, 1918, Dickson County Archives, Charlotte, TN (hereafter, *Grimes v. Blacksmith*).
13. Testimony of Patsy Grimes, *Grimes v. Blacksmith.*
14. Testimony of Wade Vanleer, *Grimes v. Blacksmith.*

CHAPTER 5

1. Edward Carmack, "The Race Problem," *Olympian* 2, no. 4 (Oct. 1903), 308.
2. Pauli Murray, *States' Laws on Race and Color* (Athens: University of Georgia Press, 1997), 438–41.
3. Louis R. Harlan, ed., *The Booker T. Washington Papers*, vol. 3 (Urbana: University of Illinois Press, 1974), 583–87.
4. Social Explorer Dataset (SE), Census 1900, digitally transcribed by Inter-university Consortium for Political and Social Research. Edited, verified by Michael Haines. Compiled, edited and verified by Social Explorer. https://www.socialexplorer.com/data/Census1900.
5. W. E. B. Du Bois, "Of Mr. Washington and Others," *Souls of Black Folks* (Project Gutenberg, 1996), https://www.gutenberg.org/files/408/408-h/408-h.htm#chap03.
6. For more on Black migration to Kansas, see Nell Irvin Painter, *Exodusters: Black Migration to Kansas After Reconstruction* (New York: W.W. Norton, 1992).

CHAPTER 7

1. Letter on Nathan Bowen, 1875, Governor James D. Porter (1828–1912) Papers 1875–1879, GP 24, Box 10, Folder 1, Tennessee State Library and Archives, Nashville, TN.
2. Dickson County Circuit Court Book G, 1884–1889. Dickson County Archives, Charlotte, TN.

CHAPTER 8

1. Essie V. Gilbert, 1990 Bowen Family Reunion Journal, unpublished booklet, Charlotte, TN, 1990.
2. "Dr. Watts" hymn singing was a tradition of African American song styling derived from hymn texts written by the eighteenth-century theologian Isaac Watts. "Dr. Watts Singers," Mississippi Folklife Directory, accessed June 4, 2025, https://msfolkdirectory.org/dr-watts-singers.

CHAPTER 9

1. "US Register of Officers and Agents, Civil, Military, and Naval, in the Service of the United States, 1863 to 1959," Ancestry.com.
2. Schedule "C" 1 Oct 1859 - A list of negro slaves owned by Woods Yeatman & Woods Lewis and Co. at Cumberland Iron Works Stewart County Tennessee, Ancestry.com.
3. Jewel Gilbert, "My Ole Mule," St. Louis, MO, 1949.

EPILOGUE

1. Social Explorer Dataset (SE), Census 1870, digitally transcribed by Inter-university Consortium for Political and Social Research, edited, verified by Michael Haines. Compiled, edited, and verified by Social Explorer. https://www.socialexplorer.com/data/Census1870.
2. William H. Frey, "A 'New Great Migration' Is Bringing Black Americans Back to the South," Brookings Institute, Sept. 12, 2022, https://www.brookings.edu/articles/a-new-great-migration-is-bringing-black-americans-back-to-the-south.
3. Dr. Sokoto Fulani interview by Learotha Williams Jr., November 21, 2015, Promise Land, TN.

REFERENCES

GOVERNMENT DOCUMENTS

1850. US Census. Slave Schedule. Davidson County, TN.

1860. US Census. Population Schedules. Dickson County, TN.

1861. Constitution of the Confederate States of America.

1861. Tennessee. Public Acts of the State of Tennessee, Passed at the Extra Session of the Thirty-Third General Assembly, April 1861. Nashville, J.O Griffith & Co, Public Printers, Union and American Office.

1863. United States. Lincoln, Abraham, *Emancipation Proclamation*, January 1, 1863.

1868. *Acts of the State of Tennessee Passed at the First Session of the Thirty-Fifth General Assembly for the Years 1867–68*. Nashville: S. C. Mercer.

Dickson County Circuit Court Book G, 1884–1889. Dickson County Archives, Charlotte, TN.

COURT CASES

Dickson, Tennessee. *Bill and Patsy Grimes v. John Blacksmith*, October 1917–May 31, 1918. Dickson County Archives, Dickson, Tennessee.

ONLINE DATABASES

Ancestry.com. "U.S., Register of Civil, Military, and Naval Service, 1863–1959," online database. Ancestry.com, 2014.

Social Explorer Dataset (SE), Census 1870. Digitally transcribed by Inter-university Consortium for Political and Social Research. Edited, verified by Michael Haines. Compiled, edited, and verified by Social Explorer. https://www.socialexplorer.com/data/Census1870.

Social Explorer Dataset (SE), Census 1900. Digitally transcribed by Inter-university Consortium for Political and Social Research. Edited, verified by Michael Haines. Compiled, edited, and verified by Social Explorer. https://www.socialexplorer.com/data/Census1900.

NEWSPAPERS

Christian Recorder

Nashville Daily Union

Nashville Globe

Nashville Union and American

National Era

Richmond Enquirer

PERSONAL LETTERS AND OTHER ARCHIVAL SOURCES

1875. Tennessee. Letter on Nathan Bowen file, 1875, Tennessee State Library and Archives, Nashville, Tennessee.

Gilbert, Jewel. "My Ole Mule," St. Louis, MO, 1949.

Schedule "C" 1 Oct 1859 - A list of negro slaves owned by Woods Yeatman & Woods Lewis and Co. at Cumberland Iron Works Stewart County, Tennessee.

Williams, Learotha, Jr. Dr. Sokotu Fulani Interview. November 21, 2015. Promise Land Heritage Association, Promise Land, Tennessee.

SECONDARY SOURCES

Carmack, Edward, "The Race Problem," *Olympian* 2, no. 4 (Oct. 1903): 308–16.

Cornish, Dudley Taylor. *The Sable Arm: Negro Troops in the Union Army, 1861–1865*. New York: W.W. Norton, 1966.

Douglass, Frederick. *Narrative of the Life of Frederick Douglass Written by Himself.* Edited by David Blight. Boston: Bedford St. Martins, 1993.

Du Bois, W. E. B., "Of Mr. Washington and Others," *Souls of Black Folks*, Project Gutenberg, 1996. https://www.gutenberg.org/files/408/408-h/408-h.htm#chap03.

Frey, William H. "A 'New Great Migration' Is Bringing Black Americans Back to the South." Brookings Institute, Sept. 12, 2022. https://www.brookings.edu/articles/a-new-great-migration-is-bringing-black-americans-back-to-the-south.

Harlan, Louis R. ed., *The Booker T. Washington Papers*, vol. 3. Urbana: University of Illinois Press, 1974.

Lincoln, Abraham, "Letter in Reply to Horace Greeley on Slavery and the Union—The Restoration of the Union the Paramount Object." The American Presidency Project, accessed on May 6, 2025. https://www.presidency.ucsb.edu/documents/letter-reply-horace-greeley-slavery-and-the-union-the-restoration-the-union-the-paramount.

Murray, Pauli, *States' Laws on Race and Color*. Athens: University of Georgia Press. 1997.

Painter, Nell Irvin, *Exodusters: Black Migration to Kansas After Reconstruction.* New York: W.W. Norton & Co., 1992.

Parson, Elaine Frantz, *Ku Klux: The Birth of the Ku Klux Klan during Reconstruction*. Chapel Hill: University of North Carolina Press, 2015.

Patterson, C. Perry, *The Negro in Tennessee, 1790–1865*. University of Texas Bulletin, no. 2205. Austin: University of Texas, 1922. Repr., New York: Negro Universities Press, 1968.

UNPUBLISHED WORKS

Gilbert, Essie V. "1990 Bowen Family Reunion Journal." Unpublished, Charlotte, TN, 1990.

NAMES INDEX

B

Bartee, Maggie Gilbert 149, 151
Bates, Leon 47
Bell, Alice 54
Bell, Montgomery xvi, xvii, xviii, 3, 28
Bennett, E. Jewel Bowen 146
Blacksmith, Agnes 59
Blacksmith, Bob 55
Blacksmith, John 59, 63
Blacksmith, Katie 55, 57, 58, 59, 60
Blacksmith, Mary 58, 63
Blackwell, Agnes 59
Bly, Lovey 59
Bly, Wash 59
Bowen, Bertie Vanleer 75, 123
Bowen, Farmie Della Vanleer 20, 78, 84, 100, 127
Bowen, George Washington 20, 34, 78, 84, 91, 100, 127, 134
Bowen, Greeley Horace 110, 112, 113, 121
Bowen, Hattie Gilbert 148
Bowen, Jesse J. 113, 156
Bowen, Leander (Lee) 116, 118
Bowen, Lucy Carr 70, 100, 109, 116, 127
Bowen, Molly 18, 31
Bowen, Nathan xi, 22, 23, 30, 70, 75, 100, 102, 104, 108, 109, 115, 126, 127
Bowen, Richard (Dick) 120, 126
Bowen, Thomas 87, 109, 110
Britt, Levi 22
Britt, Robert 22, 102
Bryant, Della Gilbert 23

C

Clemons, Ellen 40, 53
Collier, C. C. 42
Collier, Elisha 52
Collier, Hannah 11
Collier, Jane 59
Collier, Jordon (Cardell) 52
Collier, Judy 52
Collier, Leona 52
Collier, Marshall 58, 59
Collier, Martha 58, 59
Collier, Nobie 52
Collier, Nora 52
Collier, Riley 59
Corlew, Violet 49
Cunningham, Beasley 24
Cunningham, Beatrice 24
Cunningham, Betty 11, 58
Cunningham, Elvie 23
Cunningham, John 23
Cunningham, Lev 11, 84

Cunningham, Mandy 11, 84
Cunningham, Noye 11, 12
Cunningham, Panthera Vanleer 83
Cunningham, Sol 11, 84, 106

D

Driver, Idessa Canara 52
Driver, Kelly 52
Drouillard, James Pierre 3, 45

E

Easley, Hulda Bowen 108
Easley, Willis Buck 102, 108
Edmondson, Betty Ruth 43
Edmondson, Charlotte Bowen 21, 22, 87, 126
Edmondson, Earl 51
Edmondson, Emma Hutton 18
Edmondson, Eolie 51
Edmondson, Hester 51
Edmondson, James 23, 24, 162
Edmondson, James (Jim) 126
Edmondson, Jeff 17, 19, 22
Edmondson, Jefferson I 126
Edmondson, Jefferson II 126
Edmondson, John 51
Edmondson, John Wesley 17, 18, 20, 21, 22, 51, 126, 156
Edmondson, Josie Gilbert Armstrong 19, 21, 23
Edmondson, Lesley 51, 131
Edmondson, Lizzie 53
Edmondson, Pearl 51
Edmondson, Robert 51
Edmondson, Sallie Suggs 65, 87, 126
Edmondson, Susan 51
Edmondson, Theo 142, 153
Edmondson, Theodore 23
Edmondson, Violet Gilbert 17
Edmondson, Wesley C. 136, 148

F

Fulani, Sokoto (Charles Nesbitt) 33, 34, 42, 162

G

Garrett, Clark 7, 20, 27, 34, 36, 37, 48, 50
Garrett, Ethel 11
Garrett, Gertrude 49, 50
Garrett, John 20, 21, 49, 50
Garrett, McPherson 49
Garrett, Sally Edmondson Vanleer Suggs 21
Garrett, Violet 50
Garrett, Washington 49
Gilbert, Essie Vanleer Kirkman 129, 148, 163
Gilbert, Mark 149, 155
Gilbert, Priscilla Redden 25, 96, 109, 148
Gilbert, Rita 148
Gilbert, Robert J. T 136, 148
Gilbert, William 25, 50
Gilbert, William I 148
Gilbert, William II 148, 150
Gilbert, William Jewel 139, 148
Gill, Wed 22
Grimes, Alberta 54
Grimes, Alfred (Elbert) 34, 53, 54, 55, 58
Grimes, Arthur Lee 58
Grimes, Dan 56, 57, 61
Grimes, Dess 58
Grimes, Eddie 54
Grimes, Emerson 54
Grimes, Emma 54
Grimes, George W. Jr. 58
Grimes, Henry 54
Grimes, Irene 54
Grimes, Isaac P. 54
Grimes, James 54
Grimes, Jane 57

Grimes, John (the first) 54, 55, 56, 58, 61
Grimes, John (the second) 55, 57
Grimes, John B. 55, 56, 61
Grimes, Katherine 58
Grimes, Mary 54, 57
Grimes, Miller 54
Grimes, Minnie Johnson 58
Grimes, Patsy 57, 58, 59, 60, 61, 63
Grimes, Percy 54
Grimes, Priscilla Horner 58
Grimes, Rosie 54
Grimes, Sam Blacksmith 54, 55, 57, 59, 61, 62
Grimes, Samuel 54
Grimes, Susie 54
Grimes, William (Bill) 58, 59, 61, 63
Grimes, William (Dess) 58

H

Hampton, Bob 151
Hampton, Fannie (Toad) Gilbert 25, 155
Hannah, Ellen Vanleer Majors (Sis) 77, 78, 79
Harris, Juanita Bowen 118
Hickerson, Mahalia Tennessee 44
Hooper, Bud 25
Hooper, W. H. 42
Hutton, Althea 18
Hutton, Josephine Snowden Bowen 122
Hutton, William (Will) 10, 18, 32, 122

J

Jackson, F. 61
Jackson, Francis Talley 14
Jackson, Hagar 56, 57, 59, 61
Jackson, Hershell 20
Jackson, Katie 56, 57, 61
Jackson, Leroy 20
Jackson, Lias 7, 12, 14, 15
Jackson, Lula 31
Jackson, Mary Bea 20
Jackson, P. 61
Jackson, Priscilla Vanleer Greer 95
Jackson, Pugh 20
Jenkins, George Clayton 50
Jenkins, Richard 14
Johnson, Alfred 46
Johnson, Minnie 58

K

Kirkman, Hersey 51
Kirkman, Lizzie 43
Kirkman, Mary Florence 3, 45
Kirkman, Mary Francis 52
Kirkman, Paton 51

L

Lanier, McPherson 42
Leech, Isham W. 44
Leech, R. L. 59
Loggins, Sack 57, 61

M

Mallory, Claytee 51
Martin, Rosetta Garrett 31, 49, 50
McCauley, Susan 51
McKinley, John 46

N

Nesbitt, Allen 39, 44
Nesbitt, Arch xi, 11, 27, 33, 34, 36, 44, 45, 46, 58, 85
Nesbitt, Babe 43
Nesbitt, Beatrice 52
Nesbitt, Bettie 46
Nesbitt, Billy xvi
Nesbitt, Bob 43
Nesbitt, Charles (Fulani, Sokoto) 33, 34, 42, 162
Nesbitt, Charley 24, 31, 42, 43

Nesbitt, Charlie 24
Nesbitt, Earsley 43
Nesbitt, Ellen 33, 44
Nesbitt, Elzie 43
Nesbitt, Ernest 23, 31, 43, 128
Nesbitt, Gracie 43
Nesbitt, James 43
Nesbitt, Jettie 43
Nesbitt, John xi, 11, 23, 24, 27, 31, 33, 34, 36, 39, 41, 43, 44, 53, 71, 80, 106, 150
Nesbitt, John Henry 43
Nesbitt, Johnny 46
Nesbitt, Joseph 43
Nesbitt, J. P. 33
Nesbitt, Kittie 43
Nesbitt, Lemuel 43
Nesbitt, Lizzie Vanleer Kirkman 131
Nesbitt, Mahalia Tennessee 46
Nesbitt, Manuel 43
Nesbitt, Mary 43
Nesbitt, Minnie 43
Nesbitt, Nancy 42
Nesbitt, Nara Vanleer 85, 129
Nesbitt, Susan 43, 53

O

Overton, Ben 60

P

Primm, Harry 46
Primm, Tamar 23
Primm, William 23

R

Redden, Annie Stringfellow 25
Redden, Charles 25
Redden, Eddie (Ed) 25, 26, 151, 155
Redden, Milley Vanleer 20, 89, 90
Redden, Plummer (Boss) 89
Redden, Rachel 25
Redden, William Plummer (Boss) 19, 20, 89, 90, 109
Reddon, George Bernard 46
Richbourg, Flora Redden 110
Roberts, Alice 45
Robertson, Baxter 16, 23
Robertson, Calvin 22
Robertson, Hattie Redden 24, 25
Robertson, Hersey 24, 25
Robertson, James xvi, 3
Robertson, Ruby 23, 25
Roberts, William 45

S

Sherman, William T. xv
Smith, Niva Driver 52
Stansfield, J. 31
Stansfield, Nonie (Bradley) 31
Stone, E. H. 60
Stout, J. W. 59
Suggs, John 21
Sweat, Benessa 50

T

Travis, William T. C. 32

V

Vanleer, Addie 51, 52
Van Leer, Anthony xviii
Vanleer, Anthony Wayne 3, 45, 51, 56
Vanleer, Bessie 53
Vanleer, Daniel (Dan) 21, 65, 80, 87, 110
Vanleer, Earsley 53
Vanleer, Edward (Ed) 23, 34, 36, 37, 50, 52, 53, 126
Vanleer, Elzie 53
Vanleer, Fannie 53
Vanleer, Isham 80, 83, 88
Vanleer, Jetti 53

Vanleer, Joe W. (Lil Joe) 73
Vanleer, John 53
Vanleer, John Thomas 22, 84, 123
Vanleer, Joseph Washington (Joe Wash) xi, 5, 20, 22, 46, 70, 73, 89, 92, 100, 106, 110, 116, 123, 127, 135
Vanleer, Laura 53
Vanleer, Lizzie 51
Vanleer, Lou 51
Vanleer, Mary 51
Vanleer, Nara 46
Vanleer, Ransom 34
Vanleer, Rebecca Stokes Leech 70, 71–73, 77, 78, 95, 100, 135
Vanleer, Sarah 51
Vanleer, Susie/Fanny 23, 51, 53
Vanleer, Thomas 52, 53

W

Washington, Sally 48
Weakley, Georgia (E) 20
Williams, Alex 47
Williams, Beverly Gilbert 146, 148
Williams, Harriet 47
Williams, Hyburnia 146, 148
Williams, Landers, Jr. 48
Williams, Landin/Landers 23, 27, 34, 36, 37, 47, 127
Williams, Landy, III 48
Williams, Mary 47
Worley, James xvii

Y

Young, Sarah 59
Young, Turner 59